WAR AS RISK MANAGEMENT

This book analyses the reconfiguration of war as risk management in the post-Cold War, post-September 11 era. Despite the new strategic context established by 9/11, it is suggested here that warfare, as currently practised by the West, is characterized by continuity as much as change. Confronted with ill-defined 'wars' against security risks such as terrorism and WMD proliferation, the book adopts an innovative inter-disciplinary approach to the 'transformation of war' debate. As the study of risk management has helped fields such as criminology and sociology address new policy challenges, the book explores how International Relations could benefit from inter-disciplinary cross-fertilisation. Yee-Kuang Heng begins by systematically analysing how concepts such as proactive anticipation, the precautionary principle and appreciating 'non-events' might help scholars to reconceptualise war in its contemporary risk-management form. Through this new conceptual framework the book then analyses three recent military campaigns: the Kosovo Campaign, the Afghan Campaign and the most recent war on Iraq. These case studies, placed within a broader theoretical and historical perspective, help bring the debate on managing risks from sociology into strategy and conflict.

This book will be of great interest to all students and scholars of strategic studies, war studies, international relations and globalisation.

Yee-Kuang Heng received his PhD in International Relations from the London School of Economics and Political Science, and is curently lecturing at Trinity College Dublin. His research interests include the security implications of globalisation and the transformation of war.

'Yee-Kuang Heng writes with great verve and an obvious enthusiasm for his subject. He will be readily understood by specialist and non specialist alike. *War as Risk Management* is a fascinating book that represents a major scholarly contribution to the literature on risk, in an area: international security which has been 'off limits' to the sociologists who have so far dominated the field. In this respect, it will considerably enrich our knowledge of risk, as well as the management of risk in the debates which are currently proving so divisive in the transatlantic world, the war against terrorism being at the head of the list.'
Professor Christopher Coker, London School of Economics and Political Science

'This is a very impressive book which makes a compelling and original case. The argument applies ideas of risk to strategy and security. In so doing Yee-Kuang Heng manages to reconceptualise war as risk management rather than threat response. This is an important move, which is accomplished in a convincing and sophisticated manner.'
Professor Colin McInnes, University of Wales, Aberystwyth.

WAR AS RISK MANAGEMENT

Strategy and conflict in an age of globalised risks

Yee-Kuang Heng

Routledge
Taylor & Francis Group

LONDON AND NEW YORK

1006960827

First published 2006
by Routledge
2 Park Square, Milton Park, Abingdon, Oxon OX14 4RN

Simultaneously published in the USA and Canada
by Routledge
270 Madison Ave, New York, NY 10016

Routledge is an imprint of the Taylor & Francis Group

Transferred to Digital Printing 2009

Typeset in Times New Roman by Taylor and Francis Books

British Library Cataloguing in Publication Data
A catalogue record for this book is available from the British Library

Library of Congress Cataloging in Publication Data
A catalog record for this book has been requested

ISBN10: 0–415–37589–4 (hbk)
ISBN10: 0–415–54499–8 (pbk)

ISBN13: 978–0–415–37589–4 (hbk)
ISBN13: 978–0–415–54499–3 (pbk)

Taylor & Francis Group is the Academic Division of T&F Informa plc.

CONTENTS

ACKNOWLEDGEMENTS

Many people and organisations have helped in the writing of this book. I would like in particular to gratefully acknowledge the assistance and encouragement of Andrew Humphrys, the military and strategic studies editor at Routledge, as well as the editorial and production talents of Marjorie François and Jason Mitchell respectively. Certain sections of Chapter Five are also reprinted by permission of Sage Publications Ltd from Yee-Kuang Heng, 'Unravelling the war on terrorism: a risk management exercise in war clothing?', *Security Dialogue*, Volume 33, No. 2, pp. 227–42, June 2002, Copyright International Peace Research Institute, Oslo (PRIO), 2002. Some issues raised in this book are also touched upon in Yee-Kuang Heng, 'The Transformation of War Debate: Through the Looking Glass of Ulrich Beck's *World Risk Society*', *International Relations*, Volume 20, No. 1, 2006, Sage Publications.

The inspiration and guidance of Christopher Coker has been indispensable to developing my thinking and writing about society, war, strategy and international relations. For this I am eternally grateful. Colin McInnes was as always cheerfully forthcoming with insights and comments on earlier versions of this book, which were put to good use. The support of Michael Clarke further made the task of writing seem lighter. Errors remain mine alone. I would also like to express thanks to my colleagues at the Department of Political Science, Trinity College Dublin, for their advice and creating such a hospitable climate for research and writing.

Finally, this book would have been impossible without the loving support of Dad, Mom, Hiroko, Chihiro, and my family. Last but not least, a word of appreciation for my other half, Akiko, who made life generally better just by being there.

ABBREVIATIONS

APM	Anti-personnel Landmine
CIA	Central Intelligence Agency
CJTF	Combined Joint Task Force
DoD	Department of Defence (US)
FBI	Federal Bureau of Investigation
IISS	International Institute for Strategic Studies
ISAF	International Security Assistance Force (Kabul)
JCS	Joint Chiefs of Staff (US)
J-STARS	Joint Surveillance Target Attack Radar System (US)
KFOR	Kosovo Force
MANPADS	Man-portable Air Defence System
MoD	Ministry of Defence (UK)
NATO	North Atlantic Treaty Organisation
NGO	Non-Governmental Organisation
NSC	National Security Council (US)
OSCE	Organisation for Security and Cooperation in Europe
PGM	Precision-guided Munitions
PMC	Private Military Company
QDR	Quadrennial Defence Review (US)
RMA	Revolution in Military Affairs
RUSI	Royal United Services Institute for Defence Studies
SAM	Surface-to-air missile
SDR	Strategic Defence Review (UK)
UAV	Unmanned Aerial Vehicle
UNMOVIC	UN Monitoring, Verification and Inspection Commission (Iraq)
UNSCOM	UN Special Commission (Iraq)
WHO	World Health Organisation
WMD	Weapons of Mass Destruction

1

THE RECONFIGURING OF WAR

When I was coming up, it was a dangerous world and we knew
exactly who the they were. It was us versus them and it was
clear who them was. Today we're not so sure who the they are,
but we know they're out there somewhere.

George W. Bush, 2000[1]

The survival of liberty in our land increasingly depends on the
success of liberty in other lands ...... America's vital interests
and our deepest beliefs are now one.

George W. Bush, January 2005 Inauguration Speech

To what extent is war itself becoming a risk management strategy? This
book is a study of emerging patterns of contemporary warfare that have
significant implications for grasping the changing character of war. After
all, the West has 'a real problem with the concept of war these days'.[2] While
the modern era was characterised by war or the threat of war between Great
Powers, contemporary conflict involved mostly failed, destabilised or rogue
states and non-state actors. Overturning conventional logic and historical
patterns, these relatively 'weak' entities, rather than powerful ones now
posed primary strategic concerns to the West in an age of globalisation,
contributing to what some see as a new American way of war.[3] Addressing
such conceptual issues as part of the ongoing 'transformation of war'
debate, this book puts in broader perspective Anglo-American campaigns
over Kosovo, Afghanistan and Iraq from 1998 to 2005 that are in some
important aspects not yet fully understood in their entirety.

To begin with, George W. Bush's first set of sentiments quoted above
encapsulated Washington's strategic conundrum perfectly, despite his infamous tortured syntax. Bush and his predecessor Bill Clinton deployed the
greatest military machine in history without the previous Cold War template
to go by, yet myriad elusive enemies remained. The overhauling of doctrinal
and strategic concepts seemed an especially urgent task after the September
11, 2001 terrorist attacks (hereafter 9/11). Yet even before 9/11 fuzzy outlines

1

of a reworked strategic template were already discernible to some extent, albeit in rudimentary form. In a sense, 9/11 only helped consolidate nascent strategic concepts that had previously been emerging. Even legal arguments for action against Iraq in March 2003 exhibited striking continuity with those suggested in December 1998. It did not seem to matter if US Administrations were Republican or Democrat.[4] Throughout the late 1990s and arguably even more so after 9/11, the Clinton and Bush Administrations had in fact waged military campaigns against Kosovo (1999), Afghanistan (1998, 2001) and Iraq (1998–2003) consistently employing the same strategic premise. Clinton's last years in office were spent lobbing cruise missiles at these countries, causing great consternation at the UN – not unlike his successor. Globalised security 'risks' in all three cases had to be tackled proactively declared both Administrations, essentially echoing each other's rationales. Interestingly, this implied continuity in strategic thinking where one might expect discontinuity given the different Administrations and strategic contexts involved.

Furthermore such 'risks' – even catastrophic terrorism – did not constitute existential survival threats equivalent to what the West faced before. The Cold War had generated well-established concepts such as containment, deterrence and 'net assessment' of quantifiable material threats in terms of capabilities and intentions. Bureaucratically, the Pentagon even had its very own Office of Net Assessment under the legendary Andrew Marshall; an indicator of how ingrained the concept was. In contrast, corresponding doctrinal and conceptual approaches to managing hard-to-quantify post-Cold War security risks remained relatively unexplored. This book's main goal is thus to investigate contemporary warfare from a risk management perspective of proactively averting probabilistic scenarios, leading to preventive strategies. This is in contrast to a more orthodox understanding of war involving 'net assessment' and reacting to more 'real' or imminent material threats. This perspective will be illustrated through three case studies – Kosovo, Afghanistan and Iraq – of conflict and strategy in an age of globalised risks.

The second of Bush's statements quoted above is a useful marker for illuminating the ideological development and solidification over four years of his Administration's self-proclaimed mission. Ironically, candidate Bush on the 2000 campaign trail was sceptical of overseas crusades to spread democracy and nation-building, preferring a 'humble' foreign policy. The Bush Administration of 2005 seemed to exhibit exponentially greater clarity of purpose, strategic direction and possibly even suggested that US foreign policy now involved spreading democracy for its own sake, 'unmoored' from the war on terror.[5] Others claim to discern broader political-religious traditions informing the Bush policy's 'utopian' themes of perfecting human life and limiting evil.[6] Nevertheless, closely intertwined with this clearly more messianic tone was a self-interested concern with amorphous dangers essentially akin to that espoused in his first statement about not knowing who the 'they' were now in a time of globalisation. Paradoxically, the more powerful America became the more paranoia and fear seemed to mark its relations with enemy 'others' in distant lands seeking to endanger it.[7] More cynical observers would even suggest that renewed emphasis on freedom and democracy was simply a direct result of Washington's failure to uncover weapons of mass destruction or terrorist links in Iraq, which were the primary justification for war.

Despite its renewed ideological zeal, it may be more accurate to characterise the Bush 'vision' as a blend of opportunities to spread democracy and dangers to manage which are not necessarily exclusive. Its almost Wilsonian 'grand strategy' arguably sees no contradiction between power and principles, tying the spread of democracy with security interests especially after 9/11 in a stable globalised world.[8] These two crucial dimensions of American foreign policy – spreading democracy and managing globalised security risks – are unfolding simultaneously and affected by each other, creating both tensions and synergies. The exigencies of managing risks, for instance, required coddling undemocratic actors such as the Afghan Northern Alliance and Pakistan. Bush was also allergic to 'nation-building' in Afghanistan in that campaign's opening salvos. On the other hand over the longer-term, spreading democracy in the Middle East – 'countries of great strategic importance'[9] according to Bush – forged a synergistic relationship with managing risks by also under-mining the political 'tyranny' that spawned Islamic fundamentalism. Advancing democratic ideals in distant lands had become an 'urgent requirement of our nation's security', given the impact of globalisation.[10] Notwithstanding lofty 'freedom' rhetoric, safety concerns arousing fear and anxiety about vague distant dangers in an age of globalisation remained a powerful undercurrent in 2005 – as they did throughout the 1990s. This book concentrates on these persistent negative undertones to Bush's newfound idealism via a longer-term historical perspective tracing how the Clinton White House through to Bush's second term militarily confronted such risks.

Additionally, conceptual notions in the West commonly associated with expectations of how and what war is *supposed* to be, appear out of sync with the ongoing transformation of war. The iconic image of US Marines victori-ously raising the Stars and Stripes over Iwo Jima after titanic struggles is perhaps one. This public tendency and natural desire for closure mirrors some but fortunately not all military planners and officials. Donald Rumsfeld, one of the more discerning policy-makers who sidestep this conceptual pitfall, suggested that conventional notions of war such as massed armies fighting spectacular decisive battles do not apply to the war on terror and the campaign in Afghanistan. A new vocabulary was needed to reconceptualise war.[11] This was not uniquely a post-9/11 issue. Rumsfeld's predecessor William Cohen noted the Kosovo campaign too fell short of a 'classic definition of war' and struggled to characterise what was actually happening.[12]

The murky realities of war are clearly more complex: there were certainly numerous 'small wars' such as counterinsurgency campaigns or brushfire wars in the past 200 years that did not satisfy such ideal-type criteria. Nonetheless the reification of 'classic' wars endures, explaining current analogies to Pearl Harbour and World War Two. This is of concern, as Rumsfeld noted, not only for simplifying the complex messy realities of wars past and present. Political and strategic ramifications also lurk in failing to come to grips with less than ideal features of contemporary warfare. For instance, public expectations of swift decisive visible successes might be unrealistically high. While there are always entirely valid lessons to be learnt from history, having done that we should jettison misleading historical analogies and comprehend things differently as Rumsfeld suggested.

Two closely related questions flow from these issues:

i   The primary focus of this study is, given the lack of existential survival threats, can Washington's rather frequent campaigns against Kosovo, Afghanistan and Iraq from the late 1990s to 2005 be construed as risk management? Thus, the core hypothesis to be assessed is that, under specific parameters, these wars bore distinctive hallmarks consistent with risk management strategies in terms of impetus, manner and modes of implementation, and outcome evaluation.

ii   The secondary related hypothesis suggests that risk management features define contemporary wars rather than ideal-type notions.

If these claims are to be sustainable, recent wars ought to manifest indicators of risk management concepts and strategies intended to highlight and reduce security risks. Policy-makers should for instance display deep concern for uncertain globalised risk scenarios and adopt precautionary strategies over conventional 'net assessment'. If so, we could then have viable explanations for the reconfiguration of war as risk management. Social science, in developing knowledge to understand important issues should be guided by precision, logical consistency, originality and empirical validity.[13] This opening chapter, and indeed the book as a whole, aspires to these criteria. The task of this chapter is to set out the case for reconceptualising the age-old concern of war. Research parameters are signposted more precisely, to avoid analysis being misapplied where it is not suitable. Finally, I justify the selection and use of case studies that offer insights into the issue at hand.

OLD WINE IN NEW BOTTLES?

For much of the twentieth century, major war between Great Powers was the central security concern most feared and analysed, culminating in worries about nuclear Armageddon. This type of war now appears obsolete.[14]

Great Powers apparently no longer war among themselves. The West was still in the 'war' business but the business at hand had changed significantly. Wary of the changing forms of war, respected military historian John Keegan refrained from defining war in his 1998 BBC *Reith Lectures.* He would only define it minimally as 'collective killing for collective purposes'.[15] The monumental challenge of defining war is beyond our purposes here. Our aim is more modest: simply to explore how war has changed for the West.

John Mueller postulates that the legitimacy and appeal of war in the conduct of relations by and between 'war-averse' Great Powers in the West is in freefall. This was due to a confluence of various trends: economic prosperity, shifting societal attitudes, democracy, new devastating technologies, international norms and institutions, not to mention peculiarities of the post-Cold War international structure.[16] China and Russia were more interested in economic growth than posing existential threats. War for the West has become increasingly remote and distant to the extent of it becoming almost a 'spectator-sport'.[17] It was in the process of being revalued due to deeper shifts in society's moral, philosophical and social basis in a post-metaphysical era.[18]

With the erosion of its romantic appeal and acceptability, the nature of war practised by the Western world became increasingly utilitarian and instrumental, rather than existential or expressive of one's purpose. The idea of fighting for some 'noble' cause was also undermined.[19] War, once a distinct component of modernity and even a proactive historical instrument to bring about human perfection, was no longer seen as such to the same degree.[20] In its day, Pearl Harbour was relished by some as 'the hour for elation', a chance for America to fight for creation of a better world.[21] Although some neo-cons might now see the same opportunity, such self-confident sentiments seem rather alien to the contemporary *zeitgeist.* Pearl Harbour's oft-cited contemporary equivalent 9/11 evoked instead huge doses of anxiety, uncertainty and worst-case risk scenarios.

Rather than major inter-state wars, what we have left, if Mueller is correct, are war's remnants, 'residual warfare' and conflicts within states such as terrorism and ethnic instability.[22] Not strictly speaking wars by Mueller's narrow definition, they do pose policing problems for the West. Indeed, through globalisation, such apparently 'internal' conflicts can easily become internationalised through transnational mechanisms.[23] Given the relative lack of Great Power animosity and immediate survival threats, military action relabelled as 'policing' by the American 'sheriff' to rein in potentially disruptive elements in the international system might well become commonplace in the twenty-first century.[24] This is a significant departure from the past centuries' overriding concern with Great Power rivalry and its consequences. Yet as Lawrence Freedman suggests, 'the strategic language required to describe and analyse such new situations has only developed slowly'.[25] Since they no longer 'do' major wars among themselves, it is suggested in this book that Great Powers like Britain and the US now talk the language of risks and 'do' risk management instead against those entities who pose all the security risks today: destabilised/rogue states and terrorist networks. War is being regrounded in terms of managing risks. So should the appropriate strategic language of analysis.

Recent campaigns over Kosovo, Afghanistan and Iraq certainly have raised issues going to the heart of how we conceptualise war. Although NATO forces were taking and returning fire, the main lesson in Kosovo for Tony Cordesman was 'that war can no longer be called war'.[26] Supreme Allied Commander Europe (SACEUR) General Wesley K. Clark claimed it was 'not really a war'. Clark felt the air operation violated all known principles of war as we know it.[27] If not a war, what was it then? By the 2001 Afghan campaign, US Defence Secretary Donald Rumsfeld was advocating a paradigm shift in conceptualising a new type of war with unseen successes and no clearly defined end in sight. Rumsfeld neglected to note that Washington had already embarked on that war in August 1998 with cruise missiles targeting Afghanistan's terrorist infrastructure – Operation *Infinite Reach*. The 2001 campaign in fact 'bore many hallmarks of Western military operations in the 1990s'.[28] America's first full-scale pre-emptive war on Iraq in 2003 stoked massive controversy over the lack of an imminent threat – a 'smoking gun'. Yet most commentators seemed to overlook similar criticisms about abstract dangers first levelled over Operation *Desert Fox* in December 1998. Rather than simply anomalous occurrences, these examples taken on the whole suggest a need for an overall explanatory framework to rethink these intriguing aspects of war.

This arises also partly because long-held models of war in the West provide a useful, but rather inaccurate 'straw man' as a starting point for analysis of recent wars:

i   the US and UK normally tend to go to war in responsive mode,[29] in response to aggression or well-defined threats, though this has not been the case recently;
ii socio-moral determination, willingness to sacrifice for 'heroic' purposes;
iii rapid decisive battles in titanic force-on-force warfare;
iv visible, preferably spectacular successes and clearly distinct end-points.[30]

To be sure, there are of course differences between America and Europe. America's great wars in the past century might have been all-out wars against adversaries treated as immoral unscrupulous criminals to be totally destroyed. This differed from European conceptions of a more gentlemanly contest between respectable state parties.[31] Nonetheless, taken together these notions served to provide the Western mindset with an intuitive feel of what war should be but one that is prone to mislead. The appeal of such norms derives not only from its black-and-white simplicity but also from the possibility of expecting neat outcomes at the end of it all. A proper appreciation of conceptual challenges resulting from the changing character of war confronting us can be hamstrung by this linearity of thinking. Ironically Clausewitz, from whom such notions and much Western strategic thought are supposedly derived, was a non-linear thinker in a world widely but mistakenly assumed to be linear.[32] Clausewitz's sense of war as such was not an 'idealised analytical abstraction' and neither should ours be.[33]

Notwithstanding some appreciation of 'non-traditional enemies and conflicts', the US *Joint Vision 2020* generally reflected idealised thinking. It acknowledged diverse asymmetric threats but is most applicable in 'traditional force-on force confrontations' where being 'decisive in war' is more attainable.[34] This echoed the 1993 US Army Field Manual 100–5, *Operations*, which summed up the American view of war: 'the American people expect decisive victory', and quickly too. Such views stressing decisive and immediate success of military operations continue to shape policy, despite faulty assumptions about the American people's lack of staying power or casualty intolerance.[35] Indeed this desire for closure informed Bush's ill-advised carrier landing on the *Lincoln* proclaiming 'mission accomplished'. There seems to be anticipation that familiar and preferred forms of war would essentially be replicated.

In fact, Edward Luttwak suggests that the West's 'post-heroic' wars now lack the grand national purposes embodied in the Clausewitzian paradigm. Instead they arouse little public enthusiasm. Clausewitz's Napoleonic-inspired concepts of mass, momentum and quick decisive results from set-piece battles were leading strategists down the wrong path when in fact warfare had changed. In this context, Luttwak contends that only a new concept of war could help account for less decisive cumulative forms of combat that were emerging. This would require cultivating a patient and modest strategic outlook able to appreciate partial results. In a complex globalised interconnected world, a delicate balance had to be struck between doing too much, which might be too costly and disruptive, and simply wringing one's hands, which could impair global stability.[36]

Indeed, viewed collectively, cruise missile strikes in 1998 against Afghanistan and the endless policing of no-fly zones over Iraq before regime change in fact constituted a significant digression from the past emphasis on overwhelming force and decisive outcomes: as low-key bombing became 'routine, it also became non-controversial' and even habitual.[37] Counter-terrorist operations in Afghanistan by 2005 too exhibited this feature. War had become minimalist, more modest in purpose and even routine with little public enthusiasm, creating inconclusive outcomes: all features of war that can best be appreciated through the lens of risk management. The United States has had to redefine 'victory' in these less than decisive operations, as it did three decades earlier in Vietnam. Victory meant persuading the Vietcong

that they could not win, rather than destroying its military forces.[38]
Recognising Cold War constraints and South Vietnamese politics, America
sought not to lose rather than to win. Watered-down definitions of victory
are not unique to the twenty-first century operational environment. Yet
preconceived images of unequivocal successes persist incongruent with war
in its current risk management form.

Every war has its own innate characteristics: its causes, protagonists,
terrain, technology and tactics, casualties sustained and so on. However,
perceptions tend to be influenced by imagery of earlier, especially monumental struggles like World War Two, even in supposedly 'new'
circumstances of any war.[39] As Karl Marx remarked, 'When men make
history, they don't do it in their own clothes, they dress it up in clothes of
the past'.[40] Yet as Holsti pointed out, war is in fact not unchanging but a
dynamic and diverse concept. Indeed, the forms of warfare have diversified
to such an extent that we can no longer see war as a 'single institution of the
states system'.[41] In his seminal *The Transformation of War* Martin Van
Creveld emphasised that Clausewitzian war was not war with a capital 'W'
but merely one of many forms war has assumed throughout history and that
it is changing. We might well be seeing more of non-Trinitarian warfare as
war prepares to 'enter into a new epoch'.[42] The point here is simply that war
is a multifaceted phenomenon that can manifest in various guises, and one
of its contemporary modes might be that of risk management as the West
moves ever deeper into an age of risk. To demonstrate that this is so and
how war might look like as a result is the purpose of this book.

A RISK MANAGEMENT PERSPECTIVE

Students of the 'transformation of war' debate will be mindful of how
changes in both the international structure and domestic societies affect
warfare, with both appearing to be moving in the direction of concepts associated with risk management. These will be addressed in detail in Chapter
Two. At the time of writing no international relations scholars have examined war through the specific prism of 'risk management' in the strategic
sense. Where risk is discussed, it largely involves 'tactical' issues of risk-
averse warfare such as casualty intolerance. In a recent classified study done
for Donald Rumsfeld by Richard Schultz, Tufts University expert on unconventional warfare, even US Special Forces Command was found to be
hamstrung from aggressively hunting Al Qaeda by a culture of 'risk-aversion'
and safety. Other core tactical risk priorities involved minimising casualties
and collateral damage using RMA technologies, waging hygienic 'sanitised'
wars.[43]

Technology plays important parts in contemporary war but it is the
nature of security concerns today and the way we cope with them that are

primary drivers for changes in concepts of war. Analysts for a long while, at least before 9/11, hardly broached the broader questions. Then-Commander of US Pacific Command Admiral Dennis C. Blair once chastised foreign affairs experts for not 'addressing the cosmic issue; everyone's going tactical.' Blair sought strategic guidelines on how Washington should manage its superpowerhood.[44] Rather than add to an already crowded field of tactical risk-averse war, this book considers the broader 'cosmic' question of strategic approaches to war as a tool for managing systemic risks. Such risks relate to changes in the international structure such as globalisation and the end of Cold War constraints.

War has changed substantially in recent years, propelled by transformations in Western societies, globalisation and the international system. These range from society becoming de-bellicised and hardly fired-up for wars or grand purposes, to how we now face not clear military threats from Great Power competition but serious yet ill-defined risks. It is precisely these changes that make the transformation of war debate so dynamic and multi-faceted. War was reconfiguring and reinventing itself in the process. Complex issues such as proliferation and terrorism, previously present during the Cold War, have moved up the security agenda, assuming a new dimension with globalisation and added strategic urgency. These were largely pre-existing issues given a new tinge rather than emerging from out of the blue as we sometimes mistakenly believe. The distinctiveness of issues concerned required an innovative approach more sensitive and attuned to the broader context in which governments, society and the international system have evolved.

In his *magnum opus On War*, Karl von Clausewitz emphasised historicist notions and the need to appreciate historical contexts in the study of war: 'each age has its own kind of war.... its own limiting conditions.... using different methods and pursuing different aims.... Each would therefore also keep its own theory of war'. Rather than 'anxious study of minute details', to understand war we require 'a shrewd glance at the main features.... in each particular age'.[45] Thus, eighteenth century wars to maintain the balance of power reflected a Newtonian fascination with mechanistic structures, and more generally, secular calculability of cause and effects characterising that age.[46] The Cold War too had its own peculiar mode of strategic thinking reflecting ideological struggles of that time.[47] In the post-Cold War era, different analyses of war resulted depending on which features of the age were highlighted. Broad changes in economic and social structures of the West towards a knowledge economy generated what the Tofflers called Third Wave war-forms.[48] The idea of 'post-modern war' on the other hand was anchored in the wider discourse system of 'post-modernity'.[49] Clausewitz's emphasis on the holistic analysis of war and historicism certainly stands the test of time. Such a holistic approach would not be complete without incorporating the foremost concerns of the age: risk.

In October 2002, *Washington Post* columnist Robert Samuelson observed that terrorism, economic uncertainties and war on Iraq were stark 'metaphors for the defining characteristic of our new era.... It is *risk*'.[50] Crucially, does this imply then that recent wars reflect a predominant logic of thinking about the world in terms of managing security risks? Clausewitz's most quoted statement that war is simply the continuation of politics by other means still rings true, even if some aspects of his thought might no longer do so. As Colin Gray, Clausewitz's staunchest defender, argued 'nothing vital to the nature and function of war and strategy changes, in sharp contrast to the character of war'.[51] Political goals have always been central to war despite the different ways we fight. Perhaps war now served as the instrument for political goals of risk management.

Examining policy documents and official justifications for recent wars, a pattern began to emerge – stretching across two very different US Administrations and strategic circumstances – of evidence indicating broadly similar underlying premises. Policy-makers employed the same catch-all phrase 'the risks of inaction outweigh the risks of action' from Kosovo in 1999 to Iraq in 2003. The conventional measurement of threat – capability plus intent – applied to the contemporary security environment provided few answers. While potential peer competitors like China or Russia may eventually develop military forces with intent to harm the West in future, they do not pose an immediate existential threat.[52] Yet many security challenges remain.

Given the difficulties and inadequacies of traditional threat assessments, uncertainty and risks have permeated major American and British defence guidelines. NATO's first post-Cold War *Strategic Concept* in 1991, the UK's 1998 *Strategic Defence Review* (*SDR*) (updated in 2002 after 9/11) and the 2002 US *National Security Strategy* are significant examples. The 1998 *SDR*, for instance, shifted its focus from 'threats' towards 'risks and challenges' such as WMD proliferation, regional instability, massive humanitarian suffering, rogue regimes and terrorism. Britain and its allies had to contemplate 'active management of these risks'.[53] By late 2003, Donald Rumsfeld famously was rapped on the knuckles by the Plain English Campaign for mouthing concepts such as 'unknown unknowns' and 'known unknowns' in his survey of the post-9/11 security environment and the war on Iraq, earning him the 'Foot in the mouth' accolade.[54] Rumsfeld, to the contrary, was speaking cogently in the language of risk and precaution and made perfectly crystal clear sense to students of risk. In fact, it is clear from the somewhat unwarranted condemnation of Rumsfeld that what is lacking so far in public understanding and scholarly analyses of recent wars is due recognition of the role of risk management in its impetus, prosecution and outcome evaluation. Highlighting the presence of these recurrent trends in a systematic manner enriches our understanding of contemporary war.

An analytical framework incorporating risk concepts was thus called for. This appeared to lie outside the field of international relations in sociology and criminology. After all, students of strategy should at least be interested in the ways in which societies conceive and provide for their security.[55] In contemporary Western society, risk management strategies appear most prevalent in crime control. Indeed prominent sociologists Ulrich Beck, Anthony Giddens, Niklas Luhmann and others suggest that the international system itself has become a globalised risk society. Of particular note is Beck's 1992 *Risk Society* and 1999 *World Risk Society* highlighting 'risk management' as a key organising principle in response to new policy challenges. This is intuitively appealing, given the increasing attention paid by mass media and policy-makers to notions of globalisation and reducing risks in all aspects of everyday political life from crime, health and food safety to environmental and economic concerns. Beck further suggests himself to this study for deliberately casting the post-Cold War world in terms of risk and this provides much insight into the complex interplay of risk and international relations. More concerned with global ecological and technological risks, and addressing the terrorism issue only after 9/11, Beck even then said little about war.[56]

Indeed he has been strikingly silent on this issue and, as Hans Joas points out, Beck has not even constructed a bridge between Risk Society's basic features and narrower sociological approaches to war such as the civil-military gap, much less the broader transformation of war debate we are concerned with here.[57] For this reason, following in the spirit of Joas's criticisms of Beck, it is appropriate and timely as well as legitimate to postulate throughout the rest of this book how such a link might look and make the connection to war and international relations.

This emphasis on risk is admittedly not new to military and government analysts; policy documents cited above have reached the same general conclusions as Beck. 'Risks' have long been discussed in defence circles throughout the 1990s under the guise of 'new non-military threats'. Yet this is unsatisfactory, diluting the conventional essence of threat: military capabilities, while misconstruing those of risk. Christopher Dandeker, for instance, suggested that confronting post-Cold war 'risk complexity', it is difficult to specify how a 'bewildering array of risks' (defined as capabilities not matched to intent or vice versa) might become identifiable threats.[58] Dandeker's analysis is more nuanced than most but ultimately still derived from threat benchmarks of capabilities and intents. Celeste Wallander and Robert Keohane also distinguished between risk and threat and how this affects security institutions such as NATO.[59] Risk in their context of institutional alliance theory, largely refers to risk of disputes among members to be managed through better transparency and information. Their understanding of 'risk' describes a situation where states do not threaten due to lack of intentions or capabilities. They similarly fail to make the leap conceptually from components of threat to those of risk (probabilities and consequences).

World Risk Society took the crucial step forward from simply non-military post-Cold War 'threats', into the broader emerging academic discourse of 'risk' emphasising probabilities and consequences, and globalisation. To a greater extent than other analyses, it especially highlighted the probabilistic and anxious ethos, the *zeitgeist* of our globalising age. The result is an anticipatory yet dystopian approach to managing risks of all sorts. It furnishes possible guidelines on how we conceptualise and manage risk, the ethos and strategies adopted and nature of outcomes to expect. Beck has a profound grasp of how society and the globalising world around us are shaped by the dynamics of thinking about and managing risks. His is a 'diagnostic sensitivity to the age' and the sense of an epochal rupture in our time.[60] Military and defence analysts did not provide an equivalent deep-rooted multifaceted framework for conceptualising risk.

Unfortunately, no off-the-shelf 'risk management' framework suitably adapted for the study of war as yet exists. The method employed here therefore seeks to explicate one from sources outside of international relations, such as criminology and sociology, where risk has already been widely studied.[61] This framework is then tested on case studies of recent wars. Risk, according to Anthony Giddens, illuminates core elements of modernity. For our purposes, it can also serve as a useful mode of entry for investigating central features of war as risk management. Risk Society concepts have not yet been applied systematically to war although a research programme on 'reflexive security' is slowly moving beyond the embryonic stage, applying sociological insights from Risk Society to new discourses and practices of international security.[62]

The focus so far by scholars such as Mikkel Rasmussen has been on reconstructing NATO's security policies in terms of risk or the 'securitisation' of risk.[63] These largely constructivist approaches say little about the reinvention of war in managing risks, and furthermore tend not to differentiate clearly enough between 'threats' and 'risks'. Even a more sophisticated analysis, like Chris Coker's 2002 Adelphi Paper *Globalisation of Insecurity: NATO and the management of risk*, appeared more concerned with NATO's transformation to a 'risk community' due to globalisation's security implications. Coker did not focus specifically on how war itself is being transformed. Furthermore, the notion of 'managing risks' in international relations so far implied using institutional membership to entice peacekeeping, negotiations and third-party mediation in dealing with 'risky states' in Bercovitch and Regan's parlance.[64] They did not relate this notion to military force.

RISK SOCIETY'S RISK MANAGEMENT WARS

How then might Risk Society wage war as risk management? Risk Society, broadly speaking, is organised in significant ways around the concept of risk in an age of globalisation. Thinking and decision-making in terms of risk and risk management is an ever-present exercise. A 'reflexive' rationality has emerged, preoccupied with *averting* an array of possible adverse undesirable consequences that may or may not materialise. This is in contrast to the previous more direct linear 'instrumental' rationality, which emphasised calculating and matching means to *attain* desired goals. This implies a significant shift in society's normative basis. Preventively managing globalised risks to calm widely felt anxieties has supplanted the previous concern with producing and distributing goods. The complexities of this framework are not discussed in detail at this stage but one should stress that it is neither particularly attuned to international relations, nor is it solely derived from Beck.

Indeed Beck is certainly not without his flaws. The prophetic tone of his diagnosis of contemporary society is its main appeal but should also be taken with caution as Hans Joas reminds us. Beck's statements are generalised, sweeping, hardly nuanced and to a certain extent exaggerated, giving very short shrift to opposing trends. He stresses epochal breaks in historical continuities at the expense of logical consistencies, and more academic definitional and conceptual issues.[65] Indeed, as will be shown in later chapters, Beck himself hardly supplies an acceptable definition of 'risk'. These posed obstacles to operationalising theories for international relations purposes.

While Risk Society provided the overall context and ethos fuelling its prominence, Beck only emphasised risk management's core importance and broad principles without providing specifics. Perhaps fortunately it is late-modern criminologists who have beat international relations to the post, having already utilised Risk Society ideas to explain the rise of proactive risk management strategies in policing and crime control. Thus, policing concepts from criminology and more specialised risk management textbooks were available to be consulted in consolidating an analytic framework for our purposes. The associated concepts are so broad that it is impossible to assess the various claims advanced. Even defining the slippery terms of risk and risk management itself is a matter of debate to be addressed in detail in Chapter Three. What can be attempted, however, is to identify a group of principles and concepts that collectively constitute 'risk management', as the term is understood here, derived from academic sociological and criminological sources. This aids in development of the following operational indicators with which to evaluate telltale risk management features in war:

i   The impetus for military action arose from pre-existing security risks aggravated by globalisation and end of Cold War constraints. Risk components of probabilities and consequences are increasingly relevant to security planners, undermining 'net assessment' of threats – capabilities and intent.

ii   In implementing risk management, 'active anticipation' and 'reflexive' consideration of possible adverse consequences that have yet to occur drives preventive policy. The precautionary principle guides policy-makers in managing ill-defined risks. Surveillance serves to obtain information as a contributor to preventive action. Minimalist goals involve simply trying to prevent the worst, rather than attaining something 'good' such as 'justice'. 'Reshaping' the environment emphasises reducing opportunities for harm over addressing causes. This papers over moral questions such as justice, guilt and motivations of 'high-risk' individuals, or rehabilitation of failed/failing states. These utilitarian 'safety-first' aspects may even coexist uneasily and conflict with broader ideological narratives such as spreading democracy. Managing risks is a patient ongoing process, which should be as routine as possible.

iii In outcome specification, the minimalist aim of risk management is not to provide perfect solutions, but more modestly to reduce risks and prevent hypothesised future harm. Non-events are thus indicators of success, but risk managers must beware the 'boomerang effect' where action to manage risks can create new unintended ones. The process is dialectical and cyclical rather than linear with clear end-points.

The purpose here is not to reify any 'risk management' model or Beck's works in particular. Rather they provide, like all frameworks, simply the conceptual lens through which deeper dynamics of military campaigns can be methodically analysed. No sustained comparison or critique of contending approaches – such as for instance the continued relevance of Realism in the post-9/11 era[66] – is attempted. The goal here is not so much to assess the ability of competing theories to explain facts. Instead, it is to critically analyse evidence for the ability of risk management to account for specific emerging aspects of contemporary wars by providing a richer framework for discussion, transcending the disciplinary boundaries of international relations.

RESEARCH PARAMETERS

This book is limited to Western wars. For other parts of the world, it should be noted, war for states and non-state actors still involves core values or survival threats rather than security risks to be managed. There is additional need to distinguish between what Colin McInnes termed the transformation of war debate and the Revolution in Military Affairs (RMA) debate.[67] Set squarely within the former, this book analyses how broader changes in the international system and societal trends in the West relate to war, rather than technological innovation. It attempts to advance the transformation of war debate by critically examining trends in recent campaigns that reflect changes with regard to risk management. As with all generalisations, the view of war propounded here requires qualification.

Risk management assumes fundamentally that it is feasible and desirable to proactively reduce risks to a greater extent than during the Cold War, without bipolar constraints and concerns about nuclear escalation. This general assumption underpins our analyses. Thus, Iraq was 'manageable' by force to the extent North Korea was not, given Pyongyang's more advanced nuclear and conventional capabilities.[68] Managing risks ideally entails multiple methods. While diplomacy, poverty, development programmes and other non-military means are equally important, the focus here is on military force. The notion of security risks and thinking in terms of the concept of risk is peculiar to material and historical conditions in the West. However claims of a clear-cut paradigm change where the previous paradigm has been completely displaced must be taken with caution. Threat assessment certainly remains valid, gauging possible peer-competitors like China and Russia and states like Iran and North Korea where possible. The point here is simply that in a globalising world without immediate survival threats, the West has also emphasised elusive security risks.

No paradigm is eternally or universally valid. Only specific case studies from 1998 to 2005 are assessed. Understanding war's underlying features at any given moment in time does not mean it cannot suddenly or even subtly shift to a hugely different pattern. Given the temporal proximity to events in question, caution also needs to be sounded about lacking the considerable benefit of hindsight. As Mao Zedong remarked on the impact of the French revolution in 1789, it was still too early to tell.

The framework applied here inevitably underemphasises certain aspects of wars. Identifying a tendency towards risk notions certainly does not imply an exclusive relationship precluding other motivations. A complex issue like war cannot be simplistically reduced to a 'single factor' explanation; competing rationales often exist. But for the framework to be useful and tested, parameters had to be set. The issue is not whether it explains all anomalies and idiosyncrasies but whether it can explain selected aspects well. The aim is simply to bring to attention in an intellectually engaging manner the relevance of risk notions to understanding war. This book does not assess whether it was somehow 'right' to fight the wars in question nor does it seek to investigate whether risk management was consciously constructed or stumbled into on an ad hoc basis.

Although I discuss the rationale policy makers put forth for war, the finer points of decision-making analysis are not addressed. Instead, the goal is a broader one, to determine if specific repetitive aspects of recent military campaigns such as surveillance operations and 'reflexive' rationality plausibly fall within a conceptual framework of risk management. Furthermore statements by key officials cannot always be taken at face value. There is no sure foolproof way of getting around this methodological issue; policy-makers could be using carefully crafted words to advance other agendas or depict themselves in a more appealing manner. Methodical, systematic and rigorous analysis can at best minimise this problem, but not eliminate it. This is another reason why statements from different sets of officials from different US Administrations from 1998 to 2005 pertaining to the same case study were examined within an overarching framework to demonstrate conceptual consistency in approaches to war. The logic and premise of thinking about risk was essentially the same regardless of the Oval Office's occupant.

Lastly, London and Washington do not necessarily share all common premises nor is it realistic to assume so. Nonetheless, a risk management perspective can demonstrate the similarities they do share. After all, undertaking military operations, often in coalition warfare with both Clinton and Bush, Tony Blair has assumed the mantle of most interventionist post-empire British Prime Minister. Although analysis is inevitably skewed to a large extent towards the American perspective as the 'senior partner', sentiments in London are incorporated to the fullest possible.

AN INTERDISCIPLINARY APPROACH

This book is additionally a response to the high profile of risk management in contemporary society and the wider social sciences. International relations and strategic studies, which have always been interdisciplinary, should incorporate such developments.[69] Kenneth Waltz's *Theory of International Politics*, for instance, demonstrated how concepts from microeconomic theory could be gainfully employed in international relations, despite its flaws. Given new developments in theory and the international structure, international relations could benefit through reconnecting with the research agenda of general social sciences.[70]

Risk studies too is integrating interdisciplinary approaches. It has expanded its original focus on health, personal and environmental risks to genetic and cybernetic technologies but not yet to international security risks.[71] As Johan Eriksson observed, since risk currently dominates and legitimises politics and society, it would 'definitely be an achievement' if specialised scholars in their own sub-fields were able and ready to cross disciplinary boundaries through theoretical cross-fertilisation.[72] This book seeks that sort of academic bridge-building, between thematically related but academically dissociated fields of international relations, sociology and criminology.

CASE STUDIES

To determine the empirical validity and logical consistency of the framework developed, three case studies are examined. Each opens with a short historical primer, and discusses particular conceptual issues. A structured comparison approach to all cases is then applied using a common set of structured questions to key issues, assessing if results match predictions. This helped ensure consistency in analysis but is not infallible as sometimes outcomes may be driven by independent variables omitted, or other non-comparable aspects of cases. The aim here is not to produce claims covering all possible scenarios but to generate contingent generalisations, within specific parameters stated. Thus it might be more precise to classify the analytical perspective adopted as a 'framework' rather than a 'theory' in the positivist scientific sense, generating deterministic law-like statements. These can be counterproductive and lead to a mechanical, inflexible mentality that is easily overwhelmed by fluidity of events.[73] Furthermore case studies do not cover all aspects of events, only those relevant to the research agenda.

To assess the broadest possible applicability of the risk management framework, case studies were deliberately chosen spanning different strategic circumstances (before and after 9/11) and geographical regions, across different US Administrations. The UK Blair government, in office throughout the period in question, served as a useful constant in the analysis. Case studies were selected where there was sufficient documentation to analyse, and controversies surrounding them were most illustrative of the new security environment: globalisation, destabilised states, rogue states and terror networks. The Kosovo and Afghanistan campaigns in particular went beyond the traditional strategic focus of US planners on Western Europe, East Asia and the Persian Gulf. These implications have yet to be clearly sketched. Case studies also involved probabilistic worst-case scenarios, and dramatic media-enhanced consequences of possibly catastrophic scale. Risk theorists suggest these fulfilled criteria that would garner the significant 'attention of policy-makers.

Numerous instances abound of Western military intervention in the 1990s. The three cases selected, however, further satisfied a key criterion. Relatively intense and sustained levels of lethal military force were clearly employed from the beginning. These cases also approximated most closely to 'war', and were commonly labelled as such by commentators. This meant omitting comparatively short and sharp uses of force such as Operation *Deliberate Force* over Bosnia in 1995 (certainly sustained for a month but relatively less intense than Kosovo and not as commonly referred to as 'war') and Sierra Leone in 1999; or the Somalia intervention in 1992–4, which evolved from a feeding operation to a more military one. Kosovo was thus chosen based on the sustained period of military force employed from the onset, being NATO's largest operation ever. Afghanistan and Iraq, apart from being the focus of significant and sustained US military action, additionally were examples of military action spanning two Administrations – Clinton and Bush. This helped to identify common characteristics and shared rationales, which endured beyond the changeover in Administrations.

17

The Kosovo campaign of 1999 introduced valuable variables into the analysis, undertaken by a different US Administration under President Clinton in greatly differing circumstances. This case involved a state racked by internal strife rather than a rogue state or terror networks. One can also assess applicability of the conceptual premises of risk management prior to 9/11. Risks in Kosovo were not as interconnected as Iraq and Afghanistan were in terms of terrorism. Yet while concerns about ethnic cleansing and humanitarian intervention are of a somewhat different strategic mould, they still fall under the broader rubric of systemic risk conceptualised through the prism of globalisation. Kosovo also shared similarities with Iraq in 2003, undertaken without explicit UN Security Council authorisation.

Events in Iraq from 1998 to 2005 contained significant implications for concepts of war. Overlapping time frames across the Clinton and Bush Administrations complicated analysis but it also strengthened the analysis presented here by introducing a longer-term perspective rather than a stand-alone one focused only on immediate events. Methodologically, Iraq posed significant challenges to the hypothesis examined here, introducing a powerful set of different variables into the equation. It involved campaigns prosecuted by two Administrations – from *Desert Fox* through the no-fly zone skirmishes, to regime change in 2003. It concerned more strategic than humanitarian motives of Kosovo; garnered much less legitimation than the 2001 Afghan campaign; and involved a far narrower coalition. Security risks evolved from simply WMD proliferation to include terrorism as well after 9/11. Most significantly, Bush moved further along the 'escalation ladder' towards regime change and democracy-building that could nullify what is being claimed here. Elimination and grand narratives are not normally part of the risk management repertoire. How would the framework fare given these developments?

As the foremost example of globalised security risks from terrorism, Afghanistan was selected not simply because it formed part of President Bush's 'first war of the twenty-first century', where Donald Rumsfeld and America's top soldier General Richard Myers called for 'new thinking'. Afghanistan had also been target of cruise missiles before in 1998 under Clinton and this again provided important historical perspective to more recent events. For methodological purposes, as a control mechanism it also introduced different variables to the equation to see if this would alter predicted outcomes. It was more or less sanctioned by UN Security Council authorisation, had broad international political, legal and military support, in response to a direct attack on the US homeland. Afghanistan seemed to be more a war of 'no choice' than the 'war of choice' that Kosovo and Iraq seemed to be. Yet operational indicators unearthed in all three campaigns according to the framework of risk management remain broadly similar. Perhaps the time of risk had well and truly descended upon us, casting its long shadow and extensive influence over the art of warfare in the West too.

2

THE DAWN OF A RISK AGE
From Cold Warriors to risk managers

RISK IN OUR WORLD

With the end of Cold War ideological conflicts followed by the events of September 11 2001, concepts, policies and trends relating to risk have become more pronounced in both domestic societal issues and those of international relations. In some cases, these became especially amplified after 9/11. Precisely what these developments are and how they might have bearing on specific aspects of recent military campaigns remains to be systematically mapped, given our intention to contribute to the 'transformation of war debate'. To place this book in its international and domestic context and suggest how Cold War mentalities might be giving way to risk-oriented thinking is thus the task of this chapter. One needs first of all to be conscious of historical precedence in the Cold War to what are sometimes touted as 'novel' features of the contemporary strategic landscape. This makes for a more nuanced and circumspect analysis. After which it is appropriate to consider changes in the nature of post-Cold War security challenges and the impact of globalisation on strategic thinking. The shift in emphasis from 'reactive' containment and specific 'threat-based' approaches, towards 'preventive' policies and more ambiguous 'risk-based' scenarios — is certainly suggestive of policy space opening up for rethinking war as proactive risk management.

It is not international relations scholars, however, but sociologists and criminologists who have so far dominated policy studies on risk management and globalisation through seminal texts such as *Risk Society* and related concepts of reflexive modernity. These will be examined in detail here. Yet being more concerned with societal contexts, they have not forged the link to war, a topic for which tantalising implications can be drawn but which remains somehow strangely distant for sociologists. International relations should thus make the opening move, for key emerging sociological and criminological ideas about risk are calling out to be applied to the study of war. As will be shown, the timing is certainly right.

STRATEGIC TRANSITIONS

This is not the place to examine Cold War strategic thought in detail. What follows is a brief, and necessarily crude, summary. The purpose here is to stress that apparent strategic transitions should not be construed in simple black-and-white tones. Bipolar certainties, nuclear deterrence, bloc discipline and arms control were major regulating instruments of the Cold War. In its aftermath, neat bipolar symmetries have supposedly been replaced by 'strategic uncertainty' and 'asymmetry' in US policy documents.[1] That said, one should not exaggerate relative clarity of the Cold War. Precise assessment was elusive, and as now, we also tended towards worst-case scenarios — most notably the alleged Bomber Gap, Missile Gap and windows of vulnerability. In fact, there was much more indeterminacy and an 'American tendency to exaggerate' threats.[2] As Senator Vandenberg suggested to President Truman in 1947, the best way to mobilise the American people against communism was to 'scare the hell' out of them.[3] This sounds very much like a tactic straight out of today's rule-book. At least in the Cold War, there were concrete enemies embodied in a physical territory and real material military threats to calculate and assess. Now both are elusive, given the focus on probabilistic risk scenarios.

Deterrence and containment as major Cold War policies translated into largely reactive strategic postures. Deterrence was founded on calculation by adversaries of a possible nuclear response to aggression. It entailed no active measures.[4] Despite containment's numerous mutations, its essence was also clear. Argued historian John Gaddis, it 'implied a defensive orientation, *reacting* to rather than initiating challenges'.[5] However, current suggestions of a complete break with reactive policies in favour of proactive ones are historically inaccurate. Much as we discussed 'anticipatory self-defence' in 2003 against Iraq, this had been invoked previously before in blockading Cuba during the 1962 Missile Crisis. 'Preventive war' before Moscow became strong enough also had some credence in the Cold War.[6] John Kennedy seriously considered destroying nascent Chinese nuclear facilities.[7] Pre-emption is thus not entirely novel within a broader historical perspective.

Strategic Air Command in the 1950s had planned for pre-emptive nuclear strikes. The Grenada and Panama campaigns were partly justified on pre-emptive grounds.[8] 1998 cruise missile strikes against Afghanistan, and the 1999 Kosovo campaign were examples of pre-emption in varying degrees. Pre-emption has been around for years, employed by both Republican and Democrat Administrations.[9] These ideas clearly have historical precedence. Moscow and Beijing were however major powers seeking to retool the existing system and could pose serious threats. Today's tin-pot dictators, rogue states and terrorists do not menace the foundations of the whole system to the same extent; rather they pose systemic risks to be managed.

Furthermore, without an overarching global strategic competition to consider, proactive concepts are now more 'actionable' on a larger scale.

The Cold War's nebulous end produced no winners:[10] the US too suffered socio-economic decay, while dubious interventions undermined its moral standing then as it does now. War seemed to be the only winner as it still endures albeit in different modes.

INTO THE UNKNOWN: THE POST-COLD WAR WORLD

Two key drivers drive security thinking and in turn frameworks for conceptualising war today: post-Cold War uncertainty and the security implications of globalisation. The late Gerry Segal once remarked the 'Great Book' providing the 'Great Explanation' for the post-Cold War era still eludes us. *Foreign Policy* even offered cash prizes for a term to encapsulate this new age! In a sense this is not new: after World War Two, there was no clear framework until NSC-68 of 1950. Without serious military or ideological challenges, foreign policy lacked a 'strategic guidepost'.[11] Arguably, 9/11 has given America a new sense of direction but even the very serious challenges of catastrophic terrorism, argued neo-Realist Kenneth Waltz, were hardly equivalent to overwhelming survival threats posed by the Soviet Union.

This being the case, Colin Powell warned back in 1992 in his capacity as Chairman of the Joint Chiefs of Staff, 'the real threat we now face is the threat of the unknown, the uncertain'.[12] The Pentagon spawned 'Uncertainty Hawks' who deemed any remotely possible danger worthy of attention.[13] CIA Director James Woolsey provided another memorable description: the US had slain the Soviet dragon but now faced a jungle of poisonous snakes. President Clinton noted that NATO, the premier Cold War institution which had emerged victorious, was now reoriented towards managing vague insecure and unpredictable conditions, rather than confronting a hostile bloc.[14] In 1999, then US Army Chief of Staff General Eric Shinseki called for a shift in thinking from 'traditional enemies' to what he called 'complicators' such as terrorists. September 11 only confirmed this trend. The nature of security problems had changed; so should approaches towards tackling these problems. Cold Warriors were in need of a makeover.

A clearly identifiable Soviet threat and ideological conflicts replaced by diffuse dangers produced in its stead a vague sense of insecurity. The Cold War was at its core driven by a mutual belief in historically inevitable confrontation between alternative sets of universal ideologies.[15] Lacking ideological challengers for much of the post-Cold War era, Clintonian America wielded power globally without a project or historical purpose and 'meaning'; it appeared more inclined to manage problems with minimal sacrifices if possible.[16] Such an ethos paralleled that of risk management.

Without a greater sense of purpose or meaning, responsibilities were measured in utilitarian cost terms, especially before 9/11.[17]

America's reticence appeared to have been overcome after 9/11. As Bob Woodward noted in *Bush at War*, the President liked 'casting his mission and that of the country in the grand vision of God's master plan'.[18] Bush's belated conversion to moralistic and markedly ideological tones, it must be said, appeared to signal a return to Cold War-style moral emphases on a contest between values. This time, it was between 'democracy' and 'tyranny' in the so-called Freedom Speech at his second inauguration in 2005. Cohen and Bacevich suggest Americans had an 'unsubtle strategic culture' and do not like murky causes, but prefer clear noble objectives and enemies — an idealised notion of war as I have earlier suggested.[19] Bush in his ideological incarnation could well have given America what it wanted. Such ideological narratives retain significant and considerable political–moral clout. However, radical Islam probably does not have the same appeal beyond its own cultural areas that communism had, nor does it pose the same set of challenges.[20] Furthermore Bush's ideological turn is hardly clear-cut. His rhetoric continues to exhibit considerable anxiety about amorphous dangers in an age of globalisation.

In this specific context, the more modest, even dystopian language of risk and precaution has simultaneously assumed greater prominence. Media reports on Bush's first *National Security Strategy* (NSS), for instance, focused almost exclusively on 'pre-emption'. The NSS actually did espouse grand visions of spreading democracy and liberty as well, but 'pre-empting' dangers seemed to capture the public imagination to a greater degree — perhaps a reflection of predominant societal anxieties preoccupied more with fear, safety and risk than democratic ideals. To Mary Douglas, risk seems to have resonance with political claims in vogue, 'the language of risk is reserved as specialised lexical register for political talk about undesirable outcomes'.[21] Risk legitimises or discredits policy, and can be a political weapon to blame others for bads that happen. Politicians declaring something 'at risk' are more likely to get attention and get the nation focused on an issue. Yet risk can be equally as divisive, as intense arguments over the actual level of pre-war risks posed by the Iraq issue adequately show.

American strategists seem caught between a rock and a hard place. Playing down previous talk of pre-emption and risks, Bush's convincing re-election and championing of freedom in fact masks considerable anxiety among foreign policy elites and the general public about the direction of US foreign policy, especially after the failure to find WMD in Iraq. America is increasingly split among rural/urban, north/south, Christian evangelical/secular. Bush is perhaps the most polarising president in recent times,[22] and it is hard to say for sure how far his talk of spreading democracy goes down with such a divided nation. Indeed, recent polls seem to indicate Bush's foreign policy goals are not particularly appealing, with majorities thinking the White House's priorities were not those of most Americans.[23] As the ever-perceptive *Atlantic Monthly* drily observed, few in Congress nowadays view foreign affairs solely as an overarching moral contest of values and ideals. There is little popular enthusiasm for war as an opportunity to spread democracy and freedom. War is reluctantly undertaken with resolve but with obsessive awareness of limits.[24] A distinct lack of 'confidence in America's ability to improve the world' characterises the 'modest' wars it currently fights.[25]

The searing experience of post-war difficulties in Iraq will probably not alter this reticence. Strong presidential leadership attempted to focus the public on the broader issues of spreading democracy – public support did rise after relatively peaceful Iraqi elections were held in late January 2005. Support, however, has since plunged with the continued violence. As part of this pattern of recognising limits, European responses to African crises too have shifted from long-term development aid, towards managing conflicts. Failed and underdeveloped states are no longer seen solely in terms of their potential for progress and development. They are viewed increasingly in terms of the risks they posed from epidemics, refugees, terrorists, crime, drugs and wars, especially with the advent of globalisation.[26] Military intervention may be necessary if security risks for the West become intolerable.[27] Cold Warriors may just have morphed into risk managers.

From threats to risks

Security challenges to the West such as crime and terrorism are clearly different in nature from what it was accustomed to. The conventional 'net assessment' model of 'threat' that guided the Cold War depended on two components: assessing intentions of the Soviet Union and measuring capabilities in actuarial terms counting tanks and military hardware.[28] The groundbreaking US security document NSC-68 of 1950 described a specific threat from Moscow in terms of its hostile designs/intentions and formidable capabilities. Even with détente, threat always remained because it was defined as 'capabilities' rather than 'intent'.[29] The threat was more estimable and material; the logic behind the balance of terror ensured it was relatively calculable, according to means-end rational rules of deterrence.[30] Touting 'perfect solutions' to threats such as the Strategic Defence Initiative (SDI), America could in theory be made invulnerable to the dangers states have historically faced from conventional military attack.

Strategic planning in the Cold War largely focused on either repelling Soviet armoured thrusts through the Fulda Gap or nuclear deterrence. The rules of the game were relatively established. As Paul Wolfowitz lamented, 'during the Cold War, our security environment had an appearance of predictability'.[31] The twenty-first century risk age is not nearly as clear. Both sides during the Cold War at least possessed greater amounts of what

Giddens called ontological security — the knowledge of roughly what to expect.[32] School children practised drills for nuclear fallout. In contrast, 'living in an age of constructivism', the future is now viewed in unpredictable terms of multiple, even infinite probabilistic scenarios of what *may* or may not potentially transpire.[33] Ill-defined risk is becoming the key operative concept of Western security.[34]

Contemporary security problems are no longer addressed solely in terms of concrete capabilities and intentions. NATO's first post-Cold War *Strategic Concept* issued in November 1991 and updated in 1999 is worth quoting, illuminating the new environment of amorphous 'risks'. It described 'Security Challenges and Risks' where:

> in contrast with the predominant threat of the past, the risks to Allied security that remain are multi-faceted in nature and multi-directional, which makes them hard to predict and assess ... a great deal of uncertainty about risks to the security of the Alliance remain. [35]

Such risks included ethnic conflict, infectious diseases, economic collapse, proliferation, terrorism, crime and drug trafficking to name a few. One consequence of this was that humanitarian intervention had supposedly become in the words of Michael Ignatieff, the 'chief raison d'etre for Western armies'.[36] A combination of militarily pre-eminent America, a globalising world without clear survival threats and porous borders translated into an emphasis on such elusive risks hard to define and defend against. This arose during the Clinton administration and continued into the Bush years. Bush warned of car bombers and plutonium merchants, cyber terrorists and unbalanced dictators — sentiments that distinctly mirror the web site of the Clinton White House.[37] The Bush foreign policy circle did however initially evince a more Realist state-centric world-view focused on China, rogue states and missile defence than transnational dangers which preoccupied Clinton. September 11 recalibrated its world-view towards a greater focus on transnational challenges although it continued to highlight rogue states. By 2002, Bush's *National Security Strategy* had formally enshrined the shift away from measuring concrete threats. It noted how adversaries previously required massive military and industrial capabilities to harm America. Now elusive networks of individuals could inflict devastating destruction for less than the cost of a single tank.[38]

Donald Rumsfeld even before 9/11 eschewed the previous threat-based approach focused on the Soviet Union. Instead, he envisioned a 'paradigm shift' towards addressing uncertain risks, which could not be pinpointed specifically by country. Not knowing what dangers would arise, US capabilities had to be able to handle a wide range of likely future challenges.[39] Apparently, America doesn't 'do' countries by name exclusively anymore. It also does 'uncertainties'.[40] Grappling with uncertainty has been installed as 'a central tenet in US defence planning.'[41] As Paul Wolfowitz declared after 9/11, 'the era of invulnerability is over'.[42] Perfect security is even more of a chimera with globalisation and uncertainties. Thinking about safety in the West today, notes Ole Waever, is more about managing risks than achieving perfect security.[43]

Reactive versus proactive strategies

How might this have affected security policy? In the Cold War, Washington relied on containment and designed its military forces to *react* in case it failed.[44] Its strategic orientation was essentially reactive. In contrast, Bush's watershed *National Security Strategy* officially crystallised the proactive calculus of risk. Declaring the obsolescence of a 'reactive posture' of containment and deterrence, it plumped instead for anticipatory actions 'even if uncertainty remains as to time and place of the enemy's attack.'[45] Cold War deterrence, it argued, was effective against a status quo enemy who viewed nuclear weapons as last resort. It fails against an enemy seeking wanton destruction and martyrdom.

In the absence of imminent clearly defined Cold War threats, proactive policies have come to the fore addressing more amorphous concepts like 'danger'.[46] Such 'dangers' should not be mismanaged and allowed to develop into full-scale threats. The emphasis should be on forestalling such risks through what Carter and Perry termed 'Preventive Defence' using a whole array of policy tools. Furthermore with globalisation, dangers stem from diffused processes rather than traditional premeditated aggression. Strategies of 'prevention' are more suitable than 'reaction'.[47] Issues such as proliferation, environmental decay and diseases require prevention since it is relatively more difficult to clearly identify a particular agent to *react* against, compared to traditional aggressors.

The term 'pre-emptive' however is not unique to the Bush Administration. In December 1993, then Defence Secretary Les Aspin, unveiling the Defence Counterproliferation Initiative, was widely seen as suggesting that Washington could deal with rogue states in either a reactive or pre-emptive mode.[48] Loosening nuclear use was not initiated by the Bush Administration. During the Clinton era, it was already being suggested that nuclear weapons could be used to deny states with only 'prospective access' to WMD.[49] Mutually Assured Destruction no longer applied between Washington and potential proliferates. This removed many constraints as the RMA made force usable again without fear of nuclear escalation.[50] The Clinton Administration felt it now could militarily deny proliferants rudimentary second-strike capabilities without paying too high a price.[51] Official documents such as the Bush Administration's still-classified 2001 *Nuclear Posture Review* continue to reflect this proactive logic. Judging from snippets leaked to the media, it appeared to be pondering more scenarios for first use of new low-yield 'bunker-busters'. While counter-proliferation previously embraced diplomatic measures such as the Non-Proliferation Treaty, Washington is now apparently considering proactive risk-based military strategies.

The realignment towards 'prevention' and proactive policies has become a key theme in international relations. The notion of 'prevention' has also evolved in the process. It previously implied non-military means such as monitoring, or preventive diplomacy as an alternative to military force. As Francois Heisbourg recently pointed out, preventive actions in fact now actually entail military force to avert undesirable outcomes or prevent another party developing a threatening military capability.[52] War as a risk management strategy fits perfectly in this context with its proactive emphasis on preventing some hypothesised future harm from occurring.

Another proactive strategy favoured in Washington was to 'shape the international environment', although this officially did not mean military force. This catch-all phrase, first coined by the Clinton Administration in the mid-1990s, formed the bedrock of the 2000 *National Security Strategy* and 1997 *Quadrennial Defence Review*. The aim according to Defence Secretary William Cohen was to: 'shape other people's opinions about us in favourable ways. To shape events that would affect our livelihood and our security'.[53] The 1998 *Annual Defence Report to Congress* outlined the key goals:

i   fostering an international environment where critical regions are stable;
ii   democratic norms and human rights are widely accepted;
iii the spread of WMD is minimised.[54]

This previously meant defence diplomacy, port visits, and joint training exercises. However, Andrew Bacevich observed that the post-9/11 American reliance on using military force implied new opportunities to 'shape the environment'.[55] US military might after all has been crucial in 'reshaping the international environment' over the past five years: Kosovo in 1999, Afghanistan in 2001 and Iraq in 2003.[56] In 2002, Geoff Hoon noted in the New Chapter to Britain's *Strategic Defence Review* that expeditionary operations from the Balkans to Afghanistan had 'enabled the UK to have a key role in shaping the international security environment'.[57] More interestingly, as we shall see in Chapter Three, 'reshaping' environments is also a risk management strategy popular in criminology.

Globalisation as security paradigm

Changes in thinking about security policy highlighted above were to a large extent prompted by the recognition of globalisation's security dimensions.[58] Globalisation in particular provided the framework for thinking about elusive security risks spreading beyond boundaries. Globalisation, declared

Thomas Friedman, is not just a trend or fad but the new international system that has emerged in place of the Cold War.[59] The US National Intelligence Council report *Global Trends 2015* described globalisation as a key driver that will shape the world of 2015. Tony Blair observed in his famous speech on the *Doctrine of the International Community* that rather than clarity of the Cold War, a new framework for thinking about security and war was required. State survival for the West was hardly under threat from an external aggressor. Furthermore the world had 'changed in a more fundamental way' through globalisation. Blair warned 'globalisation is not just economic. It is also a political and security phenomenon.'[60] Many domestic problems, he noted, are caused by distant issues: Balkan conflicts also created more refugees for Britain and America. Much of the heroin on British streets came from Afghanistan. Indeed rather than states maximising opportunities for citizens in the global marketplace as Philip Bobbitt suggests, the security dimension of globalisation might mean states having to devote more resources to minimise risks instead for their peoples. The resulting 'overall security paradigm' was one where globalisation created new vulnerabilities but pre-eminent America and the West had the necessary military capacity to cope.[61]

There are however clear historical precursors to globalisation in the pre-World War One era. Indeed some claim it is hardly new in the broader historical scheme of things. After all, more than 55 years ago, Franklin Roosevelt's final inaugural address noted an individual state's well-being was dependent on nations far away. What difference does contemporary globalisation make? Furthermore, issues such as terrorism (PLO) and proliferation (India, Pakistan, Israel) existed even during the Cold War. Fears of Balkan instability date to the late nineteenth century. So does 'economic interdependence' and free trade.

Put simply, Roosevelt's point is of even greater resonance than before. Although interdependence is hardly novel, it occurs far more rapidly. Fuelled by new communication and transport technologies, increased intensity, velocity and impact of global flows of people and materials, it can be dangerous to neglect zones of instability although this does not apply uniformly across the board. Taliban Afghanistan was a case in point. Globalisation has heightened not only awareness but also potential vulnerability to indirect impact of distant events. Undermining distinctions between 'inside' and 'outside' and material threat assessments, it presents instead a difficult probabilistic dilemma of action or inaction especially if security challenges are involved. Essentially it means contemplating various what-if risk scenarios and how to manage them.

Globalisation however does not necessarily produce security risks in the first place. Ethnic cleansing did not result from globalisation per se but other issues such as tensions in Kosovo. Al Qaeda was aggrieved more by US foreign policies it detested. Globalisation does, however, exacerbate pre-existing risks. Its effects are not uniform. While many benefit, others ranging from disaffected Islamists to far-right American 'Patriots', resent its encroachment and turn it against its supporters. More ominously, globalisation provides also the means and access to potentially destructive information and technologies — previously only available to states.

Globalisation might have been largely a US initiative and benefit but also exposed it to risks by crucially providing the interface and infrastructure for security risks spreading, especially highlighted by 9/11. The December 1999 US *National Security Strategy* was unequivocal: 'globalisation also brings risks'.[62] This document, often seen as the clearest indicator of an Administration's strategic approach to the world, described risks spreading halfway around the world in the form of ethnic conflicts, weapons of mass destruction and terrorism, diseases and environmental degradation. NATO's 1999 *Strategic Concept* talked up these same security risks. Indeed the term 'proliferation' now describes any of the above transnational dangers that can spread across porous boundaries, apart from its original meaning relating to WMD.[63] Such 'systemic risks' relate to the globalised international structure and erosion of Cold War restraints.[64] These are in need of management since security is, more than ever, seen as indivisible in an increasingly interdependent world.

Even the proliferation of water hyacinths proliferating in Africa's Lake Victoria concerned US intelligence. According to the predominant probabilistic mode of thinking about worst-case scenarios, this could trigger negative chain-reactions leading to regional conflict. Indeed, depending on how nervous one is, an inclusive concept of security could include anything that causes an apparent insecurity.[65] Our current risk age is very jittery indeed. This affects how policy-makers have justified responses to risks, real or perceived. Increasing numbers of globalised contingent events can affect large numbers of people. To policy-makers, the logic of globalisation, if taken to its logical conclusion, meant that human rights abuses, war or poverty around the world could eventually have an impact of some kind. America after 1945 sought to make the world safe for democracy. In the new millennium, globalisation had to be made safe for the world, given its security implications. Events such as 9/11, and ethnic cleansing in Kosovo thus came to be seen as part of the globalisation motif. What currently animates the West's security agenda and its anxieties is the need to combat such 'security risks'.

Another key factor in the globalised strategic equation was the spectre of failed states, much talked about also during the Clinton years but placed at the heart of security policy by the Bush Administration. The US *National Security Strategy* released in September 2002 and the UK MoD's Joint Doctrine and Concepts Centre report *Strategic Trends* published in March 2003, both identified failed or failing states as primary security dangers exacerbated by globalisation, rather than powerful all-conquering states as conventional logic and historical evidence would suggest. President Bush explains: 'America is now threatened less by conquering states than we are by failing ones.... Weak states like Afghanistan can pose as great a danger to our national interests as strong states'.[66] This can be attributed to how the notion of globalised risk overturns strategic logic. Even the greatest powers like the US and UK with unassailable military capabilities now feel insecure, rather than secure, from ostensibly 'weak' actors like failed states.

UK Foreign Secretary Jack Straw, speaking at Birmingham University on 6 September 2002, introduced the 'at risk' concept, ranking states according to 'risk factors' of how likely they are to collapse. Especially after 9/11, this was a key strategic imperative. Just as multinationals and medical practitioners practise risk assessment, Straw contended that governments needed to make similar calculations at the core of foreign policy. This 'risk' concept arguably raised related questions of 'management' and what tools to adopt, including military force if necessary. Whereas ideology in the Cold War and superpower competition determined which nominally unimportant territory attracted strategic interest, now it is globalised risks. Policy-makers have started talking the talk in terms of risks. Whether they will also walk the walk by waging war as risk management is a question with far-reaching consequences for international relations.

FRONTRUNNERS: SOCIOLOGISTS AND THE RISK SOCIETY

Yet it was sociologists, not international scholars, who did all the initial running in exploring the contemporary political importance society placed on risk and risk management. These sociological trends, in combination with developments in the international structure observed earlier, in turn hold significant implications for the transformation of war debate and in particular our reinterpretation of war as risk management. The *Risk Society* thesis of sociologists Niklas Luhmann, Ulrich Beck, Anthony Giddens and others offers a core but by no means exclusive, conceptual foundation. Indeed even they disagree among themselves on certain issues. Theorists John Adams and Mary Douglas who do not necessarily fall within the Risk Society fold also made noteworthy contributions. Yet the specific connection to war as a risk management exercise remains elusive, with sociologists operating alas on somewhat tangential paths as if never the twain would they meet.

Ulrich Beck

Risk Society, which provided much of the rationale and motivation for this study, was first translated into English in 1992.[67] The foremost proponent of risk and its political impact, Beck was mainly concerned with nuclear power, radioactivity and environmental degradation. Predominantly a sociology thesis about theories of 'reflexive modernisation', it ostensibly had nothing to add to our knowledge of war. Its contents and concerns were largely not examined in detail by international relations theorists or cited in international relations literature for much of the 1990s. In fact, *Risk Society* merits much closer scrutiny. If Beck's assertion that risks have redefined the post-Cold War world is correct, the critical question that arises is whether war too is being reconfigured as risk management in the process?

It was only later that Beck's *World Risk Society* (1999) and *What is Globalisation?* (2000) related more closely to international relations.[68] These works suggested how the world was moving from clearly identifiable enemies, to dangers and risks to fill the enemy vacuum. Still a sociologist at heart, Beck dwelt mainly on the implications of a shift to a global ecological and financial Risk Society, for democratisation, politics of risk-definition, and decision-making processes within domestic society. In its focus on globalisation, this was perhaps an archetypal text of the period, although Beck adopted a rather more sociological perspective. He initially stopped short of the next logical step: namely, of analysing the refugee flows, transnational terrorism, and WMD proliferation he had already identified as new systemic risks.[69] These had broken out of Cold War security structures, aided by globalisation, constituting a 'new source of danger'.[70] However, his prescription of a transnational 'cosmopolitan manifesto' rather optimistically assumes that global risks create 'risk communities', where people negotiate rather than fight.[71]

September 11 provided the stimulus for Beck's first concerted foray into international relations, contributing to a collection of essays edited by the Foreign Policy Centre in London and an LSE public lecture on the topic. Global terror now formed one of Beck's three 'axes of world risk society' besides ecological conflict and financial crises.[72] Even then, he did not address how force might be used to manage risks. Instead, Beck continued to argue that globalised terror created new possibilities for a cosmopolitan state sharing solidarity with foreigners. This, he claimed, was the last bond in a world where God, nations and historical purpose are increasingly disavowed. Beck's laudable goal however remains distinctively long-term. It is regretfully inadequate against urgent risks posed by Al Qaeda, requiring new control mechanisms involving war as a risk management strategy.

THE RISK SOCIETY

Notwithstanding its prescriptions for cosmopolitanism being somewhat off the mark, *World Risk Society* encapsulates the current state of our world and supplies important analytical guidelines for reconceptualising contemporary war and its dynamics. What follows is thus a hopefully concise summary of its main features drawn mainly from Beck, his close collaborator Giddens, and fellow German Niklas Luhmann, which have been filtered for their relevance. The complete agenda is far broader than my present concerns for which specific concepts also had to be whittled down or supplemented. Beck and Giddens, like all academics, have their detractors. The focus here is not debating the validity of their propositions — indeed some of Beck's conclusions are inadequate, as is his very narrow definition of risk. Rather, my concern is distilling their insights for application to international relations. The following key concepts are flagged for discussion, as interlinked notions rather than strictly segregated ideas:

i   reflexive modernisation;
ii   active anticipation;
iii manufactured insecurity and global risks;
iv   Risk Society's minimalist ethos.

Risk Society, broadly speaking, is organised in significant ways around the concept of risk and increasingly governs its problems in terms of discourses and technologies of risk.[73] Rather than post-modernism, which sees politics as at an end, risk is a dynamic force for change. How we interpret risk, negotiate and live with it will structure our culture, society and politics for coming decades.[74] Politics has taken on new meaning and importance in terms of risk. Risk assessment and management have assumed almost mythical status. As a Cabinet Office Strategy Unit report noted, 'the language of risk is now used to cover a wide range of different types of issues' from terrorism to BSE, and railways.[75] Much contemporary public discourse appears geared to warnings about risks. In Britain, even gardening was labelled 'the ultimate danger sport' in March 2003 with gardening injuries reportedly soaring. In February 2005, British consumers were gripped by the latest in a long line of food scares: the Sudan-1 food dye, which was potentially cancer causing, had made its way into a wide array of everyday comfort foods.

What makes contemporary fears qualitatively different is that not only are we more aware but new types of fears have emerged. However, there is no particular consensus among sociologists, even between Giddens and Beck, on reasons behind the current preoccupation with at least six broad categories of risk: lifestyle, environmental, medical, economic, criminal and interpersonal relationships. Security risks were only recently included. We face far greater uncertainties and dangers, with globalisation of risk in terms of intensity (nuclear war), spread (WMD proliferation and ethnic instability) and more events that can affect whole populations, such as global economic collapse or global warming. Human activity and technology have also 'manufactured' risks, such as mobile phone radiation, requiring specialised scientific expertise. An increasingly affluent society is no longer prepared to accept risks or side effects that might have been tolerated in the previous struggle against scarcity.

According to Beck, the transformation into a risk society occurs when hazards undermine or elude established existing risk calculations.[76] One cannot insure against or eliminate incalculable risks eluding traditional time-space limitations such as 'mad cow disease' (BSE), global economic recession, nuclear meltdown or de-territorialised, de-nationalised terrorism. Others like ethnic cleansing are freed from previous control mechanisms of the Cold War. 'Calculating and managing risks no one really knows has become a main preoccupation.'[77] Governments have to take up the risk manager role, for the future looks increasingly ominous.[78]

Reflexive modernisation and risk-conscious modernity

The prominence of risks today is because of their global scale, but especially for Giddens, it is also worsened by increased vulnerability and ontological insecurity in a post-traditional society without previous support structures. Together with globalisation exacerbating the type and scale of pre-existing risks, a new frame of reference and a paradigm shift is needed. The idea of linear progress, certainty, controllability and security of early modernity has collapsed, replaced by reflexive fear of undesirable risks.[79] In post-traditional society, 'social reflexivity' means action is constituted by constantly renewing flows of new information rather than pre-given modes of conduct. Reflexivity arises because an agent regards its actions or inactions in terms of their potentially adverse consequences even before these have materialised.[80] Risk Society is characterised by ongoing reflexivity regarding risk assessments and management. The impetus for social and political transformation is not so much instrumental rationality but risks and globalisation.[81] Losing trust in traditional regulators, society and politicians manage risks in new ways. We continuously assess security less in terms of what is but what may yet materialise.

This is how Beck and Giddens's analyses relate to the perception of risks that prompt military force, with their focus on political consequences of the transition from instrumental to reflexive rationality. Under modern means-end instrumental rationality, achieving national interests depended on gauging capabilities of other states and assessing cause-effect relationships.[82] In war of course, as Clausewitz reminds us, the means-end relationship clearly does not unfold in a linear fashion given the constant interplay of opposing forces within the interactive nature of war. Nonetheless, the linear approach adopted meant specifying goals to be *achieved* and calculating necessary means needed. Reflexive rationality emphasises instead proba-bilistic risk calculus to *avert* adverse consequences that have not yet even happened. This posed the key question according to Niklas Luhmann: in a society that understood misfortune in terms of 'risk' rather than magic, fate or God, how would it cope with a future that is only more or less probable, intensely concerned with extreme improbabilities?[83]

Active Anticipation and Risk Society

By the late twentieth and early twenty-first century, the Western world was more concerned with *averting* possible negative futures than *attaining* histor-ically driven futures and utopias. The future, once associated with linear notions of progress, is now dominated by nightmarish visions. As Beck put it, 'the questions of development of technologies are now eclipsed by ques-tions of management of the risks involved'.[84] The ability to anticipate dangers and cope with them was increasingly important.[85] Anticipation is thus integral to risk management. Risk Society alerts us to the centrality of insecurity, risks and their management, the optimum means to pre-empt any adverse outcomes, and the tendency to imagine problems that may occur in future.[86] In this spirit, the British Medical Journal in 2001 banned the word 'accident', claiming that even earthquakes are predictable and preventable events that governments should warn us to avoid. Mary Douglas argued that risk formed part of a complex of new ideas, globalisation and heightened vulnerability to dangers.[87] Governments have to provide new forms of protection, especially in a litigious culture. Accidents like children being run over or failures in cancer screening are seen as 'avoidable failures', and the 'system' blamed for not managing risks.

Risk is thus a way of controlling or 'colonising' the future. What Beck calls the 'not-yet event' is a stimulus to action today to prevent possible problems and crises in future. The centre of risk consciousness lies in the future as unknown and unintended consequences dominate history and society. Risk Society 'marks the dawning of a speculative age'.[88] Especially when the scale of possible adverse consequences is much higher, it means adopting a future-oriented attitude to possibilities of action or inaction. Risk Society identifies dangers before they materialise, in contrast to the retrospective help offered by the old welfare state.[89] Britain's National Health Service, the mainstay of old welfarism — initially providing retro-spective treatment — now warns 'preventively' of smoking and alcohol risks. This domestic trend, as we have seen, has clear parallels in 'preventive' inter-national security policies.

Manufactured insecurity and global risks

World Risk Society highlighted the limited controllability of global risks and the crucial question of how to deal with them since traditional control mechanisms and institutions are now insufficient. These can only be managed; there are no perfect solutions. 'Manufactured' risks are created by our industrial and scientific processes. Risks, argued Beck, were previously constructed in terms of an enemy or foreign 'Other'.[90] God, nature or another human entity created an 'external' risk. With manufactured risks like Mutually Assured Destruction or pollution, for example, there is no distinction between perpetrator and victim, what Beck called the 'democratisation of risk'. However, Beck is too quick to posit sweeping changes in the nature of risk, for anxieties about risk still tend to be projected onto 'Others' posing risks such as terrorists and disease-carriers. Such groups are then subject to surveillance, and precautions taken.[91] Risk discourse positions social actors in two ways: those responding to risks identified as threatening them and undertaking risk management; and those risk-makers requiring surveillance and intervention.[92] While Beck assumes the two now merge, a practical meaningful distinction still exists.

In this book, risk is largely attributed to someone else's actions or contingent events, which we may alter to avoid harm. Beck's conceptualisation of risk as technologically manufactured is too narrow. Rather, to be 'at risk' is a condition of life, a 'free-floating anxiety' attaching to whatever danger is brought to public attention.[93] This comprises a whole plethora of non-technological concerns ranging from terrorism, ethnic cleansing and WMD to crime, food safety and child abuse. Criminologists have also incorporated Risk Society concerns, without necessarily importing 'manufactured risk' as Beck conceives it. Manufactured risk is furthermore applied inconsistently by Beck to terrorism, WMD proliferation and cross-border refugee flows. These are only tangentially linked to technology. Rather than 'manufactured' risk, the term 'systemic risk' or 'security risk' is preferred here.

The minimalist ethos of Risk Society

The 'normative project of industrial society was the ideal of equality and eliminating scarcity. In Beck's Risk Society, the 'normative counter-project' – its ideal, basis and motive force – is safety. This is a significant normative turn. Propelled by fear and anxiety, the focus is on developing new strategies of risk management to calm anxieties. The value system is largely negative, striving to prevent the worst, rather than obtaining something 'good'.[94] Industrial society concerned itself with production and distribution of goods. Risk Society by contrast is driven by managing and distributing dangers and bads, fearing harm of all sorts. A 'heroic' myth as the 'eternal truth' central to modernity no longer exists. Society is disenchanted with grand ideas of linear progress and wary of historical purpose after consequences for the environment and human health had been highlighted by, for example, the Chernobyl disaster.

Consequently, the risk management approach that arises stresses a 'utilitarian moral calculus' trumping other moral criteria such as generosity, guilt or fairness. By simply concentrating on what is avoidable, it promotes a negative if not dystopian world-view.[95] Faith in humanly engineered progress based on scientific rationality is undermined by a shift towards anticipating all kinds of risks based on 'reflexivity'.[96] This is now so pervasive that Giddens called modernity the 'risk culture'.[97] Ideological conflicts have been replaced by the discourse of globalisation and managing associated risks. Vulnerability defines the human condition.

People are no longer encouraged or willing to exert themselves to attain moral ideals. Zygmunt Bauman argued that modernity decried purposeless suffering. 'Pain, if it served purposes.... could be, and should be inflicted.'[98] Such purposes are now elusive as is the willingness to inflict and accept suffering. Historical thinking was one significant product of the Enlightenment. Geared towards purposive transformation of the human condition, it rejected the previous metaphysical system of divine revelation in favour of history and progress. In a risk age, this is replaced by the negative management of risks.

Exemplifying this are changes in attitudes toward heroism. Early twentieth century mass culture celebrated heroic deaths of soldiers with monuments. Late twentieth century Risk Society views fatalities as unmitigated disasters. Ribbons now indicate empathy with victimhood; red ones for AIDS awareness and yellow ones in the UK to show solidarity with troops during the 2003 Iraq war. Rather than flag waving for heroic soldiers felled in battle, wreaths were laid outside their bases. The politics of victimhood has to a certain extent undermined old-fashioned patriotism. The 'Unknown Victim' now has a memorial much like the 'Tomb of the Unknown Soldier'.[99] The recognition of limitations undercuts the omnipotence of heroes. The *zeitgeist* is such that victims, not heroes enjoy moral superiority. A society that no longer embraces heroism aims to avert, manage and distribute risks. The 'heroic warrior' and 'imperial self' have been replaced by the cautious 'Minimal self'.[100] Humankind has lowered its sights from grand historical purposes to preoccupation with safety. Fear of victimisation seems to be the great equaliser. Society sees itself as survivors, victims or potential victims. In this light, the Clausewitzian model of war derived from the Napoleonic era, could thus be seen as the 'maximalist' counterpart to a more 'minimalist' late-modern world. The insecure anxious Risk Society is more concerned with averting victimhood than celebrating heroism or demonstrating moral determination and social courage in war.

RISK AND LATE-MODERN CRIMINOLOGY

The domestic context and interdisciplinary ethos of this book can be further enhanced by briefly examining academic disciplines that have already started the ball rolling by incorporating Risk Society ideas into their specific research agendas. International relations arrived relatively late on the scene by comparison. Late-modern criminologists have, for instance, employed the Risk Society paradigm to explain contemporaneous shifts towards a New Penology and the rise of proactive risk management strategies in policing. This not only hints at possible implications for parallel trends in the study of war but also demonstrates the rich strands of interdisciplinary possibilities inherent in the Risk Society paradigm.

Richard Ericson and Kevin Haggerty contended in *Policing the Risk Society* that the centrality of risk assessment and management in policing strategies and legal norms reflected the institutionalisation of risk in modern society.[101] A future-oriented probabilistic consciousness obsessed with safety and security, and disillusioned with modernist notions of progress, contained in Risk Society is seen by criminologists as key to understanding the rise of risk management strategies in crime prevention. Some criminologists proclaim a New Prudentialism where responsibility for risk protection is distributed to individuals and community-based organisations as the welfare state was whittled down. However, there is little individuals can do to directly reduce systemic risks such as terrorism. After 9/11, the idea that state and politics should be replaced by the market seems unconvincing.[102] Governments have largely retaken responsibility for risk management such as airport security.

The New Penology

Paradigm shifts can be exaggerated. 'Zero-tolerance' policing for instance combines old-style disciplinary enforcement with risk-based surveillance and information processing.[103] The significance of risk should not be overstated — targeting high-risk areas may simply reflect a need to work more efficiently with limited resources.

Nonetheless, some aspects of New Penology exhibit interesting features that could be extrapolated to understanding war. Old Penology was concerned with responding to crime by diagnosis and rehabilitation of individual offenders, through establishing responsibility, causes, morals and guilt. Crime was seen as deviant, abnormal. Soaring crime rates, questionable results and declining budgets led to alternative strategies being developed. The previous concern with 'mind' in terms of understanding intentions and motivation gave way to a focus on 'body', altering structures within which individuals behave. We now manage environments and populations to reduce risks rather than intervening and treating individual offenders.[104] Conceptions of risk have largely displaced previous notions of normality and deviance.[105]

In this context, there is increasing acceptance that crime, 'given its routine social normality and presence, may be better understood as a risk to be managed'.[106] The new policy goal is identifying and reducing risks to protect the wider public rather than rehabilitative rhetoric or moral considerations.

The politics of risk and safety have to a degree overturned justice.[107] With victims routinely invoked to justify laws such as Megan's Law in the US, it is politically imperative that victims and potential victims must be protected. Former Home Secretary David Blunkett argued that we should recalibrate the whole system in 'favour of the victim, not placing the criminal at the top of the agenda'.[108] To be subject to intervention even before committing any wrong, it is enough simply to display whatever characteristics the experts have defined as risk factors.[109] In trying to anticipate future crimes, 'everyone is guilty until the risk profile assumes otherwise'.[110] Britain's new proposed Mental Health Bill thus replaces the 'treatability' criterion of an individual, with a broad category of 'high risk' offenders who can be detained without committing any crime yet. Precautionary, probabilistic calculations have in this sense replaced the moral or clinical description of individuals.

The New Penology thus views crime as 'routine, an everyday risk to be managed and assessed in much the same way we deal with road traffic'.[111] This new strategy seeks modest improvements, better management of risk, reduction of likelihood of crime, better support for victims — all 'less than heroic objectives' with little confidence to resolve permanently the problem of crime.[112] It assumes that crime occurs routinely because of criminogenic situations and opportunities rather than some moral flaws. Addressing crime before it occurs, not afterwards, situational crime prevention is a 'pre-emptive approach' that reduces criminal opportunities by 'reshaping' environments.[113] The aim is not to cure problems or address causes, but preventively reduce risks. It is managerial, not rehabilitative.[114]

Rehabilitation, the idea that people can be transformed for the better as part of a modernist metanarrative of 'progress', still endures but no longer expresses the overarching ideology. It is increasingly supplanted by strategies to manage risk. According to Gordon Hughes, offenders are treated only to the extent that it helps protect the public. Rehabilitation is now seen as part of managing risks, rather than a purely 'welfarist' or 'correctionalist' project. Probation and parole have downplayed their social work functions in favour of monitoring risks.[115]

Previously, crime was seen 'retrospectively' and individually to allocate blame and punishment. New Penology views crime 'prospectively' through calculating risks and preventive measures. There is a shift away from 'deterrent penalism' and 'reactive policing' strategies responding quickly to crime, to 'proactive' and 'preventive' policing, which predicts dangers to be prevented.[116] Risk thus arises not so much from a particular precise danger embodied in real attributes of an individual, as from a combination of abstract factors and probabilistic aggregates that might create undesirable outcomes. This promotes new-style anticipatory surveillance known as 'systematic pre-detection' to avoid facing a concrete dangerous situation.[117]

It is a future-oriented forward-looking view managing risks and preventing future offences rather than a backward-looking one focused on punishing the individual. Les Johnston concluded that the actuarial antici-patory nature of commercial risk management increasingly shapes the public police ethos. Due to risk-oriented thinking, policing has become increasingly proactive. Where reactive post hoc policing still occurs, infor-mation is collected for purposes of future risk assessment.[118] Indeed, this was 'reacting' in a 'proactive' fashion. Rather than focusing on retrospective moral concerns such as correction, justice or revenge, the proactive, more utilitarian goal is to prevent repetition if harm has already occurred.

This discussion of the ethos of proactive risk management strategies in policing and crime control bears directly on the questions posed, namely is war becoming risk management as well? Policing strategies, by this account, can be seen as illuminating possible sets of similarities that might be exhib-ited in specific aspects of war. It provides a deeper understanding of the concepts involved and ethos behind it, as well as the wider application of risk management theories in society and social sciences.

SO NEAR YET SO FAR: *RISK SOCIETY* AND WAR

The emerging international and domestic factors relating to risk that might influence the transformation of war debate, and in particular how war might be reinterpreted as risk management, is now clear. It was suggested that globalisation aggravated pre-existing security risks such as ethnic instability, WMD proliferation, failed states and transnational terrorism among others. Furthermore, the end of Cold War constraints, which might have helped keep these issues in check, complicated the risks in question. Classical 'net assessment' of threats in actuarial terms of capabilities and intentions is increasingly untenable. These new security challenges have shifted the goal-posts for evaluation, a point noted in US/UK policy documents. Uncertainty and probabilistic risk scenarios rather than the more material Soviet threat now prompt precautionary action. Today policy-makers contemplate proactively 'shaping the environment' and preventive policies rather than largely reactive strategies such as containment.

Although less prominent in international relations, sociologists and the *Risk Society* thesis provided considerable potential explanatory power for this new globalised environment even before 9/11 and especially after. The risk concept has cropped up on the radar screens of policy-makers and policy documents but no scholar (not even Beck) has adopted risk manage-ment as the centrepiece of an attempt to understand war and our world. In fact the probabilistic Risk Society and its unwavering focus on risk manage-ment holds the key to understanding the rise of war as a risk management strategy, in the same way as criminologists Richard Ericson and Kevin Haggerty argue Risk Society presages the proliferation of risk management strategies in policing.[119] The Risk Society paradigm indeed has so far been a versatile and productive analytical tool employed in different fields, begging the question why not in the study of war too. The study undertaken here is, to the best of my knowledge, the first attempt to do so.

That war is changing is not a new notion as the wider 'transformation of war' debate has been ongoing from Van Creveld's path-breaking 1991 effort *The Transformation of War* to Mueller's *The Remnants of War* in 2004. The debate hinges on how war has reconfigured itself and assumed different war forms, a consequence of broad transitions in both domestic society and the international system. One possible avenue of enquiry to be drawn from these observations is that of risk management, as risk-oriented thinking becomes increasingly prominent in societies of the West and the post-Cold War inter-national structure. 'Reflexively' managing ill-defined security risks to proactively avert possible adverse consequences by reshaping the interna-tional environment therefore seems a promising interpretation of recent wars. These concepts in fact increasingly guide the West's wars, and it is the complex nuances of risk and the analytical framework employed in this book, which remain to be addressed in the next chapter.

3

FORGING THE LINK

Risk management goes to war

> Governments are now seen to have a plain duty to apply them-
> selves explicitly ... to remove all risk or as much of it as
> possible.
>
> The Royal Society, 1992

Risk, as we have seen, ranks highly among the central guiding principles of reformed Cold Warriors contemplating the vagaries of contemporary international political life. Policing too has become more akin to proactive risk management rather than rehabilitative retrospective crime busting. These simultaneous developments on both domestic and international fronts in turn unfold promising but hitherto unexplored intellectual avenues in international relations for reconceptualising war as risk management. It is well and good that the language of risk is gaining prominence, but what might war as risk management look like in practice if talk is indeed being translated into action and an incipient link being made to war? It might be staring us straight in the face without our even being aware of it.

In order to rectify this and investigate implications for strategic studies, overarching analytical guidelines can be derived from concepts previously highlighted in Beck's *Risk Society* and its intense concern with probabilistic futures and risk management. In so doing an interdisciplinary working framework can be arrived at to help facilitate systematic analysis. However, contested concepts such as the notion of risk itself need to be unpacked, posing substantial theoretical obstacles and precluding straightforward application to international relations. This unfortunately also impedes a swift transit to our case studies. Additional careful scrutiny and refinement is therefore required before a sufficiently succinct and precise summary appropriate for international relations researchers now and in the future can be developed.

To attain greater precision and sharpen the analytical edge of the framework employed, conceptual parameters are calibrated to fine-tune its focus. Key risk terminology also needs to be defined. For the sake of conceptual clarity, I delve into the difficulties of operationalising a hugely ambiguous notion like 'risk' for analytical purposes in international relations. After demonstrating how scholars have addressed, or more commonly neglected, this issue, a working definition of risk encapsulating its core characteristics is suggested although an ideal definition admittedly is impossible. Finally, specific nuances and complexities of the concept of risk management are addressed, together with two of its key features: surveillance and the precautionary principle. Rather than furnish a watertight analytic framework, the dual purposes here are to specify the limits and difficulties of synthesising and applying an interdisciplinary study of risk to international relations; and, after so doing, to derive a logically consistent thematic matrix to examine specific aspects of war through the prism of risk management.

RISK MANAGEMENT, NOT PERCEPTION

In risk studies, risk perception and assessment have garnered most attention. For John Adams, everyone qualifies as a 'risk expert' simply because individual backgrounds and experiences influence unique risk perceptions. Perceptions also depend on how risk is shaped and occasionally misrepresented by NGOs, media, politicians, 'talking head' experts and a country's political culture.[1] Mary Douglas and Aaron Wildavsky claimed there is no increase in *real* risks, only in *perceived* risks because very influential social actors claimed so.[2] This is a complex debate beyond our present purposes. Suffice to say the politics of risk definition has assumed utmost importance, as Beck elegantly suggests, because successfully asserted definitions are a 'magic political wand' to which resources and policies must flow.[3]

There are ample international relations works and the Copenhagen School's 'securitization' approach demonstrating how risks are socially constructed through Ole Waever's 'speech act'. Rasmussen's analysis of how NATO reconstructed its post-Cold War security is another example.[4] It should be stated unequivocally that research presented here is not geared towards contributing to constructivism, risk perception or assessment. Instead, as an effort in strategic studies, its predominant concern is providing a coherent conceptual framework for analysing repeated patterns in the use of organised military force for political purposes of managing risks.

Nonetheless, risk is culturally constructed; subjective perceptions of risk vary among and within societies, and it is all-too-often contested. It is impossible to ignore this fact. Identification of risk occurs within specific socio-cultural and historical contexts, rather than now largely discredited notions that some cultures are simply more fearful than others. Beck appeared to incorporate both a realist and weak constructivist approach – there are objective 'real' risks out there, but the nature of risk is conceptualised differently in the West compared to earlier eras and other societies.[5] Furthermore, risks do not simply exist 'in themselves'. They become a political issue also when people are made aware of them by media or politicians.[6] A 'Realist constructivist' perspective is thus adopted by this book, recognising the dynamic interplay existing between material and cultural factors.

41

Risks are socially and culturally predicated in so far as we choose and define which risks to address. The focus however is Realist questions of war and security, and how policy-makers *apply* definitions of the risk scenario in waging war.

As the executive director of America's Federal Commission on Risk Assessment and Risk Management commented, numerous reports have been written and resources allocated into how to improve risk assessments. But very few addressed 'what you *do* with the risk assessment, which is the point. The goal after all is risk reduction, not developing quantitative descriptions of risk'.[7] Ultimately, Beck concedes the question of how and whether a risk is constructed or real is perhaps immaterial. What matters more is the actualisation of risk in policy-makers' minds, how it is responded to and acted upon.[8]

UNRAVELLING RISK AND ITS MANY FACES

Connotations past and present

Risk is not new nor is it a static monolithic concept. Norms and practices related to its usage have evolved according to specific circumstances. Humankind has always faced danger and uncertainty. Panics in the past could be situated within magic or a Christian context of Bible, judgement and apocalypse. These provided conceptual and behavioural means of coping with dangers such as demons, death and disease. The original meaning of risk arose in this context. Risk can be traced back to at least the Renaissance, supposedly deriving from the Italian 'risico', meaning dangers of maritime voyages from storms and rocks. The concept of risk in that time excluded ideas of human fault but was largely attributed to acts of God or *force majeure*. People saw the world in terms of fate, luck or random events beyond control. Personal decisions assumed less significance than they currently do.

Changes came with modernity and science, rationality, progress and order. Risk became probabilistic and scienticised; all probabilities were technically calculable and controllable by a scientifically enlightened humankind, confident in the powers of rationalisation. By the nineteenth century, risk extended to human conduct and society. To Beck, risk can thus be a modern notion that unanticipated results may occur due to our own activities or decisions, rather than fate or nature.

By the late twentieth century, we also confront globalised high-intensity risks such as nuclear meltdown or catastrophic terrorism as a result of human action. These are uncontrollable and unknowable and can no longer be transformed into rationalised calculable risks. Such global risks of unprecedented scale have been added on to the more personal ones of early modernity. These fuel the ever-increasing motivation to manage risks. In the West, where control over one's life course is paramount, risk has replaced older ideas about causes of misfortune such as sin, and even more secular notions of 'accidents'. More importantly, risk now assumes human responsibility for the causes of risk, and that something can be done to avoid harm.[9] This in turn influences how societies conceptualise the role of preventive military force to avert security risks.

The world faces the same old risks and many new ones. An important distinction is that of human responsibility. Even old risks such as disease, famine and floods are no longer seen as acts of God but avoidable human activities. The idea of being 'at risk' is now equivalent to being 'sinned against'. We adopt the role of 'potential victim', endangered by risks imposed by others or one's inactions, rather than, as previously, seeing one's 'sinful' actions as bringing retribution on oneself.[10] Take the age-old issue of disease for instance. The Ebola virus was attributed to the effects of human logging and deforestation. Cancer and AIDS are no longer about divine judgements but failure to manage risks. The previous no-fault paradigm of disease has been replaced by the at-fault paradigm. Potential victims have responsibility to self-manage risks. It is their fault if they fail to act preventively. In extreme cases, 'pre-emptive' surgery is prescribed to avoid high-risk cancers.[11]

Definition

Risk has clearly become the 'defining characteristic of our age', arguably one of the most powerful and widely used concepts in contemporary life.[12] Yet it remains an imprecise and slippery concept despite the rapidly growing literature and industries mushrooming around it. It manifests in varying risk domains from economic investment and accounting scandals to food safety, nuclear energy and terrorism. Furthermore, risk has acquired multiple meanings from probability (risk of terrorism), to consequences (risks to security produced by ethnic cleansing), to describing perilous situations (Saddam Hussein poses risks or is a risk to peace). Risk can form part of a strategic calculation, exist materially on its own or often overlap between the two. It can be a normative concept implying the desirability of avoidance actions or a purely descriptive one. When policy-makers warn that 'we face new risks' they are describing a situation, or they can argue 'the risks of inaction outweigh the risk of action' in normatively justifying decisions. Where possible throughout this book, it will be indicated whether risk is used as a descriptive term, a normative one or most commonly a combination of both. A rigid usage of risk will not be helpful to understanding the multiple real-life conditions where it has been employed in various guises. Instead, a measure of conceptual precision can be attained by defining its essential components as theoretical guideposts while utilising the multi-faceted concept in a broad manner reflecting its complexity and richness.

Fortunately, international relations has always dealt with what W. B. Gallie called 'essentially contested concepts'[13] such as national interest and power. International relations has thrived partly because such concepts stoke debate and controversy. Arnold Wolfers' article 'National Security as an ambiguous symbol' warned that the concept of security 'may not have any precise meaning at all'. Security, notes Barry Buzan, while 'weakly conceptualised' is nonetheless a politically powerful concept, which can provide a useful perspective to international relations.[14] To Buzan, these are as imprecise as they are influential concepts that deserve study, requiring additional analysis to identify conceptual boundaries, internal contradictions and relevance of new developments.

With regards to the notion of risk, Beck appeared more intent on understanding its implications and political significance than defining the concept. However, it is worthwhile dissecting the concept in some detail. Although precise definitions are elusive, one will be suggested here not hoping it will garner universal agreement (an impossible task) but simply as a foundation stone. By providing reasonably clear markers of risk features and refining its various forms and meaning within specific international relations contexts in which we may use it, lack of an overall universally agreed definition should not put off analytical enterprise or empirical verification.

Some suggested definitions

Little is precise about 'risk' and no commonly accepted definition can exhaust its meaning and usage. However, all risk concepts share one common element: the distinction between reality and possibility.[15] Risk is thus associated with the possibility that an adverse state of reality may occur as a result of natural events or human (in)action. Risk would be irrelevant if the future was fated or independent of human action. It implies contingent losses resultant from contingent events. These consequences are, more importantly, viewed from a non-fatalistic viewpoint. They can theoretically be altered through either modifying the initiating activity or mitigating its impacts.[16]

In the 1920s Frank Knight suggested a distinction between the concepts of uncertainty and risk. The classical technical meaning of risk lay in formal probability theory within economics and decision analysis. It depended on conditions in which probability estimates of an event and all possible outcomes are known. But this is only one meaning of risk. In many other cases, such as 'social risks' or 'security risks', assigning probability figures is impossible. By contrast, uncertainty meant immeasurable probabilities since the theoretical and empirical basis for assigning probabilities was unknown. Uncertainty meant knowing neither the odds nor outcomes, while risk meant knowing the odds and possible outcomes but not exactly what would happen. 'Risk' and 'uncertainty' were nominally and formally separate ideas, but each is now associated with the other. This contemporary colloquial synonymous usage of the terms has created confusion as their strict formal definitions have become largely obscure.[17] The formal distinction between risk and uncertainty now appears untenable and makes no practical sense applied to ambiguous and unquantifiable security risks.

Furthermore, the previously two-dimensional concept of risk used in economics and marine insurance incorporated probability of both losses and gains. It had a positive dimension of investment decisions, financial gains or psychological thrill-seeking; and a negative element of endangering safety. Lacking its previous positive connotations, risk now largely means simply unacceptable danger and negative outcomes to be avoided, without the original number-crunching of probability multiplied with magnitude of losses *and* gains.[18] Risk in this sense embodies the fundamental premise of probability and magnitude found in quantified technical definitions of risk but does not insist they be precisely knowable, an impractical proposition.[19] In lay parlance, risk is now used to describe phenomena that have the potential to deliver substantial harm, regardless of whether probability of harm is estimable.[20] This definition is adopted here, and as noted earlier is a broader understanding of risk than Beck's narrow techno-centric focus on 'manufactured' scientific risks.

Types of risk and their characteristics

A by no means exhaustive list of risks might comprise:

i   socio-political risks from internal or external foes (human behaviour);
ii   economic risks;
iii natural risks from ecological dangers;
iv   technological risks.

These often overlap. Human behaviour can combine technology and WMD. Social risks include negative externalities from the choices and actions of one party creating risks for others. Terrorism and drunk driving are common externally imposed risks.[21] There is another crucial difference. Ecological and financial risks are largely *unintentional*, whereas terrorism *intentionally* produces bads. Some risks are knowable and can be perceived through scientific and mathematical knowledge (using a microscope to see bacteria or economic data indicating possible economic risks). Others, such as rock climbing or extreme sports, can be perceived directly. Most controversial are 'Virtual Risks' ('risk of a risk' or 'unknown unknown') where experts cannot agree or do not know enough. These include BSE, global warming, mobile phones and terrorism. The figure below demonstrates the often interlinked nature of risks.[22]

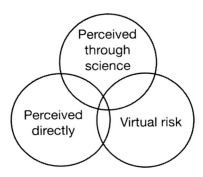

Figure 3.1 Risks.

Approaches to risk

Many differing approaches to risk exist. Cognitive psychologists focus on perception; professional risk assessors and insurers prefer quantitative approaches; sociologists study the broader political significance of risk. Institutional approaches address rules and norms in how organisations manage risk. The emphasis placed on particular aspects varies according to concerns of analysts and inherent limits of case studies.

As Paul Slovic argued, where experts describe 'real' or 'scientific' risk in 'objective' narrow quantitative ways through formal technical mathematical models, the public has a more complex qualitative approach. There is no 'single correct perception of risk'. Slovic, the father of risk perceptions, outlined three dimensions:

i   the dread factor (lack of control, catastrophic potential, fatal effects, unfair distribution);
ii   the unknown factor (risk tends to be overestimated if it is novel, unobservable with relatively unknown consequences);
iii scale of risk (the number of people exposed).

Risks due to human action (e.g. terrorism) or novel technologies (e.g. weapons of mass destruction) are especially feared. This 'contextualist view of risk' is subjective, value-laden and multidimensional.[23] Not only does it embody traditional risk parameters of probabilities and consequences, but it also takes into account individual or collective risk, catastrophic potential, voluntariness, dramatic coverage and so on. A narrow definition of risk confined to numerical models is sufficient only if probability and consequence are well known. Yet we now face 'hard-to-manage risks' rather than 'quantifiable risks'.[24] After 9/11, the private insurance sector cannot insure risks that are infinite and impossible to price.[25] A taxonomy of risk could look like this:

More acceptable risks	Unacceptable risks
Voluntarily undertaken	Involuntary
Individual control, 'extreme sports'	Loss of individual control
Naturally occurring risks	Artificial, a result of human activities or
Latent, slow-developing or ongoing	science and technology
long-term harm of low impact such as	Catastrophic potential, sudden and
car accidents	dramatic such as terrorism
Reversible impacts	Irreversible impacts

Source: Professor Rod Smith, 'Risk and Society – Is Science dangerous?', Imperial College and LSE Joint Lecture Series, 11 March 2002, London School of Economics, London.

It is essential to specify carefully what risks are addressed in this book since risk is complex and multifaceted. The risks in question cannot be measured precisely in quantitative formal mathematical terms. Thus a qualitative social science approach is adopted. These risks possess 'tombstone-ability': the capacity to produce deaths or victims through dramatic catastrophes that command media coverage and focus public opinion. These provide 'policy windows' for changes.[26] Security risks were selected based on criteria deemed as most unacceptable to society and which would attract policy-makers' attentions:

i   incertitude on probability of occurrence;

ii   dramatic and catastrophic potential outcomes;

iii involuntary and imposed, collective rather than individual;

iv irreversible harm, difficult to control;

v   adverse consequences for which decision-makers think they will be held accountable;

vi where future outcomes are hard to predict, risks that are analogous or uppermost in decision-makers' minds might be extrapolated to the original risk in question.

Two sets of risks are normally discernible in international relations: systemic risks such as proliferation, terrorism and ethnic cleansing; and tactical risks incurred by a policy response. These sets of risks are dynamic and can evolve in intensity according to circumstances. An ostensibly 'tactical' risk such as incurring friendly or civilian casualties ('collateral damage') could have 'strategic' impact if policy-makers lose public support, political office or change the direction of a military campaign. Nonetheless, we are mostly concerned with what Ulrich Beck and Tony Blair's Cabinet Office Strategy Unit termed 'systemic risks', which are currently dominating the agendas of many countries.[27] Systemic risk arises from peculiarities of the international structure where ethnic tensions, terrorist flows, or destabilised or rogue states have broken free of Cold War control systems and are aggravated by globalisation.

'Risk', 'Threat' or 'Hazard'?

'Hazard' is often used in health and safety and the environment while 'threat' is commonly associated with security. Yet these terms are often used interchangeably and loosely by policy-makers and scholars, further complicating what is already a hugely dense subject matter. Scholars such as Yaacov Vertzberger, Mary Douglas and Deborah Lupton seem to think that risk in everyday language now simply means 'danger', 'threat' or some unhappy event that may occur. Beck's definition of risk (as 'a systematic way of dealing with hazards, insecurities induced by modernisation') itself has been lambasted for creating 'unnecessary misunderstanding' given the common usage of both risk and hazard as synonyms.[28] Beck claims further that the operational criterion for distinguishing risk and threat is denial of private insurance protection. If risks that cannot be delimited spatially and temporally now elude the logic of private insurance and are no longer quantifiable, the boundary between 'predictable' risks and uncontrollable threats is breached.[29] Here Beck has muddied the waters even further, implying that risks had simply become 'uncontrollable threats'.

Clearly there is no universal acceptance of the terminologies described above. Some suggest that 'threat' implies an imminent well-defined danger very close in time and highly likely to strike. Others such as Johan Eriksson, betraying some frustration, argued that 'threats, risks, dangers – *or whatever they are called* – are social constructions'.[30] Eriksson's collaborators concurred that any difference between 'risk' and 'threat' is hardly of any practical importance. Therefore risk, hazard and threat, to them are synonyms, defined according to its everyday usage. Mikkel Rasmussen too did not explore in detail the differences between 'risk' and 'threat'.[31] Shlomo Griner's response to Rasmussen picked up subtle conceptual differences, suggesting that risk and threat are not the same, but alas provided no convincing distinction. Griner narrowly conceived of risk as something one incurred through one's own actions, suggesting incredibly that 'terrorist activity surely entails a risk, but for the terrorists *themselves*'. He emphasised internalisation of risk where agency and responsibility arise from internal processes, neglecting involuntary risks imposed by external 'others'.[32] Griner misread the complexity of the risk concept. There is a big difference between those who incur risks through their own actions or choices (this is the most common conception of risk), and more pertinently in our context those who feel they are involuntarily victimised – or put at risk by other risk-makers and thus seek to undertake preventive action.

Risk is therefore a broader complex concept, incorporating the likely scale of unwanted consequences, probability, frequency and duration. Thus, Giddens suggested that 'risk' should be separated from 'hazard' or 'danger'. Risk implies probability that an action or inaction may produce undesirable outcomes. Risk implies things where humans have potential control, actively assessing and managing future dangers as societies try to shape future outcomes. Choice is also intrinsic to risk. There are no 'risk-free choices, even the decision not to decide. Avoiding active decision may entail more risk than making an active choice.'[33] Niklas Luhmann further distinguished between 'risk' and 'danger', noting that 'risk' involved potential loss as a consequence of decision or non-decision, invoking a concept of attribution. 'Danger', for Luhmann, is something that occurs externally regardless of our decisions or non-decisions, actions and non-actions. The novelty of the risk phenomenon is that we are transforming more and more 'dangers' into 'risks' as an expanding array of dangers like terrorism or technological hazards are attributed to decisions or indecisions.[34] Clearly there are differences in terminology and to employ them accurately, there is a need to delineate them more precisely.

Threat and risk: conceptual components

Perhaps the best way to differentiate threats and risks is through their respective components. Both imply different ways of conceptualising danger. Risk emphasises the *probability* and *magnitude* of *consequences*. In international relations under the Old Security Paradigm, the conventional notion of threat was usually defined narrowly in military terms composed of assessing an opponent's *intentions* and military *capabilities*. Strategic studies was thus preoccupied with reducing very concrete military threats of nuclear confrontation with missiles facing off across Europe, and analysing the impact of weapons systems like SS-20s on the strategic balance. Threat was defined largely by notions of military power, power-resources and means of power rightly or wrongly perceived as overwhelming or not. 'Without power, there will be no threat'.[35] Security was usually seen as derivative of power where the actor with the strongest power capabilities would theoretically feel secure. A Weberian means-end rationality approach assumed the realisation of a state's interests depended on the balance of capabilities between that state and others.[36]

A new paradigm based on risk would in contrast revolve not on power capabilities and intentions but rather dangers considered at the level of their potentiality and probable magnitude of consequences. Dangers now stem not from powerful states but failed and destabilised states posing risks through globalisation, terrorist and refugee flows, or diseases. These dangers are conceptualised as risks in terms of their probabilities and consequences, since their material power capabilities or intent are impossible to gauge or even non-existent.

The 1997 US Presidential/Congressional Commission on Risk Assessment and Risk Management defined how risky a particular situation is as a product of two factors: probability of occurrence of adverse event; and extent and magnitude of that consequence. In this respect, rather than 'danger' or 'hazard', risk should be associated with ideas like chance and probabilities.[37] Given that the present structural novelty means we cannot know the future, the future can only be 'perceived through the medium of probabilities to provide the present with some basis for decisions'.[38] The popular usage of risk thus reflected the impact of a late modern way of 'probabilistic thinking' on our culture, regardless whether this probability is quantifiable or not.[39] Consequently, a previously deterministic rationality of science is being replaced by 'conditional, probabilistic rationalities'.[40] The concept of risk thus implies probabilities and consequences; threat involves capabilities and intentions.

Action-reaction dynamics

Another way of distinguishing between threat and risk might be the ways in which they elicit different action dynamics. Threats constitute an 'action-reaction' relationship as an output of policy (making threats against others), or input upon policy to be reacted upon (threats from others). In strategic theory, the threat concept is often described as a necessary reactive answer to aggressive actions from an adversary. The nature of 'threat-avoidance' policy normally saw threat as an impact on the polity coming from the outside to be 'reacted upon'.[41] John Hertz's Security Dilemma highlighted the action-reaction dynamics involved in an anarchic system as states seeking to increase their own defence capabilities incurred even more suspicion from other states responding in kind. This manifested during Great Power arms races but hardly applies when dealing proactively with terrorism or destabilised weak states. The term 'threat' thus normally meant imminent and well defined to some analysts; something to which we normally have to react.[42] Risks on the other hand are much more imprecise and uncertain, requiring proactive management.[43]

Fear versus anxiety

Threats generate fears; risks fuel anxiety. This suggests a final subtle distinction between the two concepts. With huge social changes ranging from gender roles to individualisation, most sociologists agree we are living through a period of acute insecurity and high anxiety.[44] Public controversies about health and environmental dangers which do not yet exist or about which we simply do not know enough create a 'generalised climate of risk', in turn generating vague anxieties.[45]

Sigmund Freud suggested that there is a distinction between fear and anxiety. Fear requires a definite object of which one is afraid; it tends to be more immediate, specific and focused. Apprehension (anxiety) implies a certain condition of expectation of danger. People experiencing anxieties generally tend to feel threatening uncertainty about the future and are troubled when the cause and nature of anticipated danger is unclear. It has a 'quality of indefiniteness and lack of object'.[46] Although the number killed on 9/11 was less than 10 per cent of the annual highway fatalities in America, it aroused anxiety because it was dramatically reported by the media; it was unexpected and random, creating unfocused vulnerability and a sense of stepping into the unknown.

Admittedly, in everyday language, it is hard to maintain a consistently clear distinction between fear and anxiety. Yet it appears the key difference between them is the amount and quality of knowledge we possess. Anxiety thrives on tension between knowledge and ignorance of fearful situations. With fuller understanding, vague uncertainties of anxiety can be transformed into known objects of fear.[47] The significance today of uncertain knowledge of risk lies in the extent to which it engenders more anxiety about a threatening future.

DEFINING RISK MANAGEMENT

Governments as risk managers

Given the levels of anxiety today, it is perhaps unsurprising that risk management is increasingly politicised and institutionalised. 'Risk bureaucracies', such as the Food and Drugs Administration and Homeland Security Department in the US, have sprung up. Britain has its Health and Safety Executive, the Food Standards Agency and the Civil Contingencies Secretariat. Most industries have safety watchdogs, while consumer groups from rail passengers to mobile phone users demand and monitor regulation. Organisations must be seen to do everything possible to protect the public. Even school trips now have 'safety supremos', while local councils and hospitals have 'risk managers'.

Downing Street was certainly monitoring this development. In November 2002, its Cabinet Office Strategy Unit published a study on risk, with a foreword from Tony Blair emphasising his concern to manage risks better. It argued, 'handling risk is increasingly central to the business of government' and that 'explicit consideration of risk should be firmly embedded in government's core decision-making processes'.[48] Rising public expectations for governments to manage risk are set against a backdrop of declining trust, and increasing activism around risks amplified by the media. Furthermore, many risks such as terrorism are global and transnational, beyond individual scopes of action. With safety and well-being established as top political imperatives in a Risk Society, there is an increasing need to address the notion of risk management.[49]

Indeed some risks are the reasons why we have government in the first place: to protect persons and property from villains within the country and outside.[50] Yet international security risks form an under-researched part of an expanding set of risks subject to government intervention, from finance, GM food, transportation, environment and new technology to terrorism. Risk management policy can be 'any government activity designed to reduce risk or reallocate it'. Yet it is not generally studied as a governmental function.[51] Relatively little is known about public risk management, compared to its private sector equivalent. Governments possess special risk management qualities from their monitoring capacity to enforcement ability. Public risk management policies are extensive but less tangible and apparent than other government functions such as building schools. Despite America's laissez-faire image, the Federal Government's role as what David Moss called the 'ultimate risk manager' has been crucial before and especially after 9/11. With the November 2002 Federal Terrorism Insurance Act, Washington served as 'insurer of last resort' since private insurers can no longer efficiently manage risks from catastrophic terrorism. Moss argued that since 1960, risk management had expanded from insuring businesses and workers in order to promote economic development, to simply protecting *all* citizens from an ever-widening array of risks. As people became richer, 'most fascinating of all, risk management policy in the US reflects an unmistakable shift in priorities from economic growth to security over two centuries'.[52]

Definitions and assumptions

Risk management is a complex subject with differing approaches to diverse areas from health and safety, business and finance, to terrorism and crime. There is no single generic, widely accepted definition or model of risk management, only broad principles and general methods.[53] This is especially so in international relations where research on risk management has hardly taken off. The US 2001 *Quadrennial Defence Review* (QDR) described Managing Risk as a central 'strategic tenet'.[54] Its framework, however, appeared more specifically geared toward organisational risks, balancing and mitigating operational force management, institutional risks and future challenges. This is unsuitable for our purposes, concerned with reducing international systemic risks rather than balancing them against others.

An important assumption in risk management is that it be both feasible and desirable to do so. It can be defined generally as 'a field of activity seeking to eliminate, reduce and generally control pure risks'.[55] Risks have to be continuously reduced to a level deemed tolerable or as low as can reasonably be achieved. One way, as we have seen from criminology, is to 'act pre-emptively upon potentially problematic zones, to structure them in such a way as to reduce the likelihood of undesirable events or conduct occurring'.[56] Reducing likelihoods is fundamental to the concept.

Risk management features competing world-views between 'anticipationism' and 'resilience'. Anticipationism is related to the precautionary principle, as proactive risk management is integral to the process.[57] Anticipationism is preferred here over resilience. The latter is less desirable for significant harm has already occurred and addresses consequence-management issues such as first-responders. Purely anticipatory strategies systematically survey the landscape for any risks to be managed providing the impetus for action. The UK report *Strategic Trends* released in March 2003 thus argued that 'horizon scanning' and 'assessment of likelihood' to understand future risks is increasingly recognised by governments as a 'valuable tool to reduce or manage risks'.[58] Tombstone-style strategies on the other hand manage risks that literally explode on the agenda with dramatic media coverage of catastrophic disasters like rail crashes, or terrorism. The goal is to avoid repetition.[59] A clear distinction is however untenable given the inevitable extent of overlap: tombstone risks after Srebrenica were associated with Kosovo via horizon scanning, as was Iraq after 9/11.

Various processes, not necessarily as segregated or sequential as implied here for discussion purposes, are involved in risk management. According to the US General Accounting Office (GAO), a threat analysis, the first step in determining risk, identifies and evaluates each threat on the basis of its capability and intent to harm. Risk management is then the process of understanding 'risk'– the likelihood that a threat will cause harm with some consequences – and deciding on and implementing actions to reduce it.[60] Again, the GAO formulation of 'risk' and 'threat' is by no means definitive. It merely indicates one way of approaching the problem.

This book suggests that first analysing 'threats' based on capability and intent, as the GAO recommends, and *then* the likelihood of that threat occurring (risk) is increasingly being undermined. We have skipped the first step of properly analysing threats, and instead focused simply on 'risk' in terms of likelihood and consequences. This is the logical outgrowth of a way of thinking about globalised dangers dominant in a probabilistic culture characterised by the Risk Society.

The second part of risk management involves options and implementation. The Royal Society listed four basic methods to manage risk:

i   forecasting, monitoring and the precautionary principle;
ii deploying resources;
iii laying down regulations;
iv through state organisations like armed forces, 'direct action is always important for handling some risks such as crime or terrorism'.[61]

Good risk management will be anticipatory, proactive and a 'routine' activity integrated into general management activity.[62] Another possible method involves reshaping the environment which has been employed in criminology.

Outcome specification is another crucial process. Successfully managing 'pure risks' means avoidance of loss such that no harm results.[63] This means it is difficult to quantify results. Non-events are indicators of success. Linear approaches to risk management separate assessment and management activities. However, a cyclical approach is often suggested, as Figure 3.2 below shows, emphasising the importance of feedback and monitoring mechanisms on how a particular risk evolves rather than static pre-set goals.[64] Continuous surveillance of risks is undertaken, and actions taken to reduce them if necessary. This also involves considering whether any strategy may itself create new risks: Beck's 'boomerang effect'.[65] This is an ongoing process with no finite end since risks can only be minimised, not eliminated.

International relations has clear parallels with the boomerang effect in the Security Dilemma, but the main difference lies perhaps in the nature of the problem in the first place. The boomerang effect might create new sets of risks altogether. The Security Dilemma, however, essentially perpetuates the same vicious cycle of insecurity, through states engaging in arms races as the most cited example. There is no direct equivalent to arms racing in the war on terrorism or when managing rogue states like Iraq or issues like ethnic cleansing. Instead boomerang effects can sometimes create an entirely different problem. For instance the Kosovo campaign created huge complications for NATO-Russia relations when the original concern was ethnic cleansing.

Figure 3.2 The risk management process.

Source: Cabinet Office Strategy Unit, *Risk: Improving government's capacity to handle risk and uncertainty*, London, November 2002.

Surveillance

The cyclical nature of risk management means surveillance is often the 'preferred vehicle' for doing so.[66] International relations, in contrast to surveillance studies and risk theory, has largely neglected the increasing role of monitoring power'.[67] The IMF for instance seeks greater surveillance capacities. The UN had been inspecting Iraq for much of a decade. According to the Royal Society, 'monitoring is the tool for investigating how things stand and a contributor to precautionary action in the face of uncertainty or ignorance.'[68] Furthermore, the demand for risk management is giving a big boost to surveillance.[69] Effective risk management needs to generate the necessary information on risks involved and account for how risks might change over time.[70]

Surveillance here means not simply spying but systematic bureaucratised gathering of information for management purposes. The aim is not only to watch every actual event but also to 'plan for every eventuality'.[71] What was previously the domain of police and intelligence agencies has become routine as businesses monitor consumer choices every time a credit card is swiped or an Internet site is visited. Such continuous monitoring is embedded in apparent normalcy rather than a heavy-handed Orwellian Big Brother. All sections of society from credit agencies to consumer groups now seek to manage risk by discovering as many risk factors as possible. September 11 only intensified these prevailing trends.

Surveillance is closely associated with Risk Society and the shift away from Old Penology. Rather than retrospective punishing, supervision is increasingly 'prospective'.[72] We now sort people into risk categories, using 'pre-emptive and anticipatory surveillance' to prevent something from happening.[73] It can provide advance warning, estimate consequences and fore-tell the possible occurrence of events by identifying circumstances that create undesirable outcomes.

Classical Benthamite surveillance required physical proximity. As David Lyon noted, twentieth century surveillance was limited to specific sites such as factory floors. However with new technologies, 'surveillance went global'. Rather than previously co-present with each other, employers can now monitor workers at distant locations through satellites and trans-continental fibre optic cables. Similarly, US personnel monitor Al Qaeda operatives thousands of miles away. According to Lyon, collecting information quickly at great distances is the best way to monitor and pre-empt risks by indicating where a potential offender may strike in a globalised world. Globalised, transnational policing now aimed to reduce risks through 'knowledge-based risk management'.[74]

The precautionary principle and risk management

The ultimate deadlock in Risk Society is the gap between imperfect knowledge and decision. No one really knows the outcomes but nonetheless decisions have to be made. Beck termed this the 'risk trap'.[75] One oft-cited way out is the precautionary principle, which arose in the 1970s when environmental impact assessments revealed discrepancies between significant risks of serious harm and accuracy of scientific forecasts. Now a recognised general principle of international law, the 1992 Rio Declaration is often deemed to enshrine its essence: '...a precautionary approach should be applied.... where there are threats of serious or irreversible damage, lack of full scientific certainty shall not be used as a reason for postponing cost-effective measures to prevent environmental degradation taking into account costs and benefits of action or inactions.' (Although other definitions exist, suggesting that where uncertainty exists one should not act, this view embodied in Rio is the most widely accepted.) People are thus inclined to take anticipatory action to prevent harm if something bad might happen. Precaution reorders victim powerlessness towards emphasising new mechanisms of victim avoidance and favours would-be victims rather than beneficiaries of risk-related decisions.[76] Critics say this stifles innovations.

While the principle remains linked to scientific uncertainty, it is also becoming a culturally framed concept.[77] The principle has moved from environmental, scientific and legal realms to become fully politicised, incorporating non-scientific public opinion and social values. Precaution became politically explicit in February 2000 with the European Commission noting it 'is particularly relevant to the management of risk' by decision-makers. It stated that 'absence of scientific proof of a cause-effect relationship.... should not be used to justify inaction'.[78] The Council of Ministers' Nice Decision later that year went further by accepting precautionary action without detailed scientific evaluation could be taken if the risk was urgent. Precaution occupied central place in the debate on war with Iraq.

Sometimes it is claimed that Washington favours a 'precautionary approach' over the 'precautionary principle', for fear of the latter being abused as a rhetorical weapon stifling innovation. The difference lies more in name than substance. The 1999 White House Declaration on Environment and Trade stated 'precaution is an essential element of US regulatory policy' since regulators often have to act without full scientific certainty to avert potentially serious harm. US legislation has accordingly moved from strictly requiring proof of actual harm, towards anticipating and preventing possible harm.[79]

Levels of incertitude, probability and catastrophic potential thus affect the type of risk management strategies adopted and whether they are precautionary or not. 'Normal' risks pose little statistical uncertainty and low catastrophic potential. Therefore a purely 'risk-based' management strategy presupposes that probability of occurrence and extent of damage are relatively well defined. This includes smoking and AIDS. More pertinent to our purposes are 'intermediate' and 'intolerable' risks such as terrorism and WMD proliferation, where certainty is contested and catastrophic potential may be great. Problematically, the new 'riskiness to risk' is such that it is even disputed whether risks exist at all. Such 'unknown unknowns' lie outside the boundaries of traditional risk assessment. 'Precautionary-based' risk management strategies are thus adopted where there are high levels of uncertainty about probabilities and extent of occurrences that are of catastrophic potential.[80]

The precautionary principle does not apply where likelihood and severity of impacts are well known since level of uncertainty is low. When the harm associated with risk is slight and occurrence very unlikely, little needs to be done. Precaution is triggered only when harm is severe and irreversible. Even when harm is catastrophic with little uncertainty about its occurrence, the choice of action is straightforward. The problem arises in grey areas where harm is catastrophic with significant uncertainty about its occurrence. Significant portions of political decision-making are now devoted to managing risks using precaution as a guide.[81]

It is also important to distinguish between 'false negatives' (where agents or activities were initially considered harmless until evidence of harm emerged – asbestos) and 'false positives' (where precautionary action later proved unnecessary – the Y2K bug and war on Iraq). Contemporary blame is divided into two types: blame for commission (such as polluters creating a risk) and blame for omission (for not managing risk sufficiently).[82] Policy-makers thus see incentives to undertake precautionary action especially in a litigious age. Actions to manage risks themselves generate risks and consequences but inaction can sometimes generate even greater risks. For instance, US officials rationalising the Kosovo war pointedly faced this conundrum. There is a need to balance the risks involved.[83] However, considering pros and cons is difficult. The costs of preventive action are often tangible and clearly allocated; costs of inaction are less tangible, less clearly distributed and long-term.

A THEMATIC MATRIX OF RISK MANAGEMENT

Having surveyed the intricacies of defining the notion of risk, risk management principles and concepts in the context of Beck's *Risk Society*, we are now in a position to propose an analytical perspective for international relations purposes. The redeploying of war as risk management can be understood in light of similar social, political and economic trends studied in sociology and criminology. Information presented will thus be analysed within an interdisciplinary framework. Deductive-theoretical tools will be combined with an inductive empirical approach, employing 'a parallel demonstration of theory' by first explicating a particular framework, then interrogating its utility applied to case studies of recent wars.[84] The following thematic operational indicators of risk management will guide case studies through a structured comparison approach:

1   Identifying risk as the impetus for war

i   *Systemic risk*
     Was systemic risk highlighted in terms of globalisation and end of Cold War constraints? Did these arise from 'anticipatory horizon-scanning' or a concern with avoiding repetition of 'tombstone-style risks' or a combination of both?

ii   *Risk or threat?*
     Did risk components in terms of probabilities and consequences help to conceptualise dangers?

2   Implementing risk management

i   *Active Anticipation*
     Is society's active anticipation of risks being transferred to the international scene? Have we eschewed reactive policies for proactive risk management strategies in the process? Did 'potential victims' adopt preventive victim-avoidance strategies? Was reflexive rationality evident in heightened awareness of possible adverse consequences of action or inaction?

ii   *The precautionary principle*
     How compelling was evidence for war? Were there 'false negatives' or 'false positives'? Were policy-makers concerned about blame for 'omission' (not taking precautions)? Was it purely precautionary or involved some desire to avoid repetition of 'tomb-stone' style risks?

iii *Surveillance*
     Were there continuous review processes seeking to prevent dangers in advance? Did long-term monitoring aid risk management actions?

iv   *'Less than heroic' strategies of risk management*
     To what degree did a utilitarian safety-first moral calculus override notions of democracy, or justice? Did war become an everyday 'routine' instrumental activity in managing risks? To what extent did war 'reshape' environments to reduce likelihoods of unwanted outcomes, rather than address moral issues such as causes and intentions of offending individuals or rehabilitating collapsed states?

3   Outcome specification

i   *Non-events and minimalism*
     Were non-events the intangible negative indicators of successful preventive action? Was there recognition of limits aimed at 'simply preventing

a bad' rather than complete solutions to an underlying problem or
grand narratives?

ii   *Cyclical open-ended processes*
Was risk management patient, cyclical and dialectical, or linear and
one-off? Did risks evolve and were new risks created through the
'boomerang effect'?

The three case studies will be analysed through this thematic schema. It is to
these that we now turn.

4

THE KOSOVO CAMPAIGN

War as a risk management exercise

We cannot turn our backs on the violations of human rights in other countries if we want to feel secure.
   –Tony Blair, Economic Club of Chicago, 22 April 1999

HUMANITARIAN WAR

The rhetoric of humanitarianism and humanitarian intervention clearly dominated the discourse on the Kosovo campaign but this perhaps did not tell the whole story. Without the Soviet threat and decline of ideological and structural explanations for war, David Chandler for instance felt war defined through human rights discourse was simply a fig leaf for Great Power domination over weaker states.[1] There were certainly other complex motivations involved than simply humanitarian rhetoric as Michael Mccgwire and Adam Roberts also suggest.[2] These will be discussed in later sections. Kosovo perhaps failed to live up to its billing as a purely 'humanitarian war' but as Nick Wheeler rightly argues, motivations need not be solely humanitarian for an intervention to be deemed humanitarian.[3] Indeed, that would be setting the bar impossibly high and states more often than not act on a combination of interests. Nonetheless, other less explicitly humanitarian considerations suggest there is more to it than meets the eye.

   An alternative approach not yet attempted in academic discourse is adopted here. To what extent could the Kosovo 'war' be construed as risk management? As with the later 'war' on terrorism, policy-makers and academics had difficulty categorising certain aspects of the Kosovo operation. NATO even expunged the 'war' word from its vocabulary. Although a coalition operation, the chief military contributor was America; its actions thus dominate analysis. Employing a set of structured questions inferred from the test framework developed in Chapter Three to guide analysis, observed evidence is presented to assess the framework's empirical validity and congruency. It is the contention of this chapter that trends surrounding specific aspects of the Kosovo campaign have implications for developing the broader notion of war as a risk management exercise.

In particular, it will be shown how systemic risks from ethnic cleansing were the primary impetus for war, especially when viewed through the lens of globalisation. When implementing policy remedies, policymakers consistently stressed proactive stances and employed a reflexive rationality. In this context of averting unwanted outcomes, the precautionary principle came into play while surveillance operations served to monitor the risks involved. The use of force became routinised in the Balkans as part of a reshaping strategy to reduce risks, rather than resolve them conclusively. Finally the campaign outcomes are evaluated from a risk management perspective, appreciating non-events and compromise solutions as measures of success. Unlike finite ends usually associated with war, risk management is an ongoing process.

BRIEF HISTORY

For much of the 1990s, under Ibrahim Rugova, the majority Kosovar Albanians largely adopted a non-violent strategy of passive protests and parallel administrative institutions after Belgrade withdrew its autonomy in 1989. This posed little concern to regional security. This appeared to have changed after the Dayton Accords in 1995 passed over Kosovo in the desire to get agreement on Bosnia. Milosevic also refused to discuss the issue then. To some Kosovars, the passive strategy had failed. Furthermore, the collapse of neighbouring Albania into near anarchy in 1997, led to widespread looting of army arsenals. These fell into the hands of the newly formed Kosovo Liberation Army (KLA). Significant new risks arose with the KLA and local support inflamed by brutal Serb responses. The complex historical background or possible reasons why Milosevic eventually capitulated will not be analysed. Numerous other books have done so. The detailed negotiation positions and mistaken assumptions of both sides entering the war are also not subjects of discussion. What follows is simply a brief description of the immediate run-up to the air war and its conduct.

By October 1998 diplomacy had secured a shaky ceasefire. Observers entered Kosovo and NATO aerial surveillance proceeded under UN Security Council Resolution 1199, which warned of ambiguous 'further action' if agreements were flouted. After the collapse of last-ditch talks at Rambouillet to end renewed fighting, Operation *Allied Force* was launched on 24 March 1999. Ethnic Kosovar Albanians soon started flooding into neighbouring Albania and Macedonia. The stated goals of the air campaign were to demonstrate the seriousness of NATO opposition to Belgrade; deter Milosevic from continuing attacks on civilians and create conditions to reverse ethnic cleansing; and degrade Serbia's capacity to wage war against Kosovo in the future or spread the war to neighbours.[4] Relying on air power alone and explicitly renouncing ground troops was hardly a perfect strategy and has been much criticised. Yet air power in such situations was the appropriate instrument given NATO's casualty intolerance and relative lack of vital interests. It would prove largely ineffectual against events on the ground and could not act alone without the threat of ground forces or wider diplomatic efforts.[5] However given the political realities within NATO, whereby key partners like Greece refused to countenance ground troops, Clinton chose the best 'among a bunch of bad options'. This in a sense actually represented a good strategic choice to maintain Alliance unity, while simultaneously demonstrating NATO credibility, using at the very least, air power, after repeated threats to use force. Hopefully, this 'bomb-and-pray' strategy would work.[6] Milosevic eventually signed up to a Military-Technical Agreement in June 1999 and Serb forces withdrew soon after.

CONCEPTUAL ISSUES

Much has been written criticising the motives, legality and wisdom of NATO's recourse to war: for example, Noam Chomsky's polemical *The New Military Humanism* and Ted Galen Carpenter's *NATO's Empty Victory* – a less polemical but still far from satisfactory analysis. The ethics and moral defensibility of risk-free war from afar also generated much discussion. Sometimes, the debate degenerated and 'fragmented into a series of mini-arguments about details and episodes'.[7]

Cognisant of this, the Kosovo issue is addressed here from a broad thematic risk management perspective rather than an episodic chronology, which has been well documented elsewhere. Kosovo recommends itself as a case study for several reasons. It was NATO's first major sustained combat operation without UN endorsement and the most intense use of military force in Europe by the West since 1945. Besides being the longest US combat operation since Vietnam, it also 'revealed the distinct attributes of a new American way of war'. It provided important insights into how developed countries will wage war in future and 'holds the key to understanding the decade that has just passed'.[8] Indeed, Stephen Biddle suggested that 'this curious little war' had important repercussions for US military policy.[9]

Much like Iraq in 2003, the Kosovo campaign also heralded great change in the foundations of international relations. Michael Ignatieff concluded that humanitarian intervention is now the 'chief raison d'etre' for Western armies'.[10] Tony Blair in his famous Chicago speech, argued that the campaign shifted the balance between human rights and state sovereignty. Timothy Garton Ash called Kosovo the first post-Westphalian war where neither the nation nor state had a major role. Instead, it was supposedly fought not for territory but for foreigners, the first humanitarian conflict in history.[11] Václav Havel thought human rights had been elevated above the law of states.[12] There is growing but reluctant acceptance of war as a lesser evil to address human wrongs. Kosovo was thus the first 'humanitarian war' where direct threats to vital national interests were lacking. President Clinton chose the most appropriate means, 'immaculate coercion'.[13] Clinton understood that in such wars, political support was sustainable only if it was bloodless. Values are not worth much, lamented Ignatieff, if impunity is necessary before they are defended. This was not a blanket aversion to casualties. According to Supreme Allied Commander Europe (SACEUR), General Wesley Clark, the Army preferred showdown on the Korean Peninsula or the Gulf.[14] Such interventions, serving US national interests but resulting in casualties, could be tolerated, an important caveat to the analysis presented here.

Yet, to Krauthammer, 'humanitarian war' had no future because it was a contradiction of bloodless war, no vital interests were engaged and rewards were hardly satisfying.[15] The post-war independent International Commission on Kosovo concluded that the international community willed a humanitarian end, without willing sufficient means: what Michael Ignatieff called 'our madness'.[16] Indeed it was rumoured that one Milosevic residence escaped bombing because it allegedly held a Rembrandt work. Ignatieff wrote, allowing a Rembrandt to save a criminal 'is a necessary madness, since the truth is that we are more anxious to save our souls than to save Kosovo.'[17] The tentative minimalist nature of the campaign was already evident. Although humanitarian objectives may also be considered noble and just, these do not evoke the will to sacrifice blood and treasure. There is less glory and even fewer heroes in such operations. The West intervened not for grand historical purposes or metanarratives but to manage problems with minimal casualties.[18] Victims are highlighted instead, from victims of ethnic cleansing and collateral damage to interveners shot down as victims of war. These were after all not wars of survival against clear specific threats but wars of choice against ambiguous security risks.

Furthermore, the Kosovo operation overturned Westphalian and UN legalist models of using force only in response to international aggression. It also defied the more practical military requirements of the Powell doctrine, which advocated overwhelming military force only for clearly identifiable vital interests and ends. Although the Powell doctrine was eventually validated on overwhelming force (more than 1000 warplanes were deployed by June 1999), clear vital interests and endgames elude easy definition. Andrew Bacevich was nonetheless adamant that Kosovo was an 'imperial management' strategy. Rather than protecting Kosovars, its purpose was to sustain American dominance on a continent that had 'advanced the furthest toward the openness and integration defining the ultimate goal of American grand strategy'.[19] Could risk management rather than imperial management or humanitarian intervention be the main goal instead? Kosovo may have been the last 'humanitarian war' by Krauthammer's calculation and overturned many conventional legal and practical military requirements for war. It did, however, fulfil many criteria for risk management.

Furthermore, NATO participants were not allowed to call it 'war'. Some commentators suggest NATO's operation was not really a 'war' but perhaps a 'police' operation to manage a 'condition of insecurity'.[20] Not for national survival, it was limited and carefully constrained under the media spotlight; victory was carefully defined. This, to Wesley Clark, was modern war.[21] BBC correspondent Jonathan Marcus called Kosovo the 'war that dared not speak its name'. Secretary-General Solana was emphatic: 'NATO is not waging war against Yugoslavia'.[22] Yet NATO was taking and returning fire on a sustained and large-scale basis, a war to most people. Three weeks into the campaign, Defence Secretary Cohen accepted that despite being engaged in combat, he was unwilling to pronounce whether that measured up to 'quote: a classic definition of war'.[23] British Defence Secretary George Robertson was less circumspect, 'it is not a war'.[24]

These verbal gymnastics helped maintain public and political suupport for military force. There were also legal reasons, for war is largely prohibited by the UN Charter, while only Congress could formally declare war for the US. It could also have been discomfort with what NATO had in fact started.[25] Could the conceptual confusion also have arisen since this type of war as risk management did not fit 'classic' definitions of war comprising massed fielded armies and decisive battles?

A year after the end of hostilities, NATO still clung to its guns: 'This was not a war.'[26] To General Klaus Naumann of NATO's Military Committee, Milosevic 'had accepted war but NATO had accepted just an operation'.[27] Neutral words like 'operation' and 'disrupt' suggested a purely utilitarian use of force rather than an emotive word like 'war'. Even before hostilities erupted, when asked to comment on NATO's upcoming Kosovo mission, General Sir Michael Rose pointedly noted that imposing a political settle-ment forcefully was not peacekeeping. It was war.[28] The concept of war needs to be refined to properly take account of these developments.

More telling questions have been raised over whether the campaign was a war or coercive diplomacy. General Clark felt Kosovo was the latter. It was called a 'war' (by media, not officials) simply for ease of public under-standing.[29] Ignatieff agreed that this sounded and looked like a war with the requisite imagery of bombers and destruction. In truth it was coercion designed to sway Milosevic's mind.[30] Richard Haass similarly argued that in contrast to *Desert Fox* over Iraq in December 1998, at least air power over Kosovo was compellant, linked to a specified set of demands.[31]

Thomas Schelling defined 'coercive diplomacy' as less heroic, less mili-tary, less impersonal than force used to overpower an opponent militarily.[32] Schelling distinguished between brute force and coercion. Brute force aims to deny an enemy use of certain assets by their destruction. Coercion aims to compel an enemy to do your will by threat of force, or limited force, with the prospect of more to come as its most important component.[33] However the distinction between the two is not always clear-cut.[34] Kosovo involved elements of both. The Americans and British were not totally united on the aims of bombing – there were subtle differences. Michael Clarke rightfully noted that while American statements sometimes seemed to imply that bombing was coercive diplomacy, the British took a more 'managerial' and instrumental policy of denial than coercion.[35] Defence Secretary George Robertson clarified that he did not seek to play mind games. The goal was simply to use strategic precision bombing to reduce Milosevic's ability to order ethnic cleansing.[36] The British position was therefore more conceivably a risk management strategy than coercive diplomacy.

NATO's approach involved a mix of escalation theory and hi-tech warfare. Washington never desired all-out war or the Air Force doctrine of 'parallel warfare' stressing simultaneity in attacking strategic targets and fielded forces. It opted for phased gradualism, expressing a desire to stop bombing and settle the dispute politically. What NATO fought did not resemble war apparently: 'it was not fought using all combat arms, implemented tentatively without any shock or decisiveness or simultaneity.'[37] The Pentagon noted 'this was not a traditional military conflict. There was no direct clash of massed ground forces'.[38] Others such as *New York Times* columnist Thomas Friedman, wanted a 'real air war'. Friedman found it absurd that Belgrade held concerts while other Serbs rampaged in Kosovo. Herein lies the core problem: did Kosovo not fit such preconceived notions because it was a new form of war as risk management? While there are certainly strong arguments that the campaign was more coercive diplomacy than war, risk management could provide another plausible explanation.

Two levels of risks are pertinent here. The first entails globalised systemic risks of human rights abuses and ethnic conflict. The second applies on a more tactical level, which attracted most attention.[39] Concern with tactical risks and force protection was all too obvious. Washington subcontracted to a private company DynCorp to monitor ceasefires and NGOs to air-drop food; warplanes bombed from 15000 feet, politicians promised to reduce the risks of unintended damage, Apache gun-ships were not used because of risks from Serb MANPADS. Sometimes these overshadowed the original concern with systemic risks. As General Clark later argued, occasionally even 'insignificant tactical events' (such as losing a NATO pilot) can have political or strategic consequences: a key characteristic of modern war.[40] Kosovo has been described as '*Disjointed war*' despite current emphasis on joint operations. Multiple objectives of minimising collateral damage, and avoiding friendly casualties were contradictory.[41] Clark's memoirs revealed that the first requirement was to avoid losing any aircraft, one of four 'measures of merit' he issued.[42] Unsurprisingly then, Kosovo was the first war conducted under 'post-heroic' rules: no casualties for fighting forces and no deliberate attacks on enemy populations.[43] NATO repeatedly stated that its enemy was not the Serb people but regime targets. However, our main concern here is not these tactical developments in risk-averse warfare. Despite being greatly constrained by tactical risks, the focus is on how NATO managed the systemic risks of ethnic cleansing exacerbated by globalisation.

Globalisation and systemic risks: ethnic cleansing

Systemic risks as the target for risk management action in Kosovo certainly were in abundant supply. Problematically, risks are generally ambiguous and risk perception is inherently a subjective and culturally constructed process. Different actors may perceive a risk differently. The variables are endless: from international and domestic political structures, to cultural background, cognitive mindset of decision-makers who see in information only what they prefer to see and so on. Secretary of State Albright, who lived in Yugoslavia for some time and spoke some Serbo-Croatian, was known to drive hardline US policy: journalists dubbed the war 'Madeleine's War' after the rigid manner in which she conducted Rambouillet made conflict more unavoidable. Albright repeatedly drew analogies to Hitler and past failures in Bosnia. Furthermore, other factors such as Tony Blair's alleged desire to strut the world stage interacted in complex ways with geopolitics, history, ideology, bureaucratic infighting, differences with NATO allies and domestic politics especially in Germany with its Red-Green coalition.

Nonetheless, data gathering and comparative analysis of statements can provide a useful guide to patterns and regularities to be analysed here.[44] Furthermore, our focus is not the intricacies of decision-making, which others have already competently examined.[45] Our concern relates mainly to understanding the chosen policy and its implementation/consequences, rather than detailed decision-making analysis of how that policy was chosen.

Risk is used here as a descriptive term to refer to a situation. The conflict in Kosovo entailed 'risks of horizontal escalation' spreading outwards as well as 'vertical escalation' involving ever more savage attacks on civilians.[46] Historically speaking, Great Powers have always tried to contain Balkan conflicts much like today – from the Bosnian revolt of 1876 and the Macedonian uprisings in 1903 to the Balkan wars of 1912–13. Despite Bismarck's well-known remark at the Congress of Berlin in 1878 that the Balkans were not worth the bones of a single Pomeranian grenadier, the region was to embroil Germany in World War One and again in 1999. The main aim then, as now, was to prevent Balkan conflicts destroying international stability. It was never believed they could be fully resolved, only limited.[47] There is nothing new here: Benjamin Disraeli warned back in 1878 that 50,000 crack European troops were necessary to maintain order in the Balkans.

However, mutual interests and rivalries then were dictated largely by considerations for the balance of power. Great Powers would have seen opportunities together with dangers. They would have exploited Yugoslav crises to further their own interests.[48] The concerns in 1999 were not so much balance of power and jostling for gains between Great Powers as avoiding risks of conflict spread, which could be exacerbated by the impact of globalisation. Over Kosovo in 1999, most nineteenth century members of the Concert of Europe were on the same NATO side, except for Russia. There was hardly significant concern for balance of power concepts, perhaps only on the Russian side. Rather than presenting opportunities, the Kosovo crisis presented only risks viewed with great trepidation.

What is more important now is the end of the Cold War, globalisation and associated systemic risks. The dissolution of Yugoslavia was related to the collapse of communism as forces previously holding the federation together came apart. Communist apparatchiks like Milosevic played the nationalist card to keep power. Some scholars argued the Kosovo campaign also marked NATO's blurring of its role from a military alliance into a police organisation. Its object was now to 'manage turbulence that might affect security of its members' rather than exclusively directed against an identifiable enemy such as the former Soviet Union.[49] The implications of Kosovo were furthermore viewed most importantly in terms of globalisation. Tony Blair, providing one of the more coherent justifications for intervention, candidly admitted, 'twenty years ago we would not have been fighting in Kosovo', given Cold War constraints. Instead globalisation was now the new framework for security. Speaking at the Economic Club of Chicago, the Prime Minister noted that 'globalisation is not just economic. It is also a political and security phenomenon'. Conflicts and the violation of human rights in other countries affected our sense of security.[50] The US *National Security Strategy for a New Century* in December 1999 was unequivocal: 'globalisation, however, also brings risks.' Ethnic conflicts endanger regional stability in many parts of the world.[51] This indicated a case of 'horizon-scanning' of the strategic landscape for security risks. However, it was also clear in the minds of policy-makers like Blair and Albright that a desire to avoid repetition of previous dramatic 'tombstone-style' risks such as Srebrenica motivated their actions. There was no clear demarcation as policy-makers drew analogies from past experience and extrapolated into preventing what seemed like analogous risks from happening.

Over Kosovo, the definition of 'strategic importance' changed as a consequence of globalisation. Previously, it derived from resources or geography such as access to the sea or control of trade routes. Through globalization, information technology and collapsing Cold War controls, Kosovo's significance lay more in its potential to cause damage beyond its boundaries, exporting unwanted phenomena such as chronic insecurity, chaos, illegal immigration and drug-trafficking.[52] Increasing global interconnectedness meant that instability in a relative strategic backwater like Kosovo, according to this logic, could undermine the very stability globalisation depended on. The Kosovo campaign, in this sense, served to manage such risks. Instability could spread to Europe, which was seen as crucial to globalisation and economic interdependence. Clinton seemed to acknowledge as much: 'that's what this Kosovo thing is all about'.[53]

Before *Allied Force*, Henry Kissinger wrote that Kosovo did not pose any 'threat to American security traditionally conceived'.[54] Indeed, new concepts of globalisation and risk warranted a reconceptualisation of security interests. During the Cold War, at least there were clearer ideological, economic or security interests involved from Korea to Vietnam. Post-Cold War Kosovo seemed a most unlikely place for intervention.[55] Washington's security interests in Kosovo in 1999 seemed even less important than those over Iraq or Osama bin Laden.[56] The trigger was mainly couched in terms of possible risks. In March 1998, the Council of the European Union condemned Milosevic's use of force against Kosovars for placing 'the security of the region at risk'. The Contact Group similarly warned that 'the risk of an escalating conflict requires immediate action'.[57]

Launching Operation *Allied Force*, NATO leaders repeated verbatim the purpose to avert a humanitarian catastrophe. Yet the military means employed were insufficient to attain immediate objectives of halting ethnic cleansing. Adam Roberts argued that since a humanitarian disaster was not averted in the short term, it is a 'questionable model of humanitarian intervention'.[58] NATO action included many elements that were not purely humanitarian nor did they exclusively relate to globalised systemic risks. This is hardly surprising for it is unrealistic to expect states to act purely on a single motive. Further motives ranged from guilt over earlier inaction on Bosnia, NATO's credibility, to reluctance to accept more refugees. Key considerations according to Roberts were humanity and risk to NATO credibility especially since the Allies guaranteed the October 1998 ceasefire. Foreign Secretary Robin Cook warned that NATO credibility was on the line if that guarantee was not met.[59] NATO acknowledged in its report on Kosovo one year on, failing to square up to Milosevic would have eroded the credibility of its institutions.[60] As Michael Clarke rightly noted, NATO credibility was at stake after very publicly issuing its Activation Orders (ACTORDS) in late 1998.[61] NATO's leading members did not emerge with reputations unscathed from Bosnia. Now Kosovo was a key test for both NATO's relevance on its fiftieth anniversary and the idea of 'out of area' operations.

Dana Allin concluded that NATO took action only when moral issues were reinforced by security risks relating to European stability.[62] Blair's rationale implied as much. Mass expulsion of Kosovars certainly demanded our attention, but what made this more imperative was it happening in a 'combustible part of Europe'.[63] Kosovo after all seemed to pose greater security risks than Bosnia, its closest analogous example. By autumn 1991 Washington did not act in the first phase of the Bosnian conflict because it judged that 'complete inaction did not pose the risks action did'.[64] As then Secretary of State James Baker colourfully noted, 'we've got no dog in this fight'. His deputy Lawrence Eagleburger believed the war posed risks only to those directly killing each other. NATO thus failed to act robustly until 1995 when the corrosive effect on transatlantic relations and between NATO's European members was becoming obvious. Missing from this sort of calculus over Bosnia was that inaction might entail its own risks detrimental to US interests.[65]

This calculus became more apparent over Kosovo, which was deemed a greater security concern. The so-called 'Christmas Warning' in 1992 by the first Bush Administration had earlier identified a geopolitical 'red line' over the Kosovo issue as a strategic interest if the conflict in Bosnia spread south. Milosevic was warned that if Serbia started a war in Kosovo, Washington would feel obliged to act. This was repeated by the Clinton Administration. In 1993, Secretary of State Warren Christopher cautioned that Albania, Greece and Turkey could be sucked into any Kosovo conflict. The stakes for the US were to 'prevent broadening that conflict.'[66] Kosovo and possible pan-Albanian nationalism, bordered by Macedonia, Albania, and Greece was deemed a different set of risks altogether.[67] It posed more risks to regional security than the Bosnian conflicts. Blair forewarned risks rippling across the region.[68] Apart from substantial human rights concerns, violence in Kosovo, situated at the heart of a combustible region could spread to neighbouring states and far beyond, threatening NATO's southern flank. Michael Mccgwire thus believed that the 'Christmas Warning' and fear of insecurity spreading beyond Kosovo was the key to understanding NATO action.[69] This posed even greater concern when viewed through the prism of globalisation aggravating this possible instability. Despite Clinton's contention that Kosovo was a powder keg in the heart of Europe,[70] there was in fact little real chance of triggering Great Power confrontation on the scale of Sarajevo 1914. As Kissinger derisively commented, 'Milosevic is no Hitler but a Balkan thug'. Milosevic was hardly in a position to threaten global equilibrium.[71]

Risk or threat?

This brings us to the capabilities and intentions of Milosevic in ascertaining whether he did pose a threat conventionally conceived. Milosevic's Serbia hardly constituted a direct survival threat to Britain or America. At best, he was an indirect threat. UN sanctions since 1992 had crippled the economy and its population levels; GDP had dropped sharply. Despite constant emphasis on 'degrading his military capability', Milosevic's military hardly qualified as an existential threat despite being primed for ethnic cleansing and Serb anti-air capability was certainly robust. Rump Yugoslavia had no chance militarily against a NATO boasting 35 times its armed forces, 25 times its defence budget and 696 times its national wealth.[72] Furthermore, some contended that it was not the Serbs with expansionist motivations, but the KLA seeking a Greater Albania.[73] Even if Milosevic's much touted *Operation Horseshoe* intended to create many more refugees and destabilise the region, the intention could also have been to settle his own Kosovo problem once and for all. Intelligence assessments of Milosevic's intentions were also inadequate. US intelligence was 'utterly divided' on how to read his intentions and troop movements into Kosovo in early 1999: was it purely sabre-rattling or war preparations?[74] Based on intentions and capabilities alone, the threat picture was far from conclusive or compelling.

Instead a mentality emphasising risks – based on probabilistic thinking and possible catastrophic consequences of inaction – appeared to inform policy-makers. This led Clinton to declare that security interests over Kosovo could not be assessed in conventional terms of size or distance. Instead we should contemplate possible consequences of inaction.[75] The national interest lay in ensuring the conflict would not spread. Otherwise, it could only be stopped, at far greater cost and risk, according to Clinton's logic. Upon launching air strikes, Clinton outlined two sets of 'risks of failing to act': one to the innocent people who might be killed or driven from their homes; the second related to regional stability.[76] Concern operated on two levels: the humanitarian argument and that of security risk. The components of risk were clearly present: the probability of not acting and incurring undesirable consequences. NATO's retrospective report *Kosovo: One Year On* expressed similar concern about the 'potential to spread instability to neighbouring countries in the region'.[77] This sounded like a revived version of the long-discredited domino theory. Now the concern was the potential for proliferating risks accentuated by globalisation, not communist expansionism. Furthermore, the catastrophic consequences emphasised by policy-makers drew references to genocide and possibly another Holocaust. In the Western mindset, few other stark consequences come near, although genocide does not exactly describe what was actually ethnic cleansing and enforced population displacement.

The language of risk dominated the new *Strategic Concept*, which outlined the 'complex new risks' that face NATO with the demise of communism.[78] This Concept has been criticised for a very vague definition of NATO's geographical limits. Almost anything from stalled economic reform, terrorism, to ethnic instability could be considered a potential security issue. In NATO's defence, this probabilistic mindset is a natural outgrowth of managing uncertain and unpredictable risks that might have significant consequences. There is some truth that 'new NATO is not focused on an enemy state but an enemy concept: instability'.[79] In this context, the concept of elusive risks and their management would fit like a glove.

IMPLEMENTING RISK MANAGEMENT

Active anticipation

Risk management strategies are generally proactive since the locus of action is avoiding future events that have not yet occurred. Policy-makers become 'reflexive', *averting* alternative futures through anticipatory measures without specifying in advance clear cause-effect relationships. The emphasis is less on *achieving* goals by instrumental calculation of relative capabilities of the states involved. The notion of risk allows potential victims to take avoidance action. It is true though that NATO 'reacted' to events on the ground with fighting already underway in Kosovo. The key here is how NATO reacted in a 'proactive' fashion. Its locus of action was future possible consequences and to prevent repetition of a Srebrenica-like situation, rather than seeking retrospective revenge or justice for victims of Milosevic. This is discussed in detail later. Risk here is not only a descriptive term but a normative one implying the need for preventive action. It also formed part of a strategic calculation.

NATO's post-Cold War rationale essentially revolved around two issues: enlargement and proactive 'out of area' missions.[80] In various *Strategic Concepts* and negotiating the 1997 *Founding Act* with Russia, NATO emphasised it would not attack unless it was attacked. It was a *reactive* Alliance. However over Kosovo, NATO became a 'proactive military organisation'.[81] As NATO's original mission of collective defence ended with the Soviet Union, a more proactive role developed for managing a broad array of risks. The focus became developments posing risks to members' security, rather than Article 5 events.[82] NATO's new Security Concept clearly envisions a more proactive approach: 'an important aim of the Alliance is to keep risks at a distance by dealing with potential crises at an early stage'.[83] NATO failed in preventive diplomacy in Kosovo despite numerous warnings throughout the 1990s but launched a proactive military campaign to forestall a full-blown crisis.

Even before the Kosovo war, Secretary-General Solana argued that 'security policies must become increasingly proactive', anticipating and averting new challenges.[84] After considering counter-factual and alternative course of actions, this proactive argument manifested in how both Clinton and Blair justified NATO action on reflexive terms. This was consistent with a slew of policy statements employing similar language that persisted to later wars in

Afghanistan and Iraq. On commencing air strikes Clinton concluded 'the dangers of acting now are clearly outweighed by the risks of failing to act.'[85] Blair echoed this reflexive premise: 'the potential consequences of military action are serious.... but the consequences of not acting are more serious still.... we have always been in favour of taking action sooner rather than later'.[86] As hypothesised by a reflexive rationality framework of risk, emphasis was on proactively averting possible adverse consequences of (in)action, even before these have materialised rather than more direct instrumental rationality.

Kosovo was thus the first major outing of a newly proactive NATO managing systemic risks. NATO averted 'potential victimhood' for Kosovar Albanians, and also prevented itself falling victim to adverse consequences of ethnic cleansing in the form of regional instability.[87] Clinton's final *National Security Strategy for a Global Age* noted approvingly how defensive entities had transformed into proactive instruments for meeting post-Cold War challenges.[88] NATO action in Kosovo was cited as a successful example.

Better safe than sorry?

Discussions in 2003 about a new US security doctrine of pre-emption are actually not unprecedented. Some precursors were already evident in Kosovo. It was a form of precautionary action designed to pre-empt worse atrocities and related instability, avoid possible corrosive effects on the Alliance, and 'damage Serb capacity to wage war against Kosovo in the *future* or spread the war to its neighbours'.[89]

How much did Western intelligence actually know about the infamous Operation *Horseshoe*? Was there compelling evidence about Serb plans of massive ethnic cleansing to justify military action? Or was there some semblance of the precautionary principle at work here? Some evidence suggests action was taken in spite of uncertain and indefinite proof. Tim Judah testified on the precautionary rationale for intervention, that another Srebrenica could happen at any time: 'how was one supposed to know that was not going to happen?'[90] A NATO spokesman tellingly argued in August 2000 after the International Criminal Tribunal for Former Yugoslavia (ICTY) failed to corroborate NATO claims of genocide in Kosovo, 'the point is did we successfully pre-empt or not.... We would rather be criticised for overestimating numbers who died than for failing to pre-empt'.[91] Clearly there was concern about omission, and being blamed for not taking precautionary action. During the bombing, NATO spokesman Jamie Shea suggested that Pristina football stadium had become a massive concentration camp. Inflated figures of those killed by Serb forces were provided. Before the war, President Clinton and Secretary Cohen regularly tossed out figures of 100,000 dead. [92] The State Department even upped the ante to 500,000.

In the post-war period however, the figures dropped until by August 2000, the ICTY announced numbers below 3000. Atrocities alleged at Trepca mine where hundreds of bodies were said to have been incinerated or thrown down the mineshaft, turned out to be false. Nothing was found at all. Unsurprisingly, after the war, there were calls in Britain by Alice Mahon MP of the Balkans Committee for Robin Cook to answer questions that the Government deliberately misled the public, inflating scale of deaths to justify bombing. This became a case of 'false positives' inherent in the resort to the precautionary principle. The risk ultimately turned out to be less serious than initially suggested. This set a precedent for later wars in Iraq. Christopher Layne claimed that in fact there was no large-scale organised ethnic cleansing ongoing in Kosovo until NATO intervened. Albanian refugees were simply fleeing the fighting between Serb forces and KLA guerrillas.[93]

Refugee flows, whether from guerrilla fighting or ethnic cleansing, are nonetheless similarly destabilising from NATO's point of view. Milosevic had indeed adopted brutal tactics against Albanian villagers. Figures from the UNHCR Special Envoy for the region stated that on 23 March 1999 before NATO action, there were over 260,000 internally displaced persons (IDPs) within Kosovo, over 100,000 refugees in the region and over 100,000 outside the region. Two thousand had been killed by March 1999, mostly during KLA spring and Serb summer counter-offensives before OSCE monitors were deployed in October 1998. It may seem callous to call the Kosovo air war one of precaution when in fact large-scale human suffering had occurred. Would this count as a humanitarian catastrophe justifying intervention?

Strictly speaking, Dana Allin agrees with Christopher Layne that Belgrade's earlier actions of summer 1998 were not ethnic cleansing but brutal counter-insurgency tactics.[94] Despite extreme Serb brutality, in terms of casualties inflicted and individuals at risk, the violence in Kosovo was substantially less than what happened in Rwanda and not much greater than Bosnia previously. This was deemed by Michael Mccgwire 'unsubstantial' and insufficient to justify in January 1999 summoning various parties to Rambouillet and the absolute insistence on KFOR under NATO direction. The real aim was actually to forestall a full-scale civil war.[95] Jonathan Charney argued that the NATO action in Kosovo could only be understood as 'anticipatory humanitarian intervention' since human rights violations prior to withdrawal of OSCE observers were not massive and widespread. Such intervention in absence of proof of widespread violations, the argument went, allowed hegemonic states to use force against international law.[96]

But Jonathan Charney and other critics of NATO intervention on this premise miss the point despite themselves raising the concept of 'anticipatory humanitarian action'. Surely a more credible argument, as Daalder and O'Hanlon point out, can be made that despite such claims of relatively low-level violence and that Kosovo had not (yet) become a full-fledged humanitarian disaster, 'without intervention things would get much worse'.[97] If events were allowed to continue unabated without taking precautionary action, a full-scale civil war with predictably dire humanitarian and regional consequences would occur. By then it would be no good intervening. NATO, however, initially failed to anticipate or prevent the intensified ethnic cleansing immediately after hostilities began. Over the past decade, military force on the side of 'right' against 'wrong' has a moral ring to it lacking since the colonial period. Even humanitarian NGOs like Médecin Sans Frontières are lobbying for pre-emptive humanitarian intervention by force. Its founder and later administrator of Kosovo, Bernard Kouchner, argued that Western states have the right to 'intervene as a preventive measure to stop wars before they start and stop murderers before they kill'.[98] In other words, precautionary use of force was justified.

Most recently, various commentators have stated that, after passing several criteria and preconditions, anticipatory military action can be legitimate 'in response to clear evidence of likely large-scale killing or ethnic cleansing'.[99] The requirement for clear evidence went somewhat contrary to that of the precautionary principle operating under much more uncertainty. NATO also moved quicker than before, perhaps learning from previous experiences in Bosnia. This is suggestive of a 'tombstone' style approach to risk management, seeking to avoid similar dramatic disasters garnering media attention rather than a purely 'precautionary' stance.[100] Blair warned of men being singled out by masked paramilitaries without anyone knowing what happened afterward: 'recall that at Srebrenica they were killed'.[101] There were historical precedents and somewhat less uncertainty than a purely precautionary approach would suggest. Nonetheless, the basic premise of 'better safe than sorry' encapsulated in the precautionary principle was reflected in NATO action.

Surveillance

Surveillance is the vehicle of risk management, collecting information on risks and assessing whether they require more management action. During the Cold War, NATO had mechanisms designed to provide advance warning of Soviet military moves. These consisted of 'indications' of steps an adversary had to take to prepare military action. This system focused largely on quantitative military developments and more concrete capabilities. However, the post-Cold War security environment has extended beyond traditional aggression, to unconventional risks such as ethnic instability.

NATO normally obtains early warning through the Euro-Atlantic Partnership Council as well as internal bodies like the North Atlantic Council and the Political and Military Committee. Additionally, a New Intelligence Warning System (NIWS) has been developed. The NIWS is a much more inclusive system developed to take account of risks such as ethnic cleansing identified in the 1999 Strategic Concept during the Kosovo campaign. It is based on the *qualitative* informed judgement of analysts as opposed to the more mechanistic *quantitative* approach of the Cold War. It continuously monitors and assesses a wide range of risk indicators not only for NATO, but around the Euro-Atlantic periphery, rather than enemy military capabilities.[102] As suggested by the test framework, a continuous review process of risks is in place anticipating possible dangers, rather than more concrete measures of observable military capabilities.

In the run-up to the air campaign proper, there were already precursor surveillance operations in place. Together with unarmed OSCE monitors on the ground, Operation *Eagle Eye*, the NATO Air Verification Mission, aimed to verify Serb reduction of troop levels and compliance with UN Security Council Resolution 1199, assess and report on developments. The Clinton Administration, ever so concerned about risk management down to the tactical level on the ground, even subcontracted the high-risk task of monitoring Serb withdrawal to a private military company, DynCorp. UAVs such as the Predator and manned surveillance platforms such as the U-2, RC-135 Rivet Joint and RAF Canberras were involved. Such surveillance helped provide contributory information on the risks, and action that turned out to be necessary.

Verification flights ended on 24 March 1999 with the launch of Operation *Allied Force*, but surveillance flights continued to support NATO targeting and monitoring Serb ethnic cleansing in real-time. In Kosovo, the use of UAVs for surveillance avoided losses of manned aircraft without forgoing benefits of loitering and low-altitude flights. As one senior military officer noted, 'UAVs died for their country and no one mourned'.[103] On 1 April 1999, human rights groups and religious organisations asked the Clinton Administration to release satellite and UAV imagery of atrocities to the International Criminal Tribunal for the Former Yugoslavia. Washington, recognising the public relations value, promptly released images of possible mass graves, including Glodane, Velika Krusa and Glogovac. The availability of satellite imagery to the public was unprecedented.[104] It was also hoped, perhaps naively, that making the Serbs aware of such surveillance might help reduce the risks by discouraging ethnic cleansing.[105]

Tracking the civilian toll had high stakes in a war supposedly fought for moral values, as well as monitoring the systemic risks of refugee flows destabilising neighbouring Macedonia and Albania. If the risks were deemed intolerable, further management action was then taken transferring displaced Albanians to countries like Germany to relieve the burden on Macedonia. Military action was also ratcheted up a notch to include strategic targets as well in Belgrade, partly in response to intensified ethnic cleansing. As Paul Virilio observed after the campaign, the all-seeing 'Eye of humanity' now went roving across the world with satellite surveillance, manned and unmanned aircraft.[106]

After KFOR entered Kosovo, UAVs were re-tasked to force protection and area surveillance missions. The outbreak of fighting in Macedonia and increased levels of risk in March 2001 saw the despatch of more Predators to provide surveillance. A Florida-based private military company, AirScan Inc., was also involved in monitoring security risks such as smugglers and terrorists trying to cross the border, locating weapons stashes and watching suspect premises. In March 2001, with increasing tensions in Presovo valley in north-east Kosovo, the OSCE Spillover Monitor Mission to Skopje, originally established in 1992, enhanced its activity along the Macedonia-Kosovo border to collect more information. As predicted by the test framework, every time a security risk in Kosovo from ethnic cleansing, terrorists and smugglers to tensions along the border is identified, surveillance and monitoring is undertaken to assess it. Despite more than five years of international administration, Kosovo remained subject to risk surveillance. From January 2002 to May 2003, the UN Development Program's Kosovo Early Warning System provided integrated assessment and forecasting capacity of factors that might affect Kosovo in the near future and sought to forecast and prevent potential crises. Four risk areas were continuously monitored: socio-economic stability; political and institutional stability; ethnic relations; personal and public security. Anticipating possible risk scenarios and indicators was now the uppermost concern rather than a concrete military danger.

UTILITARIAN 'LESS THAN HEROIC' STRATEGIES OF RISK MANAGEMENT

'Routine' war

Some observers suggest war has become simply 'a housekeeping arrangement, a series of more or less routine tasks'.[107] Did such routine chores extend to managing systemic risks over Kosovo? After all, risk management manuals tell us, good risk management should be routinely integrated into general everyday activity. Was ethnic cleansing seen, like crime, as an everyday risk to be managed? War became routine in two senses: it became familiar, and also instrumental to manage risks. Kosovo did not engage the passions of the American people; instead the Dow Jones closed above 10,000 for the first time ever. The economic boom went on as usual unperturbed.[108] People watched from the comfort of their living rooms, giving 'virtual consent' according to Michael Ignatieff, as long as no one got hurt, on both sides if possible. The act of war had become an emotionally detached, utilitarian instrument to manage risks.

Risk management in Kosovo also helped keep the Balkan house in order through almost routine applications of force. By the late 1990s, naval deployments to the Eastern Mediterranean in support of Balkan operations exhibited a clear 'routinisation of what would otherwise be legitimately known as crisis response'.[109] Clinton suggested that previously diplomacy and force were used to end the war in Bosnia. Now conflict in neighbouring Kosovo jeopardised the region's people again.[110] There seemed to be a resigned familiar ring to it. So, the argument went, the same model of military force must be employed against what seemed to be seen in Washington as an almost commonplace occurrence of the 1990s: the risks ethnic cleansing posed for Balkan stability and beyond.

We have grown accustomed to cruise missiles lifting off, often at night for dramatic effect; or cockpit gun camera footage. As Andrew Bacevich observed, since 1993 from Somalia to Haiti to Iraq and Afghanistan to Kosovo, the Clinton Administration had 'made the use of force routine'.[111] Bacevich felt this demonstrated how Clinton had adapted preponderant American military power to the post-Cold War world. The quasi-imperial Clinton administration had used improving capabilities in air power for purposes far removed from traditional national security requirements. Such new requirements involved managing systemic risks. In the six months before Kosovo, the Clinton Administration had 'managed' three countries: cruise missile strikes against Afghanistan and Sudan; Operation *Desert Fox* against Iraq; and the low-level air war over no-fly zones. This series of events is revealing for it illuminates how air power was being used to manage security risks in a 'routine', almost nonchalant manner. Kosovo was simply the latest in a line-up of risks to be managed.

Bacevich argues that a new military doctrine no longer reliant on brute force has developed in using precision-guided air power for carefully calibrated, long-range strikes with little risk of friendly casualties.[112] Luttwak concluded that such one-sided combat against enemies who could hardly react also constituted more of a 'management' challenge than war.[113] The vague language used – 'degrading' until NATO achieves desired levels of 'degradation'[114] – could of course, as Bacevich pointed out, simply be a face-saving tactic for the White House to declare victory without admitting failure. 'Degrading' also sounds less spectacular, signalling less of a departure from everyday operations than 'war' might imply. Such language helped the Kosovo campaign seem more like a routine chore.

Personifying risks

War as risk management should theoretically be managerial in nature, not correctional. As with recent developments in criminology, the focus should be utilitarian, and more modestly managing the risks posed by a person to a wider population, rather than trying to reform that person. It should also not be too concerned with questions of justice, right or wrong, or morality. Was there any evidence of this in Kosovo? Recent advances in air power allowed for greater precision to target the enemy leadership, no longer the state or its society and citizens. Wesley Clark's briefings constantly employed pronouns alluding personally to Milosevic in describing 'his' air defences, 'his' storage plants. The Serb leader was also personally indicted for war crimes at The Hague. While special envoy Richard Holbrooke negotiated with Milosevic in the run-up to the air campaign, some US Senators and the State Department had misgivings about lending legitimacy to the authoritarian leader. Yet there was no real prospect of regime change; Holbrooke was convinced that Milosevic held the key to peace.[115]

Milosevic was often identified as the root cause of the Kosovo conflict. Secretary-General Solana stressed that the person responsible 'is President Milosevic, not NATO'. Secretary of State Albright had her spokesman James Rubin declare that 'Milosevic is not part of the problem. Milosevic is the problem.'[116] A callous, ruthless political operator, the West over the years has both demonised him and found him indispensable to Balkan problems.[117] Milosevic did not actually create the problem and there are many other factors, such as history and latent Serb nationalism; but he did exploit the situation for political purposes. Some such as Herbert London, Professor of Humanities at New York University, complained that as long as Milosevic was in power, there was no 'victory' despite NATO achieving most of its goals.[118] A Radio Free Europe/Radio Liberty report found the war in Kosovo 'disappointing' because it resulted in a 'Saddam Hussein peace' much like that after the 1991 Gulf War, similarly leaving Milosevic in power.[119]

Furthermore as Edward Luttwak observed, the paradox of strategic air power is such that the bombing may be precise yet ineffectual from the perspective of enemy leaders. Perhaps Milosevic saw air campaigns as useful or neutral in keeping him in power.[120] Vastly superior NATO forces did not seek 'regime change' or battlefield defeat of the Yugoslav army (VJ). Instead, the goal was to diminish and degrade its capabilities. This was perhaps a reflection of the limited and indirect security interests in the region as well as the fact that Milosevic was seen as potentially influential in ending the violence.[121]

On the other hand, risk management does not seek correctionalism: seeking Milosevic's removal misses the point somewhat. Rather the goal is managerial and more modest. It is fundamentally utilitarian. As long as the risks are managed to a sufficient degree, it is enough to stop hostilities. Compromise deals have been struck with him from Dayton to ending hostilities in Kosovo. Demonising Milosevic may have made the war easier to prosecute for public opinion purposes, but it diverted attention from the complex nature of the Kosovo problem and Serbia did indeed have some legitimate interests there. Western governments might well have decided after the campaign ended to engineer Milosevic's ouster through economic sanctions, diplomatic isolation, aid to opposition parties and democracy programmes.[122] It was significant though that the war itself left him in power.[123] Just as justice has been overshadowed by utilitarian risk management in crime control, this suggested that NATO did not seek redress for the many victims of Milosevic's political agenda. Nor did NATO unbendingly insist he face war crimes charges. Instead, the overriding utilitarian goal appeared simply to manage the systemic risks involved.

Reshaping the environment

Given that Milosevic was not apprehended or killed, reshaping the situation suggests another risk management tool to reduce opportunities for harm rather than focusing on individuals. Some commentators have labelled the Balkans a 'reshaped region' that served American imperial interests.[124] This mistakenly ascribed a grander vision guiding military action rather than the hesitant one exhibited in the campaign. NATO, in fact, waged a 'Goldilocks war' — neither too hot nor too cold.[125] The initial worry was not causing too little damage to Serbs but that too much damage might help the KLA. NATO did not seek Milosevic's removal or even conquest; it simply altered his operating environment, constraining his freedom of action. As Clinton argued, without NATO intervention the Serb offensive would have gone on unimpeded. In explaining NATO's inability to account visibly for destroyed Yugoslav tanks, General Clark redefined success in terms of keeping Serb heavy equipment 'in hiding, under wraps, ineffective', and thus restricting the ability to attack Kosovars.[126] This redefinition was couched in terms of reducing the conditions of instability largely fuelled by unrestrained Serbs, rather than traditional terms of destroying enemy military capability.

All-out war it certainly was not. Lord Robertson reiterated one year after the operation that its intention was to disrupt Serb violence in Kosovo, not to 'militarily defeat Yugoslavia'.[127] NATO fought to 'establish conditions' rather than 'win in the classic sense' of destroying the opponent's military.[128] Such conditions included one whereby Milosevic would no longer be able to violently persecute Kosovars unhindered. War apparently now implied reducing opportunities for inflicting harm rather than a Clausewitzian-style decisive battle. The Pentagon described the earlier preventive deployment in Macedonia as part of 'Shaping the International Environment' since it 'lessens the conditions for conflict'.[129] Fittingly, the Clinton Administration's final *National Security Strategy* described military operations over Kosovo as a good example of 'shaping'.[130] The campaign can thus be seen as Washington's shaping strategy in action, although the original concept emphasised peacetime military activities. By 'reshaping' the Balkans first in

Bosnia and then in Kosovo, NATO denied Milosevic opportunities to implement his nefarious plans and thus reduce the security risks, rather than removing him outright.

Nation-tending

Old-fashioned imperialism could overcome the problem of human rights abuse by simply eliminating Milosevic, conquering and imposing civilised standards. Yet victory and empire are no longer tenable in a post-imperialist age.[131] The air campaign itself certainly did not contain a grand narrative for rebuilding Kosovo. Indeed, the Clinton Administration lacked a broader political vision.[132] Ideally, as Zygmunt Bauman argues, 'a globalising war' such as that fought over Kosovo by a postulated international community would be a hit and run affair. Eschewing territorial conquest, it would be like nomadic warfare, without taking responsibility for consequences.[133]

This ideal situation cannot happen simply because to walk away could leave the original systemic risks that triggered intervention to bubble up again. Instead, we have 'nation-tending' efforts designed simply to keep the situation from boiling over without solving the underlying problem. For example, in February 2000, after being attacked while searching Serb parts of Mitrovica, US troops no longer deployed outside their own secure sector. French forces soon followed suit, causing 'post-heroic multinational troop degradation'.[134] Indeed when American forces did venture out of their heavily fortified camps, it looked like the 7th Cavalry.[135] They were dubbed Ninja Turtles, more concerned with force protection than peacekeeping and foot patrols. The UN Balkans human rights envoy blamed KFOR for being overly hesitant and unwilling to risk anything to fulfil its mandate.[136] Indeed the West's approach to Balkan crises has been unheroic, seeking the least risky avenue. A main reason for this could be simply because there was no international consensus on Kosovo's final status. This will be discussed later.

Enmeshing NATO allies and the UN to provide administrators and legitimacy helped reduce the prominence of the US role. This might prove the best model for reconstruction by a nation 'ill-suited for empire'.[137] UN Transitional Authorities also provided a useful stopgap measure. Municipal elections bought time, satisfying demand for non-violent political engagement without actually confronting Kosovo's status.[138] Kosovo remains in limbo, while Washington's staying power, resources and interest are being strained by issues elsewhere, like Iraq and the war on terror. Rumsfeld for one certainly seemed to think US forces in the Balkans could be better deployed in more 'critical' missions like the war on terrorism.[139] Nation-tending seemed more appropriate than heroic nation-building.

A VICTORY... OF SORTS? DEFINING SUCCESS

Non-events and the minimalist criterion for victory

A war to manage risks hypothetically would conclude with a reduction of risks, and success defined minimally through non-events such as avoiding risks occurring. Almost all the wars in historian A. J. P. Taylor's *How wars end* concluded with a great peace conference to settle issues. But twentieth century wars have had a nasty habit of eluding neat conclusion. Yet, we still cling to idealised notions of formal declarations, peace treaties, victors and defeated.[140]

Unfortunately, this ideal state of events did not happen in Kosovo either. Clinton was right that this (Allied Force) is not a 'conventional thing', where there would be one winner and one loser.[141] The nebulous end to hostilities had both sides claiming victory. Milosevic retained power (initially), and kept Kosovo under formal Yugoslav sovereignty. Militarily, NATO launched some 38,000 sorties and dropped 26,000 bombs or missiles with only 2 non-combat losses and about 20 cases of collateral damage. This was an impressive technical achievement.[142]

On the strategic and political side, the eventual KFOR deployment to Kosovo came as more of a relief than an ecstatic victory. General Clark noted, 'it didn't feel like a victory.' Victory parades were not planned. There was simply relief the campaign was over.[143] This empty feeling was alien to previous wars but would become commonplace as the West undertook war as risk management. War had become more utilitarian than emotive. Victory meant being Kosovo's guardian indefinitely, the 'most thankless and most pointless task imaginable'. Others think the only winners were the Albanian mafia *fares* criminal clans.[144] The views of Michael Mandelbaum and Charles Krauthammer are not untypical. Mandelbaum saw a 'Perfect Failure' where consequences were all opposite of NATO intentions, from exacerbating Kosovar suffering to alienating Russia and China. Krauthammer observed that humanitarian intervention merely freezes the status quo, since the West is not prepared to brutally pacify and control anymore. Occupying dangerous regions peripheral to strategic interests is the reward.[145]

The only clear victory lay in ultimately returning refugees to Kosovo and securing Serb withdrawal. Otherwise, much was ambiguous from the eventual settlement to the grand prize of having Kosovo as a de facto international protectorate indefinitely. NATO accepted a Military-Technical Agreement specifying Serb withdrawal but left ambiguous the status of the territory over which war was fought. The victory was 'virtual', producing no regime change or final political settlement.[146] Several important aspects were diluted in a 'Rambouillet-lite' accord: there was no more mention of

KFOR's 'right to unrestricted passage' throughout the FYR contained in Rambouillet. There was also no reference to a three-year transition period or referendum on Kosovar independence. KFOR was deployed under UN, not NATO auspices. NATO did however gain the withdrawal of all Serb forces; this was not the case before. The tortured legal situation was such that in 1999, Washington did not recognise 'rump' Yugoslavia, yet Kosovo independence was opposed in favour of autonomy within this state.[147] The reasons given are largely negative – fear of secessionism or ideas of Greater Albania destabilising the region. (Although there are some positive arguments that partition would undermine the European notion of multicultural, multi-ethnic states.) There was also no international consensus on the final status of Kosovo. This was hardly a comprehensive settlement, leaving the ultimate distribution of political power unresolved. It was not a perfect solution but a compromise one that sufficiently managed the risks. That is indicative of risk management that accepted limits.

Why was such an ambiguous result – described colourfully as 'the mother of all compromises'[148] – accepted despite overwhelming military odds in NATO's favour and the ultimately impressive display of aerial firepower? Despite later Battle Damage Assessment revealing that NATO exaggerated its battlefield success, Lord Robertson retorted that 'relying on numbers misses the point.'[149] This was a concept of war where success is not measured by destroying enemy military or producing clear winners but by non-events. The view encapsulated by the title of Daalder and O'Hanlon's *Winning Ugly* is illuminating. The outcome achieved, while imperfect, was an improvement over what had happened before, and certainly over what could have happened without NATO intervention.[150] Such non-events were the key to defining success. Clinton's final *National Security Strategy* in December 2000 defended NATO action as having 'prevented the real risk that violence in Kosovo would create turmoil throughout the region.'[151] Two of General Clark's so-called 'measures of merit' that guided the operation actually focused not on achieving objectives but on preventing bad things from happening.[152] Preventing a risk occurring and the non-events alluded to above are precisely the minimalist criteria for assessing risk management. By this count, despite initially placing great strain on Albania and Macedonia (admittedly a failure), the fact that the region as a whole had *not* been destabilised was a success in itself. Leading US Senators lamented the price of winning: occupying Kosovo indefinitely at huge costs. Real defeat would have been much worse for NATO, the transatlantic security relationship and regional stability. The least bad outcome was thus defined as a victory.

The fudge on Kosovo created continued tension. Yet to do more than that in itself risks encouraging further Albanian expansionism. The KLA's declared goal of Greater Albania comprised parts of Macedonia (including its capital Skopje), Greece, Montenegro and the fringes of southern Serbia.

After all, Kosovo's status had been ignored partly because a viable permanent solution such as partition or independence could destabilise the fragile inter-ethnic mix in the region. Ironically, after intervening on behalf of Kosovar Albanians, NATO now had to restrain their sentiments and protect Serbs instead. Edward Luttwak argued that uninterrupted war without outside intervention would have created some sort of peace. Ceasefires and imposed settlements only allow recuperation and prolong wars indefinitely.[153] This argument however ignores systemic risks involved in letting wars burn themselves out. Rather than a perfect solution, the minimalist outcome is something NATO had to accept, given prevailing conditions.

Today, ethnic tensions are still high, with effective partition of cities like Mitrovica. The myth of multi-ethnic administration remains elusive. In Serb enclaves in Kosovo such as Strpce, teachers and municipal workers draw salaries from both Belgrade and UNMIK. Yugoslav dinars continue to be used together with the official currency, the euro. These dual structures serve little function other than to support Belgrade's claim of sovereignty. Yet the international community refuses to confront the possible solution of partition.[154] There remained no freedom of movement, nor guarantee of security for non-Albanian populations. NATO's first air war ended with a damp squib not a bang, symptomatic of risk management. Compromise results and non-events rather than complete solutions are to be expected.

An open-ended process

Problematically, public patience in the West wears thin quickly – the inevitable public wobble in any campaign. Much as President Bush two years later was to call for patience in Afghanistan, Clinton during the Kosovo campaign reminded us 'this air campaign is not a 30-second ad'. Senior officials warned there was no silver bullet to stop Serb aggression immediately.[155] Furthermore, war as risk management leads to open-ended operations that have to continually manage new risks or resurgent old ones. There is no clean end associated with classical concepts of war. Instead, KFOR's mission elided from military into a 'perpetual police' operation, with each role blurring into the other.[156] Since risks cannot be totally eliminated, risk management is best described as an ongoing cyclical dialectical process rather than a linear one towards a clearly defined end goal.

Evidence seems to suggest that as long as there are low casualties, not concentrated in the space of a few days, the American public can tolerate open-ended commitments. The foreseeable future will only see NATO soldiers on 'near-permanent' sentry duty in the Balkans.[157] While exit dates from Bosnia initially of one year were promised and then broken to Congress, the Clinton team wisely avoided such specific deadlines for Kosovo. With the quandary over Kosovo's ultimate political future of partition or independence unresolved, the most likely result will be a quasi-protectorate for indefinite periods of time. Perhaps the commitment to stay is reflected by Camp Bondsteel at Urosevac – the largest US base built since Vietnam, housing 5000 troops with a helicopter base and all the amenities of home.[158]

Despite KFOR's entry, systemic risks were reduced but not eliminated. In March 2001, patrols along the Kosovo-Macedonia border sought to manage fresh risks to Kosovo's shaky peace as fighting flared between Albanian separatists and Skopje. On launching Operation *Essential Harvest* to collect demobilised weapons, NATO Secretary-General George Robertson argued in predictably proactive fashion, 'there are risks involved ... but the risks of not sending them are far greater'.[159] In May 2001, Serb forces re-entered the Ground Safety Zone established as a buffer zone between Kosovo and Serbia. NATO troops unwilling to interdict Albanian separatists dumped the task onto Belgrade. What was previously concern for regional stability and ethnic cleansing became, after 9/11, considerations of 'potential for terrorist activity emanating from the Balkans'.[160] Although there is no concrete evidence at present, the region exhibited risk factors: large numbers of Western troops in a largely Muslim land populated with many mujahidin, and with porous borders and loose immigration controls in the region. KFOR will have to undertake open-ended continuous monitoring and management.

In August 2002, *Jane's Intelligence Digest* warned that 'risk of far wider instability remains a key concern' especially over the failure to resolve the so-called Albanian question of Greater Albania and its impact on Macedonia.[161] Clearly the problem over Kosovo is by no means resolved; only the risks managed to an appropriate degree. Risks furthermore tend to evolve. Five years after the entry of KFOR, risks remained for Balkan instability, which could still punish Western inattention.[162] Kosovo remains an 'unfinished peace'.[163] By February 2005, warnings were being sounded again about Kosovo as the 'black hole of Europe' with possible violence erupting again.[164]

Given that risk policies operate under conditions of high uncertainty, they also create what Ulrich Beck termed the 'boomerang effect'. An initial action to tackle a risk could generate more unintended consequences and risks. The Kosovo air war brought about new risks, which themselves had to be managed: the tidal wave of refugees (which paradoxically strengthened NATO's political will) strained relations with China and Russia; the KLA emerged with greater credibility and legitimacy than Rugova. As Michael Mandelbaum ruefully mused, although every war has unplanned outcomes, in Kosovo almost all the major political effects were unanticipated and undesired.[165] It illustrated clearly the dialectical nature of war, even more so in its incarnation as risk management.

Despite being surprised by the intensity of ethnic cleansing after bombing began, NATO generally coped well with the refugee outflow that was the most visible unintended consequence. NATO had pre-positioned 13,000 troops and humanitarian aid, and then proceeded to build refugee tents. During the campaign, NATO would feed and shelter 850,000 people for three months. Kosovo became the only case in modern history where systematic ethnic displacement was reversed.[166] However one could question the price: about 2500 people had died in Kosovo before NATO intervened. In 11 weeks of bombing, although precise figures may never be known, an estimated 3000 died, mostly Albanians killed by Serbs together with about 500 civilians in the air campaign.[167] Depleted uranium projectiles and unexploded cluster bombs remain, posing significant risks to peacekeepers, civilians and the environment, which we will not go into. Generally, the 'boomerang effect' was relatively well handled and NATO-Russian relations were back on an even keel soon afterwards.

WAR AS A RISK MANAGEMENT EXERCISE

Although proponents of the Kosovo campaign think it could herald a new doctrine of humanitarian intervention and a new dawn in the protection of human rights, it might well turn out to be a strategic anomaly in that respect. Despite some controversy over whether the Kosovo operation should be classified as 'war', 'coercive diplomacy' or something else, what it does demonstrate is the extent to which war for the West is becoming a tool to manage systemic risks from its impetus, manner and ethos of implementation, to outcome evaluation.

Evidence presented in this case study demonstrates that characteristic indicators of risk management such as anticipatory action and tendencies toward 'overestimating the worst' latent in the precautionary principle (albeit not fully formed) were present. Official rhetoric and documents clearly appealed to the need for proactive action on addressing risks. Rationales for intervention put forth by senior policy-makers suggested a 'reflexive' rationality was in operation. The concern and emphasis had more to do with averting possible adverse consequences of inaction. This meant elevating probabilistic scenarios of instability spiralling out of control over prior clearly defined cause-effect relationships. However a case certainly could be made that coercing Milosevic into submission involved instrumentally calculating what was to be achieved in a linear fashion and that continued violence could certainly have the predicted effect of instability. As predicted, there was evidence of surveillance activity and continuous monitoring of risks as a precursor to action. The utilitarian nature of war as risk management was also apparent, notwithstanding emotive appeals to notions of human rights. War had become detached and distant for the West, unwilling to sacrifice to prove the courage of its moral convictions on human rights. Andy Bacevich, for instance, saw use of force over Kosovo as simply part of a routine series of 'housekeeping tasks'. Good risk management practices after all should be as routine as possible. Once again, as with Saddam Hussein in the 1990s, Milosevic personified the risks. Yet he was managed by reshaping the environment in which he operated rather than removed from power directly. Managerialism trumped correctionalism or notions of justice for his many victims, although he was later arrested and put on trial for war crimes.

In defining success minimally and through non-events, a risk management perspective further fosters understanding of the ambiguous end of hostilities and the open-ended commitment involved in Kosovo. This could help dispel criticisms of NATO and the US being bogged down by interminable missions without clear end-points. After all, risk management lends itself to such ambiguous outcomes, especially given the need to ensure risks remain continuously reduced to a tolerable level. In this aspect, risk management also helps explain the dialectical nature of the conflict given its appreciation of the boomerang effect. NATO had to constantly monitor evolving security risks and undertake further management action if necessary. There was no conclusive solution to the problem of Kosovo's status, partly due to failure of the main multilateral partners (UN, NATO, EU, Contact Group, Yugoslavia) to agree on its future. This unresolved problem continues to plague the region's prospects for the future. Huge issues remain to be managed such as organised crime, illegal immigration and simmering ethnic tensions. Nation-tending could help keep these risks in check given that proper nation-building is difficult, especially so long as Kosovo remained formally under Belgrade's sovereignty. Nonetheless, there were earnest reconstruction efforts largely due to the multinational nature of the intervention.

Taken together, these aspects allow reconceptualising war as risk management, further accentuating the West's utilitarian, instrumental approach to war in the twenty-first century. For an anxious democracy in a globalised risk age seeking to manage systemic risks with minimal costs, the blueprint unearthed in Kosovo could well recommend itself to future wars such as Afghanistan in 2001, to which we turn next. Indeed the similarities are startling.

5

THE AFGHAN CAMPAIGN AND THE WAR ON TERRORISM

Risk management vindicated?[1]

Risk managers face challenges of bracing for the unimaginable –
New York Times, 20 October 2001

A WAR BY ANY OTHER NAME?

After the September 11 (9/11) attacks, policy-makers have waxed lyrical about a 'war' on terrorism. In the West, it fuelled unrealistic public expectations. 'War' terminology spawned inaccurate analogies with war in its 'classical' form rather than the risk management variety suggested here. This can go some way towards comprehending a strange conflict where enemies are elusive networks, the goal is simply avoiding harm with little prospect of closure, and success is defined more by non-events than by what is visibly verifiable. In so doing, the validity of the analytical framework developed in Chapter Three can again be assessed, this time with a different case study and context. The same set of structured questions and predictions generated by the framework guides empirical analysis of evidence presented. The task is to scrutinise the Afghanistan campaign in particular, and more generally the struggle against terrorism, for operational indicators illuminating the possible reinvention of war as risk management.

The nature of the beast confronting us needs at the outset to be dissected. Globalised systemic risks stemming from terrorist activity in Afghanistan are pinpointed as the stimulus for action. Only then is it possible to analyse modes and ethos of policy remedies by examining the precautionary principle and how policy-makers justified the proactive aspects of military actions through a 'reflexive' rationality and risk calculus. Other outstanding areas of concern include the surveillance of risks, 'reshaping the environment' and to what extent operations in Afghanistan reflected a 'routine' use of force. Finally, results and outcomes remain to be assessed. Non-events like avoiding any future terrorist outrages are the negatively defined benchmark for success, rather than the perfect solutions or decisive outcomes implied by 'war' terminology. The open-ended nature of risk management might also explain a dialectical struggle with terrorism where disrupted networks regroup and new ones constantly emerge. This differs from the finite ends normally associated with linear notions of war.

A BRIEF HISTORY

The Afghan campaign is scrutinised here from a risk management perspective rather than via a lengthy chronological narrative. Only a short historical primer is provided, setting the general background. The Western intelligence community has long warned of security risks posed by terrorism. In particular terrorist sanctuaries in Afghanistan have concerned US administrations before. In August 1998, President Clinton launched Operation *Infinite Reach*, cruise missile strikes on terrorist facilities in Afghanistan after US embassies in East Africa were bombed, allegedly by Al Qaeda. On 21 September 1998, President Clinton urged the UN General Assembly to place terrorism on the 'top of our agenda'.

This ominous warning rang true on September 11 2001, when terrorist hijackers crashed two planes into New York's World Trade Center, toppling the twin towers, and another into the Pentagon. A fourth crashed into a Pennsylvania field after passengers on board apparently wrestled for control with the hijackers. The horror and outrage invoked an unprecedented wave of solidarity with the US. UN Security Council Resolution 1373 authorised action to combat terrorists endangering international security. On 7 October 2001, American and British forces launched Operation *Enduring Freedom*, the military phase of the war on terrorism. Campaign aims were initially unclear. The official stated aim and especially language used was similar to that of Kosovo: to 'degrade and disrupt' terrorist networks and 'prevent further terrorism'. At the onset, it seemed the Taliban were to be coerced into handing Bin Laden over and expelling Al Qaeda. Eventually the goal became regime change. US ground forces were also not inserted in large numbers initially, delegating ground combat to local allies the Northern Alliance, following the Kosovo model, while relying on air power. Sceptics decried a 'Kosovo Redux'.[2] This allegedly allowed Osama Bin Laden to slip the dragnet at Tora Bora in December 2001 as well as many Taliban/Al Qaeda in the Shah-I-kot valley in the last set-piece battle, Operation *Anaconda* of March 2002. At the time of writing, sporadic skirmishes continue.

CONCEPTUAL ISSUES

Two levels of analysis are relevant here. The first comprises the rhetorical war against 'terrorism' (a common noun), which by definition can never surrender, like 'war' on crime. Critics were right in this respect: that Bush should have declared war not on 'terrorism', but on Al Qaeda. Bush himself in August 2004 appeared to accept 'we actually misnamed the war on terror' and suggested it was more accurately a struggle against extremists who use terror as a weapon.[3] Terrorism is technically speaking more a concept, phenomenon or method of political violence, than a clear set of adversaries. It has no territorial boundaries, flags or capitals to be captured. Yet American Presidents since Johnson have declared 'metaphoric' wars since the first one on poverty in 1964. It is militarily impossible to attack an 'ism'. Terrorism the 'concept' cannot be physically combated, but terrorist groups that pose risks can. In this way, the war on terrorism currently translates into conflict with transnational Al Qaeda networks.

The second level of analysis involves more concrete manifestations of warfare against Al Qaeda and Taliban in Afghanistan: almost a 'conventional' war against states (a proper noun, which can surrender) and perhaps the only phase in the campaign that can properly be called a war.[4] Yet, in Afghanistan capturing Bin Laden and destroying the Taliban too have been sidelined in favour of less visible results such as preventing further terrorism generally. There were no surrender ceremonies or declarations of final victory either. The Afghan campaign has been subsumed in this sense within the broader war on terrorism so much so that the two seemed to intertwine. These two levels are combined by extrapolating features of risk management from military action in Afghanistan that might be relevant to the broader campaign against terrorism and vice versa. Furthermore, very few military operations have been conducted explicitly within the conceptual framework of 'counter-terrorism'. Thus few lessons can be drawn from the past.[5] More often, it fell within the broader and tested framework of 'counter-insurgency' or as is suggested here, risk management.

Momentous change in international relations was arguably in the works, with new ideas of sovereignty where states unable to rein in terrorists are liable to outside intervention. If other states fail to protest vehemently, that might imply acquiescence in yet another modification to customary international law.[6] Many claimed Washington finally had its defining mission after ten years of drift. US forces established Central Asian bases for the first time ever, with Moscow's tacit consent. Globalisation also reared its dark head, subverting conventional net assessments of material power capabilities, as failed states thousands of miles away, rather than powerful ones, now posed risks. We face the globalisation of insecurity in the first 'major war in the age of globalisation'.[7]

The 'war' on terrorism is an interesting case for reconceptualising war for several reasons. As Michael Clarke noted, this conflict was extremely unpredictable and had much potential for unintended consequences in the international system. We had to expect the unexpected.[8] Breaking with precedents set in Kosovo, policy-makers were quick to employ the word 'war'. Yet, explicitly using the word created more problems than answers. It was the 'wrong concept' to use according to Giles Andreani.[9] It implied overemphasising military force and gave legitimacy to terrorists for instance. Susan Sontag decried the use of a phantom 'war' as a metaphor with no foreseeable end.[10] Given these conceptual difficulties, it was no surprise that in late September 2001, Rumsfeld observed that the war on terrorism was 'very, very different from what people think of when using the word "war" or "campaign". We need to fashion a new vocabulary and different constructs for what we are doing'.[11] The language of risk management might serve this purpose of understanding George W. Bush's 'first war of the 21st century'.

America's war on terror is open-ended, ill defined and lacks specific parameters. Although the Bush Doctrine pursues 'every terrorist group of global reach', the predominant focus is Al Qaeda. US Defence Secretary Donald Rumsfeld too accepted that eliminating all terrorism would be 'setting a threshold that is too high'.[12] Al Qaeda's agenda and reach is exclusively global compared to 'traditional' terrorists such as the IRA. Furthermore, the dangers posed by Al Qaeda far exceed the IRA. The main aim of defeating Al Qaeda should not be distracted by targeting other terrorist organisations not involved with it. [13]

A central difficulty of terrorism is defining the amorphous concept. Attempts to do so are often inconclusive – 'one person's terrorist is another's freedom fighter' – and is not our central concern. The US State Department report *Patterns of Global Terrorism* defines terrorism as 'premeditated, politically motivated violence against non-combatant targets by subnational or clandestine agents, usually intended to influence an audience'. Al Qaeda's brand of terrorism however aims to destroy, not influence an audience. Combating terrorism involves political, military, diplomatic, financial, intelligence and police tools of statecraft. It is multifaceted: addressing root causes, prevention and preparedness, and strengthening the international framework for multilateral action. Military force is admittedly a blunt instrument; its hierarchical structure unsuited for tackling fluid networks. It might also be counterproductive, fuelling more hatred. Emphasising military tools may neglect equally important issues like poverty, political repression and intercultural dialogue. These are rather more long-term goals.

However, short-term urgent risks are posed by Al Qaeda's religious absolutes, which cannot easily be swayed by political negotiation. As a former State Department counter-terrorism czar observed, it was futile discussing root causes with Bin Laden: 'He doesn't like America. We are the root cause'.[14] We face what Michael Ignatieff termed 'apocalyptic nihilism', where terrorism is not linked to political demands but simply ever-escalating violence. These cannot be reasoned with but can only be fought.[15] Furthermore, ex-CIA chief George Tenet's Congressional testimony in February 2002 emphasised that it was impossible for intelligence to provide 100 per cent predictive capability on terrorist events. Where terrorists want to destroy, not bargain; and intelligence and diplomatic cooperation cannot be foolproof, military tools have to be resorted to.

However it is not the main purpose here to discuss in detail the pros and cons of responding to terrorism as 'war' but to understand how such a 'war' might be interpreted since the term is now so deeply ingrained in political consciousness.[16] Terrorism is difficult to conceptualise purely as war, yet this is not a new problem. In August 1984 Robert Sayre, State Department anti-terrorism director, called terrorism 'low-level warfare' but preferred to deal with it as a police matter. George Shultz, then Secretary of State, more cate-gorically insisted terrorism was 'a form of warfare'.[17] Part of the rhetorical campaign since the 1980s has been to call it war.

To Sir Michael Howard, using the word 'war' normally implies spectac-ular military action against easily identifiable adversaries – ideally states – and a clearly defined end-point producing decisive highly visible results, especially in a media age shaped by images of smart bombs in the Gulf War.[18] The context of modern war is traditionally between fixed enemies who recognise each other, like states deploying massive armies – what Raymond Aron called 'perfect' war. Such idealised abstractions contained drawbacks. Some prefer 'police action' to snatch Bin Laden. The war on terror first targeted the Taliban, hardly an established state, while Al Qaeda is a loosely organised, transnational network. There are no clear frontlines or massed forces. When states use force to destroy terrorist groups and those who harbour them, we may use the term 'war' in theory. But unlike conven-tional inter-state wars, this 'war' had no fixed set of clearly identifiable enemies even in Afghanistan.

Fundamentally, the nature of victory is unclear; outcomes will be neither easily apparent nor decisive. There will be no prospect of closure with surrender ceremonies on the battleship *Missouri*. Instead success is defined by what does *not* happen rather than what does. The language of war may serve as a semantic instrument for mobilising public support but fails to explicate the 'quirky character of this new war'. [19] Furthermore, the context of war in the West has been shifting from Great Power conflict to rhetorical 'wars' on drugs, crime and now terrorism. James Lindsay remarked that the campaign against terror 'is more like the drug war'.[20] Instead of the domi-nant connotations outlined above, it makes more sense to use the word 'war' in this way to mean mobilizing resources against a dangerous activity, which can never be eliminated but only reduced to a tolerable level.[21]

While old-style terrorism is normally inclined to negotiations, new terrorism is now seen as part of a 'war paradigm' adopted by terrorists.[22] This takes a strategic campaign-oriented view of protracted violence rather than episodic efforts in the past. Unlike the previous coercive diplomacy paradigm of terrorism, there is now no proportionate relationship between force employed and aims. It is less targeted at officials but wholesale and indiscriminate. The political goals are less explicit and sometimes overwhelmed by religious overtones. Although they still want a lot of people watching, they also want many people dead. Less restrained by political concerns about political support, the aim appears simply to inflict death. Indeed, terrorists have often declared 'war' on America before and considered themselves 'armies'. President Clinton too invoked the imagery and language of war by describing military retaliation after the 1998 embassy bombings as the 'first shot of protracted war'. This 'war paradigm' was relevant before 9/11 and it is disingenuous to claim a sudden paradigm shift in the nature of war and terrorism. If terrorists are adopting such a paradigm and becoming a major security concern, the targeted too need to adopt a 'paradigm shift', making terrorism a military problem rather than simply for policemen and courtrooms.[23] New strategies are needed to fight 'new terrorism'.[24]

Yet despite the Afghan model being touted as a new dawn in warfare, Colin McInnes noted that the decade before already contained similar talk. September 11 and Afghanistan merely confirmed these trends.[25] Although 9/11 brought war closer to the West than any other conflict in the 1990s, not much else changed fundamentally: 'the Afghan campaign bore many hallmarks of Western military operations in the 1990s'. Mirroring the Kosovo campaign, officials stressed the Taliban regime was the target, not the Afghan people. General Tommy Franks claimed this was the most precise bombing campaign in history. While tactical risks of casualties influenced the campaign, our focus is repetitive trends exhibited in managing systemic risks.

Stephen Biddle, for instance, saw more continuity than novelty in the Afghan campaign. Close quarter ground combat was still needed to dislodge Taliban positions despite innovative embedding of Special Forces forward air controllers: 'continuities were as important as novelties in the outcome.'[26] Andy Bacevich similarly concluded that the Afghanistan campaign 'bore the imprint of US military practice as it evolved during the previous decade'.[27] The interpretation of events offered in this case study is by no means definitive but suggests in the same spirit that Afghanistan also exhibited broader continuity with the earlier Kosovo campaign in terms of a strategic approach to war as risk management.

Globalisation and systemic risks: terrorism

Afghanistan was fertile ground for systemic risks as the object of risk management. The rise of the Taliban and relative neglect of the country by the West related to the collapse of the Soviet Union and systemic changes. Few strategic interests remained after Moscow withdrew, creating chaos and a failed state posing risks as a terrorist haven. After 9/11, a power with hitherto no colonial history in the region intervened. This was certainly not for promoting human rights per se, although human rights rhetoric was tacked on apparently as an afterthought to bolster political, moral and international support. The West had known of the gross human rights violations in Taliban-run Afghanistan for ages and elected to do little about it in terms of military force until after 9/11. The US intervened to manage globalisation and its associated systemic risks, rather than colonialism. Removing the Taliban and terrorist sanctuaries in Afghanistan served to reduce the risk of further terror attacks in a globalised world.

As President Clinton declared in 1998, terrorism had a 'new face in the 1990s'. Globalisation made new technologies of terror easily available to increasingly mobile terrorists. Everyone was now a 'possible victim.'[28] September 11 graphically substantiated Clinton's prediction: increasing economic interdependence also produced what Paul Wolfowitz called 'the parallel globalisation of terror'.[29] Afghan-trained terrorists from Egypt studying in Germany, funded by a Saudi, devastated New York. Terror had become 'franchised' by Al Qaeda, relying on tools of globalisation like air travel, email and faxes, free flow of people, and electronic money transfers.[30] Al Qaeda, noted the US *National Strategy for Combating Terrorism*, 'exemplifies how terrorists have twisted the benefits and conveniences of our increasingly open, integrated and modernised world to serve their destructive agenda'.[31] Senior American intelligence officials suggest the key strategic task now facing the world was to bolster positive aspects of globalisation, while reducing and managing its downsides.[32] With the impact of 9/11 fresh in their minds, the desire to avoid repetition of similar 'tombstone' style risks clearly dominated policy-makers' concerns. Anticipatory 'horizon-scanning' aspects of other possible risks however cannot be clearly delineated especially as policy-makers tend to extrapolate from analogous situations. This suggests why Bush lumped Al Qaeda and Saddam Hussein together, claiming they are 'both risks, they're both dangerous'.[33]

Risk here is largely used as a descriptive term to refer to a perilous situation, and after 9/11 the language of risk now engulfs seemingly everything: from anthrax in the post, to hijacked planes or trucks crashing into nuclear plants and 'dirty' bombs. Terrorism is not simply what has already happened, but also what could possibly happen in future, a risk so to speak.[34] Deputy Defence Secretary Wolfowitz noted 'we are in a new era, facing new risks'.[35] Terrorism has been labelled a 'strategic risk', prompting a new chapter to Britain's *Strategic Defence Review* (SDR).[36] The risks of attack have increased as 9/11 demonstrated the ease with which foreign terrorists can commit mass terrorism in the continental US. However shocking terrorist blows may be, they hardly undermine the basic foundations of their targets' global domination.[37] Kenneth Waltz also accepted that despite serious challenges of catastrophic terrorism, they hardly endanger the core fabric of a society or seriously threaten the security of a state.[38] These are dangerous times but not as dark as those of World War

Two or nuclear arms races when state survival was at stake. We face serious risks rather than existential threats.

Risk or threat?

Transnational terrorism exhibits clear components of risk: probability and consequences. We were increasingly focused on high consequence, low probability attacks even before 9/11, rather than gauging more precisely threat components relating to the capabilities and intentions of terrorists. This degenerated into limitless vulnerabilities, unspecific anxieties and over-stating worst-case scenarios shaped primarily by vulnerability assessments rather than assessing the technical capabilities and motivation of terrorists.[39]

To a degree, Al Qaeda admittedly poses an immediate serious threat rather than a risk: its intentions are clear (to cause catastrophic mayhem and death), as are its capabilities. Bin Laden has outlined his intentions clearly; acquiring WMD was a 'religious duty'. Al Qaeda also clearly demonstrated its capability on 9/11 but this is hardly conventional military capability used to conceptualise war. All it needed were simple box-cutters, not sophisticated military hardware. Terrorism is after all a weapon of the weak rather than powerful states posing 'threats' in the conventional security paradigm. Indeed, the *National Strategy for Combating Terrorism* acknowledged explicitly the difficulty of breaking down Al Qaeda terrorism into its threat components: 'the shadowy nature of terrorist organisations precludes an easy analysis of their capabilities or intent. The classic net assessment of the enemy based on the number of tanks, airplanes or ships does not apply to these non-state actors'.[40] The focus is no longer on conventional capabilities but, according to the logic of globalisation and risk, relatively 'weak' actors like Afghanistan and Al Qaeda can pose serious dangers.

In contrast, the Cold War nuclear threat was more material. People knew largely what to expect, people had drills to practise and it was more calculable. With mass-casualty terrorism, people are more anxious because they don't know what to be afraid of, with so many possible doomsday scenarios. FBI Director Mueller in February 2005 remained 'very concerned about what we are not seeing'.[41] With society becoming increasingly risk-conscious and anxious even before 9/11, it is no surprise security in an age of catastrophic terrorism is conceptualised in terms of probabilistic scenarios and all sorts of 'what-if' situations rather than more realistic evidence.

In an ill-fated attempt to scour the marketplace for assessments of the probability of terrorist events, the US Defence Advanced Research Project Agency (DARPA) plan dubbed Policy Market Analysis envisaged online trading of possible future Middle East events and terrorism. Although the plan was scrapped, the focus on probability was evident in conceptualising the dangers from terrorism. CIA officials turned to Hollywood producers for doomsday scenarios amid rumours of a resurrection of 'remote viewing' programmes in an attempt to forecast future terrorism. Even the foot and mouth outbreak in 2001 in Britain, it was argued, demonstrated vulnerability to bio-terrorism. Absent the ability to clearly identify Al Qaeda capabilities or even its members themselves, Michael O'Hanlon warned that an infinite array of vulnerabilities was stacked against us.[42] Homeland Security chief Tom Ridge conceded, 'there is a universe of potentials we have to deal with'. Attacks might occur anywhere, any time.[43] This concern with amorphous scenarios echoed Rumsfeld's sentiments to 'prepare for the unknown, uncertain, the unseen and the unexpected'.[44] The June 2003 US Government report to the UN Monitoring Committee on sanctions against Al Qaeda warned of 'a high probability' of a WMD attack in two years.[45] Emphasising catastrophic consequences such as 'dirty' bomb attacks causing mass casualties combined with myriad ill-defined probabilistic scenarios situated us squarely within the risk discourse.

IMPLEMENTING RISK MANAGEMENT

Active anticipation and reflexive rationality

Two approaches to terrorism exist. Anti-terrorism involves taking steps and measures to reduce the probability of a terrorist act occurring. It is the proactive, preventive stage and involves things like acting on intelligence and lowering vulnerabilities of installations. Counter-terrorism on the other hand involves tactical actions taken in response to a terrorist incident, including legislative efforts and consequence management. However, clear distinctions are unsustainable. The war in Afghanistan could be seen as a response to the 9/11 attacks but also in anticipation of further terrorist strikes. Risk in this context of anticipation is used not only as a descriptive term, referring to a potentially dangerous situation, but also as a normative one, implying the desirability for avoidance action. It also formed part of a 'reflexive' strategic calculation stressing the importance of taking action even without prior clearly defined cause-effect relationships, to avert adverse consequences that had yet to manifest.

Risk management's locus of action is proactive and situated in the future. It goes beyond simply punishing and retaliating, but preventing and averting as well. This involves considering counter-factuals and alternative courses of action. As Clinton observed earlier, each of us is now a 'possible victim'. As suggested by the test framework, this underlies the new security mantra of proactively averting potential victimhood. The centre of consciousness for combating terrorism thus lies in the future, reducing the risk of it occurring. Terrorism is unpredictable, dependent on the smallest whim of individuals and loosely strung groups, compared to the relatively static hierarchy of militaries that inter-state warfare implies. Planning should be based on several possible images of the future, not just a single one.[46] President Bush observed that in preparing for a variety of terrorist scenarios, the best way is to anticipate and act against them.[47]

Prevention has always been accorded a central place on the agenda. Indeed, 'preventing', 'potentials' and 'future' are key words in counter-terrorism documents. The *National Commission on Terrorism*'s top priority is to prevent or disrupt terrorist attacks through military or covert action.[48] Rumsfeld agrees 'we must be preventative'.[49] Even retrospective assessments like the joint US Congressional report on 9/11 released in July 2003 concluded that atrocity was preventable although there was no clear smoking gun. It focused on all sorts of 'what if' situations that could have prevented the attacks such as eliminating inter-agency turf struggles on intelligence. Similarly in February 2005 the US Federal Aviation Administration released its own intelligence reports on 9/11 suggesting that the chain of events that day could have been 'altered'. The onus in counter-terrorism is clearly on preventive actions.

The old approach to terrorism however viewed it as a law enforcement matter for the courts where terrorists or their state sponsors are retaliated against retrospectively after they commit terrorism. Some commentators recommend that America should now dispense with higher levels of proof needed in treating terrorism as a crime, in effect waging war. Others disagree.[50] Nonetheless, for all the controversy over a supposed new doctrine of 'anticipatory self-defence', the actual precursor can be traced back almost 20 years. In 1985, after Libyan terrorists bombed the La Belle discotheque in Berlin, the US response came to be known as the Abe Sofaer Doctrine after the official who drafted the State Department memorandum.[51] This stated that the US had a right of 'preemptory self-defence' against future acts of terrorism, when a country aids or gives sanctuary to terrorists. This doctrine was invoked in the 1986 bombings of Tripoli and again during the 1998 cruise missile raids against Afghanistan and Sudan codenamed *Infinite Reach*.

This operation set significant precedent for later operations in 2001. President Clinton justified his actions in terms of self-defence against an 'imminent threat of further terrorist attacks' and to 'prevent and deter additional attacks'.[52] Clinton, to be sure, cited specific intelligence of a terrorist meeting that day in Afghanistan to justify an imminent threat. However the real aim behind destroying the Al Shifa plant in Sudan, suggests Andy Becavich, was not so much retaliatory but pre-emptive, to deny prospective terrorists possible access to weapons of mass destruction. Using military power now indicated that the US 'intended to take a proactive approach.'[53]

After 9/11, the stakes became too high to wait for terrorists to strike first, especially with WMD. In October 2001, US Ambassador to the UN John Negroponte submitted a letter to the Security Council reporting US military action against Afghanistan. This note reserved the right in the future to initiate further actions against other organisations and states to prevent and deter further attacks on the United States.[54] This letter taken together with other statements to act against 'axis of evil' states implied that 'anticipatory self-defence' appeared to be the justification. According to FBI Director Mueller, preventing another terrorist attack was his top priority.[55] Shifting from a reactive to a proactive orientation, it now sought to prevent and disrupt terrorist plans by being 'predictive' and anticipating attacks.

Being proactive is part and parcel of the risk management paradigm in relation to terrorism. Terrorism expert Walter Lacquer recognised that preventing all terrorist events was impossible, but that we can at the very least 'reduce the risk' by keeping terrorists on the run rather than concentrating on defence alone.[56] The Council on Foreign Relations report *America still unprepared, still in danger* advised that 'a proactive mindset is key' to preventing terrorism.[57] While the Homeland Security Department reduced vulnerabilities and opportunities for terrorism by hardening 'soft' targets, the Pentagon directly reduced risks overseas by hunting terrorists and their sanctuaries. Rumsfeld described pursuing terrorists as a 'proactive' policy since it was impossible to defend against terrorists everywhere, any time. Being proactive is central to the strategies of managing terrorism.

This translates into a reflexive rationality focused on averting future attacks that have yet to materialise. Tony Blair's official statement on commencing Operation *Enduring Freedom* noted there are 'dangers in acting, (but) the dangers of inaction are much higher.'[58] Otherwise, more British lives could be lost. This sort of proactive 'reflexive' reasoning was clearly reflected in military strikes against Afghanistan three years earlier. President Clinton rationalised then that the risks from inaction surpassed those from action.[59] Senior Clinton officials Albright and Berger suggested that inaction would only invite further horror: 'it is very likely that something would have happened had we not done this'.[60] Given the difficulties of accurately calculating terrorist capabilities and intentions, policy-makers exhibited a 'reflexive' rationality aimed at averting adverse outcomes that had not yet happened.

This explains why four years later in 2002, actions such as Operation *Anaconda* were not presented as 'retribution' or 'revenge' for 9/11, which policy-makers like Rumsfeld could very easily choose to do. Indeed he explicitly rejected justification on such terms and instead the purpose of *Anaconda* served to defend America from further attacks.[61] Terrorists under pressure in Afghanistan presumably would be hard-pressed to plan strikes. Similarly, Under-Secretary of State Pickering stressed that missile strikes in

August 1998 were not just retaliation for the embassy bombings but to prevent further terrorism.[62] September 11 consolidated what had been an emerging proactive trend in reflexive Western military policies where locus of action lay in probabilistic futures that had yet to emerge.

Concern about averting possible adverse outcomes, rather than retrospective concepts like revenge, is indicative of proactive risk management's future-oriented ethos. Prevention rather than revenge should guide US military action since the central objective is to 'reduce the probability and severity of future attacks' – key indicators of risk.[63] The war on terrorism fulfilled not only a desire to hit back but also reduced the risks of further terrorism. Pre-emption, legally speaking, is not really an issue here since Washington is arguably engaging in traditional self-defence against an ongoing series of armed attacks, from the 1998 embassy bombings to today.[64] Furthermore, America was reacting to the 9/11 attacks. Nonetheless, what is more important, as seen in the examples cited above, is the 'proactive nature' of 'reacting' against terror with the main focus on preventing repetition rather than retrospective concepts like demanding revenge or justice relating to past events. These admittedly do remain important moral concerns but given the complexity and exigencies of the elusive Al Qaeda challenge, the locus of action lay more in reducing likelihood of future terrorist strikes.

Over the past 50 years, it was assumed that Washington would respond quickly and decisively to aggression but would not initiate attacks. The 2002 *National Security Strategy* argued this is outdated when terror groups operate outside control of governments and engage in symbiotic relationships with failed states. Aiming to inflict maximum death and destruction, and without any territory at stake, they appear immune to retaliation. It thus makes sense to strike first. During the Cold War, there existed the constraining factor of the Soviet Union. This no longer exists, a crucial factor making anticipatory risk management plausible. UK MoD consultations on a new chapter of its *SDR* provided similar inklings of emerging future-oriented concepts in counter-terrorism. There was to be 'more emphasis on being proactive, pre-empting problems' than sitting back waiting for them to hit us.[65]

Since 9/11 and the dawn of mass-casualty terrorism, there is zero margin for error and no chance to learn from any mistake with the benefit of hindsight, according to Bush.[66] Clearly here we are talking about 'anticipationism' rather than a reactive 'resilience' approach to risk management. Declaring that he would not be held hostage to events while dangers accumulate, the tone of Bush's 'axis of evil' speech was proactive and anticipatory, indicative of a risk manager's mindset. Colin Powell prescribed a strategy that would 'reduce the likelihood of those (terrorist) incidents' by pursuing terrorist organisations.[67] This is as clear a statement as any about proactive risk management to reduce the risks/likelihood of terrorism.

War and the precautionary principle

How much did Western intelligence actually know about Al Qaeda's role in 9/11? Was there compelling evidence, or are we increasingly resorting to the precautionary principle in responding to terrorism? Professionals in finance and economics who practise risk management now scramble to manage risks never thought possible before. Catastrophic terrorism eludes private insurance coverage. The US Terrorism Risk Insurance Act of November 2002 thus requires that the government act as insurer of last resort. However, 'terrorism is still an extremely difficult risk to predict'.[68] Preparing the nation for the worst is an act of prudence, not fatalism, notes the report *America still unprepared, still in danger*.[69] After 9/11, in the words of a World Health Organisation (WHO) spokesman warning about a terrorist smallpox attack, 'the unthinkable is no longer unthinkable and we need to prepare for that.'[70] The challenge is to properly define and respond to risk and we seem to be erring on the side of caution. The WHO felt it prudent and not alarmist to bring forward the release of its report on biological or chemical attacks.[71] A US-wide system of environmental monitors called Bio-Watch has been deployed to prepare for whatever the weapon and whomever the culprit.[72]

Authorities do not know enough about terrorist cells or sleepers and their changing tactics to assign clear probabilities, which is why precautionary-based strategies like those above are resorted to. These act amidst high uncertainty on risk potentials. It is difficult to ascertain attribution in terrorist incidents. Even if an organisation were to claim responsibility, how can we believe it? What if no one claims responsibility? No one has yet done so explicitly for the 9/11 attacks. Reliable sources are often lacking and the level of evidence is often different from that needed in a court of law or jury.[73] The UK government dossier on Al Qaeda published on November 2001 conceded that it does not constitute a prosecutable case against Osama Bin Laden in a court of law. 'Intelligence often cannot be used evidentially'.[74] Tony Blair however claimed to have seen 'absolutely incontrovertible proof'. NATO Secretary-General Lord Robertson announced himself satisfied with the 'compelling' and 'conclusive' evidence that Washington presented to NATO councils. However, what was the evidentiary test required? Communications intercepts? The US claimed that Al Qaeda and its Taliban supporters were responsible but according to lawyers failed to provide sufficient factual evidence. It only provided 'conclusory reasons and not the factual basis for them.'[75]

There was no direct information linking Afghanistan or terror groups based there to the 9/11 attacks. Evidence found in Afghanistan, however, suggested terrorist experimentation with goats and dogs using gas. Bin Laden's infamous home video was also discovered, where he was shown gloating over the 9/11 attacks and hinting at his complicity. The risks were indeed present. This implied the Afghan campaign was based less on 'false positives' in resorting to the precautionary principle than the previous Kosovo campaign. Indeed, the precautionary principle applied only to the extent that information was not perfect but was considerably more concrete than normally assumed.

Yet, with so many possible terrorist scenarios, terrorism experts desperately struggled to sieve through the sea of uncertainty. Homeland Security chief Tom Ridge cautioned that the intelligence and information he had to work with was very vague. Terrorism expert Daniel Benjamin felt 'surrounded by a cloud of unknowing'.[76] There will be an imperfect understanding of the risks involved and somehow making decisions to manage them amidst great uncertainty and inconclusive information. As Rumsfeld told NATO Defence Ministers, 'absolute proof cannot be a precondition for action'.[77] Given the elusive nature of risks today, the standards of proof demanded retrospectively for Al Qaeda's guilt may well be dispensed with in future in favour of the precautionary principle especially if the consequences of inaction are so high.

Surveillance

Surveillance is crucial to risk management strategies, collecting information on risks and assessing whether they require anticipatory action. If necessary, this is implemented. While US surveillance assets during the Cold War monitored concrete Soviet military capabilities such as missile silos and nuclear submarines, now they shifted towards identifying elusive security risks. Declassified Keyhole-11 satellite photos were used to brief media on 1998 cruise missile strikes on Afghanistan. According to Keith Hall, then Director of the National Reconnaissance Office, IMINT (image intelligence) 'helps to reduce the terrorist threat. It can help to locate terrorist camps and facilities and provide other information to track terrorists.'[78]

The US government invoked its 'shutter control' rights, buying all images from the commercial *Ikonos* satellite during the 2001 Afghan campaign, fearing that Taliban or Al Qaeda elements might use such images to locate coalition forces. A public-private division of sorts emerged on risk surveillance. With advances in commercial technology, private companies such as Digital Globe contracted to provide not only an extra set of eyes, but also the big picture, which more precise government satellites could complement. The Global Hawk strategic UAV made its operational debut as did armed Predator drones. Satellites and surveillance planes are monitoring about 15 suspect cargo ships allegedly owned or used by Al Qaeda. UAVs have been overflying the Horn of Africa for similar purposes from bases in Djibouti. As White House spokesman Ari Fleischer noted: 'we're going to be on the lookout for them when they (terrorists) emerge'.[79]

Reports suggested that Operation *Anaconda* was launched after months of monitoring Taliban/Al Qaeda regrouping. Al Qaeda's Yemen coordinator Qaed Sinan Harithi was assassinated by Predator drones after being under lengthy surveillance. Risk-makers displaying risk factors require monitoring and intervention actions if necessary, according to theories of surveillance. This then reduced the likelihood of terrorist attacks. Such capabilities to launch precision strikes within a short sensor-to-shooter time frame have been prominent in the leaked Pentagon *Defence Planning Guidance* 2004—2009.

After 9/11, Beck noted the increased importance to 'surveillance states' of the monitoring of terrorists. MI5's preferred policy of 'risk management' involves monitoring terror suspects to gather as much intelligence as possible, although it has been prodded towards a 'risk averse' policy of premature arrests.[80] The Pentagon runs an electronic surveillance programme called Terrorism Information Awareness that seeks to forestall terrorism by scanning computer databases.[81] We also need more intelligence-based 'pre-screening and monitoring based on risk criteria'.[82] The National Commission on Terrorism recommended that the Secretary for Health together with the State Department establish an international monitoring programme to give early warning of infectious disease outbreak and terrorist experimentation with biological agents. Furthermore, the nature of risks evolves and needs open-ended monitoring. The UN Monitoring Group on terrorism was thus set up to assess measures taken against terrorism and issues regular assessments. As President Bush put it, 'the war on terror will require a constant evaluation on progress' to tell us how we stand and what needs to be done.[83]

As predicted in the test framework, security risks like terrorism require surveillance to assess it and take management action if possible. This open-ended struggle will require unremitting vigilance and surveillance. Surveillance was very much in evidence with continuous review and monitoring processes trying to anticipate and forestall terrorism.

UTILITARIAN 'LESS THAN HEROIC' STRATEGIES OF RISK MANAGEMENT

Routine war

The double-edged character of this war defies conventional categories. Drafts, mobilisation, rationing or other sacrifices normally associated with war are not being considered. Exactly one month after 9/11, the American S&P 500 index was back to pre-attack levels. Within a year of Pearl Harbour – 9/11's most popular analogy – millions of Americans were fighting and dying. Instead, the White House now urged Americans to go about their routines yet maintain heightened awareness. Accounting scandals and economic problems jostled for media attention. Was terrorism, like crime before it, about to become simply a commonplace risk to be managed routinely, as suggested by the risk management framework?

War on terror in Afghanistan was becoming routine in two senses: it was becoming all too familiar, and instrumental rather than fervent. Before 9/11, Operation *Infinite Reach* was 'little more than a targeting exercise'. Unlike Clausewitzian 'real war', in which adversarial interaction is full of uncertainty, the missile strike was on American terms, eliminating any possibility of enemy surprises.[84] By 2002, American air power over Afghanistan became essentially an application of precision guidance; its pilots, technicians fighting wars mostly devoid of passion and danger. US squadrons waged war virtually unopposed – few squared off with SAMs, doing what Mark Bowden inventively called the 'Kabul-ki Dance', circling over Kabul awaiting targets to hit. 'Combat has become a procedure, deliberate and calculated, more cerebral than visceral – even if it does still have its moments'.[85] This not only reinforced the West's existing instrumental approach to war, but also reflected risk management's utilitarian ethos. The war also assumed an all-too familiar almost routine nature in Britain: it was the fifth time Tony Blair had used military force in his tenure, with the customary press briefings, jargon and cockpit imagery.

With ill-defined goals and elusive enemies in Afghanistan, by May 2002, US troops were gathered in formal 'recommitting ceremonies' to remind them of their mission. This would have been unnecessary in a heroic existential struggle. Instead, war quietly shifted into Phase 2 intelligence and police work, ammunition seizures and arrests, routine sweeps and preventing Taliban remnants regrouping. There is clear indication of 'routinisation' of this war and soon counter-terror patrols will assume the routine nature of naval drug patrols in the Caribbean. By 2005, attacks on coalition forces, engagements with Al Qaeda/Taliban elements were reported in low-key fashion, as the war appeared almost forgotten. Yet Americans will have to cope with daily risks of large-scale terrorist violence for the foreseeable future.[86] The 'war' on terrorism will become routine as terrorism comes to be seen as an everyday risk, like crime or drugs, to be managed.

Personification of risk

If a risk management approach to terrorism is becoming routine and instrumental, it also derives from a profoundly utilitarian moral calculus that effectively supersedes other moral criteria such as guilt or evil. Being managerial, not corrective, it does not address problems or causes, or rehabilitate erring individuals. Instead it simply seeks to shape environments within which these individuals operate, reducing risks to the wider population. As we have seen, the Kosovo campaign dwelt on the moral failings of

Milosevic yet left him untouched. Similarly, while Bin Laden the 'evil' one presently remains at large, the focus in Washington at least publicly has shifted from the classic Western one-liner 'dead or alive' to simply managing the risks he posed.

Shrugging aside suggestions that America's Afghan campaign had failed in its manhunt, Condoleezza Rice stressed it was more important to disrupt the operational capability of the network.[87] President Bush suggested that a fixation with any one individual misunderstood the scope of the mission. Terror was bigger than one person and Bush satisfied himself that Bin Laden was now 'marginalised'.[88] This argument amounted to the effect that Bin Laden's opportunities to inflict harm had been reduced as a result of reshaping his operational environment. Admiral Robert Natter, commanding the Atlantic Fleet, felt the key to winning this war lay not in Bin Laden's capture, but rather in keeping terrorists under pressure.[89] In April 2002, General Richard Myers, Chairman of the Joint Chiefs of Staff (JCS), announced somewhat disingenuously that the US never intended to go after specific individuals but more generally to disrupt terrorists.

The Bush Administration is not unique in focusing on disruption, not individuals. Echoes of this could be found in August 1998 after the first missile strikes against Al Qaeda. White House Press Secretary Mike McCurry similarly noted, in response to a question about whether Bin Laden was specifically targeted, that there were no individual human targets but simply an organisation and its infrastructure.[90]

Furthermore, globalised terror networks like Al Qaeda can operate without Bin Laden's physical direction or presence. It is a loose grouping of people around the world using modern technology like Internet websites to coordinate, provide general guidance and inspiration. New networked terrorist groups are less dependent on individuals than a more hierarchic organisational structure would imply. They cannot be decapitated in the conventional sense but can more realistically be disrupted. Eliminating Bin Laden, while a moral victory, would not translate into a significant pause in terrorist operations. While hugely significant, he is only one plank in a system that will survive his demise.[91] For this reason, Rumsfeld suggested it was 'unwise' to personalise the conflict.[92] Having said that, the Administration clearly downplayed the role of Bin Laden to mask its frustrations and failure at nabbing the biggest fish of all, shifting its war aims in the process. However, this raises useful implications for risk management's minimalist utilitarian perspective. It is sufficient that risks are reduced suitably, even without dishing out justice to Bin Laden. After all Bush initially promised: 'we're focused on justice'.[93]

As in crime control, utilitarian risk management slowly eroded notions of individual justice, as predicted in the test framework. Rumsfeld remarked on alleged dirty-bomber Jose Padilla that the key interest in interrogation was prevention, not punishment. The aim was simply to discover all he knew in order to disrupt other terrorist acts.[94] Brian Jenkins concurred that America's overriding aim should not be revenge or even bringing individual terrorists to justice. It was simply eliminating a terrorist outfit posing huge risks to American security.[95] This implied adopting a more utilitarian strategy over other moral concerns like justice. As with other rhetorical wars (for example, the one on crime), multi-tiered networks are the predominant form; singling out individuals through 'leadership interdiction', while an important component, will yield only short-term results with little sustained impact.[96] Plenty of middle-level operatives can still inflict real damage or replace those killed. Many cells can plan operations without much guidance. The focus should thus be on disruption, not decapitation.

Reshaping the environment

Given the difficulties in decapitation and outright destruction of elusive enemy forces, the war in Afghanistan should be ripe for 'shaping' strategies, as predicted by the test framework, in reducing opportunities for terrorism. The US campaign has certainly reshaped the region substantially to the extent needed to manage systemic risks. It is a form of active military engagement, not always assuming the conventional shape of war. A Congressional bill of April 1996 dictates use of all necessary means to disrupt, dismantle and destroy international infrastructure used by international terrorists.[97] Furthermore, more aggressive, international police and intelligence coordination have meant a less 'permissive environment' within which Al Qaeda could operate with impunity.[98] Using force and aggressive intelligence operations to reshape operating contexts can curtail opportunities for terrorists to plan and strike. Homeland Security Secretary Tom Ridge accordingly seeks to mitigate vulnerabilities, complicating terrorist calculations and making it more difficult for terrorists to strike successfully.[99] UK Defence Secretary Geoff Hoon talked of denying terrorists the 'opportunity' of surprise and hitting them in their own backyards before they can hit us, a concept known as 'up-streaming' borrowed from the global fight against drugs.[100] Wars as risk management are now into the business of denying terrorists opportunities through proactive action.

RAND counter-terrorism expert Ian Lesser recommended that 'environment shaping' around the world can reduce terror risks.[101] In the context of Afghanistan, applying Lesser's notion of environment shaping, we can diminish areas of chaos and terrorist sanctuary by destroying terror infrastructure and conditions there that make them conducive for terrorists and prevent new zones from forming. This concept is reflected in the US *National Strategy for Combating Terrorism* released in February 2003, which stated how terrorist plans are nurtured within boundaries and conditions set by the international environment. The ultimate goal of US policy is thus to foster 'an international environment inhospitable to terrorists and all those who support them' by eliminating sanctuaries, leaders, command and control, and generally unsettling their planning ability.[102] Terrorist infrastructure is important, noted General Myers, and so terrorists had to be denied 'the opportunity to continue to use them ... we are trying to set the conditions inside that country that terrorism will no longer be supported'. The net result of this, suggests Colin Powell, is to make survival far more tricky for such organisations.[103]

War now meant denial of opportunities and making environmental conditions inimical to terrorists, not just militarily defeating them in the conventional sense of a 'heroic' war against a clearly identifiable enemy or a discrete subject. As then US commander of Combined Joint Task Force (CJTF)-180 in Afghanistan Lieutenant-General Dan McNeill observed on ongoing operations in late June 2002, 'I don't have a particular name affixed to what I'm going up against'.[104] Disruption means targeting a terrorist organisation by not only stopping one of its particular operations, but rendering all its activities more difficult. US Colonel John Campbell, commander of forces in southern Afghanistan thus described his mission in late February 2003 as denying sanctuary to Taliban and Al Qaeda. By way of continued US operations and presence, this would disrupt enemy communications and planning, pressuring them into moving or hiding.[105] Constantly chipping away at Al Qaeda can at least hamper its ability to strike at will, while not yielding visible results.

Further afield, the CJTF-Horn of Africa mission statement sought to 'deny opportunity for re-emergence of terrorist groups in the Horn of Africa'.[106] The Pentagon is already contemplating bare-bones basing agreements in lawless regions in north and sub-Saharan Africa which could be potential havens. As European Command's Director of Plans and Policy noted, the last thing America needed in Africa was another Afghanistan providing conditions suitable for sustaining terrorists. This had to be prevented through reshaping environments to make it more difficult for terrorists to plan.[107]

The ability of networks like Al Qaeda to hijack weak states makes it more imperative to do so, although it is unclear what impact modern communication technologies have on the need for quasi-virtual organisations.[108] Indeed, Afghan terrorist camps were perhaps now unnecessary since Al Qaeda operated as a 'virtual entity'.[109] The only infrastructure needed was a network of safe houses. However, this obscured the importance of Afghanistan as a magnet attracting terrorists, a safe and secure location to train and recruit openly and select the best. Kurt Campbell and Philip Zelikow, leading the Aspen Strategy Group study on homeland security, emphasised that a principal achievement so far has been depriving Al Qaeda of its secure Afghan base, which provided perfect environmental conditions to plan, and harassing its operatives worldwide.

Nation-tending

Washington is famously averse to nation-building, keen on exit strategies and 'light footprints'. Tommy Franks quipped in November 2001, 'this is a conflict that probably has the easiest exit strategy in years'. In Afghanistan, Franks felt America only needed to destroy terrorist networks with global reach and their supporters – in this case the Taliban who provided support architecture.[110] There was initially no hint of any need for reconstruction. As Bush suggested, 'we're not into nation-building'.[111] Resisting the international peacekeeping force beyond Kabul, Washington's overriding priority remained the hunt for terrorists rather than more heroic nation-building. Washington spends $10 billion a year on the 17,000 American troops chasing Taliban/Al Qaeda remnants in eastern and southern Afghanistan but less than $1 billion on reconstruction since 2001, although Congress has authorised more.[112] Britain's former top soldier Admiral Michael Boyce criticised America's 'single-minded aim' of destroying Bin Laden in a 'high-tech Wild West' operation, ignoring rebuilding.[113]

Utilitarian safety-first security concerns in Washington overrode other moral reasons for reconstruction. Rumsfeld's goals were first and foremost to ensure no more terrorist havens or sanctuaries emerge; averting further terrorist acts was the overriding priority.[114] As a US diplomat reportedly quipped, 'we go in, we hunt down terrorists, and we leave as if we'd never been there.'[115] After 9/11 reconstruction implied greater national interest than previously thought. The 2002 *National Security Strategy* clearly stated that America felt more threatened not by conquering states but failing ones, especially with destructive technologies in the hands of the embittered few.[116] There was, however, little talk here of nation-building in the conventional sense but rather what Michael Ignatieff called 'nation-building lite' to safeguard strategic interests and stability at lowest possible cost.[117]

Simon Chesterman suggests the US effort was one of 'accidental nation-building' as circumstances changed. It was not planned for from the beginning.[118] President Bush did shift gears and his position later and begrudgingly accepted the need for 'so-called nation-building', but preferred calling it 'stabilisation of a future government' that would be inhospitable to terrorists. As likelihood of Bin Laden's capture diminished, attention began shifting to the plight of the Afghan people and ensuring post-conflict stability to prevent terrorists returning. Chesterman argues that justifying nation-building as part of the war on terror lowers standards for reconstruction. The minimum level of security to prevent terrorists returning is not the same as the higher standards required for concerted economic growth and development. This meant elevating military goals over political and moral priorities. The American reliance on local warlords without substantial peacekeeping beyond Kabul has improved life marginally but promises of financial aid and reconstruction have not been met.

Despite successfully organised elections in October 2004 and the apparent progress of democracy, Hamid Karzai's writ does not run throughout most of Afghanistan. Feuding warlords benefited the most from economic reconstruction, creating huge inequalities. The UN in February 2005 released the first-ever Afghan Human Development Report, which found some progress but that serious security problems remained. The nation could all too easily collapse into a state of chaos, becoming a terrorist haven again. Life expectancy, literacy and conditions for women and children, and poverty rates were among the most deplorable in the world. It lambasted the US for spending one billion dollars a month on fighting terrorism but much less on poverty alleviation and social injustices. It also found majorities of people feeling pessimistic that reconstruction was not reaching them.

This seemed to be a case of 'nation-tending' rather than 'nation-building'.[119] Just as classical rehabilitation in the modernist sense in criminology has given way to rehabilitation only to the extent that it manages risks, this is paralleled in Afghanistan. The 2002 *National Security Strategy* noted it will rebuild Afghanistan so its people are never again abused, its neighbours are not threatened, and no haven for terrorists exists.[120] Utilitarian concerns about security and terrorism appear foremost in this argument rather than moral concerns or obligations for reconstruction. Pentagon officials insisted the US role in Afghanistan is not about nation-building simply for the sake of it but about security-building.

Similarly, strategically marginal Somalia was abandoned in 1994 only for Washington to worry after 9/11 that it had terrorist bases. The Horn of Africa has been identified as another dangerous place. Instability breeds terror, intoned Geoff Hoon. The West had to prevent these conditions developing or alter them if they already existed. This would minimise risks to UK interests.[121] Renewed interests in Africa appear based more on utilitarian concerns to prevent terrorist sanctuaries than on moral concerns to rebuild weak or failed states. The re-elected Bush Administration might however well see the consolidation of democracy in Afghanistan and elsewhere as increasingly consistent with its world-view of reinforcing vital security interests, and undertake more extensive nation-building programmes.

DEFINING SUCCESS

Non-events and the minimalist criterion for victory

Hypothetically, war as risk management could conclude when the risks are reduced to a tolerable level with success defined minimally in terms of non-events such as avoiding undesirable risks occurring. Yet risks cannot be eliminated and have to be constantly managed. In contrast, success in conventional war is normally defined by desirable outcomes like defeating a fixed identifiable enemy, taking its capital or surrender ceremonies. It has a visible finite point. Attacking terrorism spawned from foreign countries has the best chance of being called 'war'. But the practical aim of military action remains more the effective suppression indicative of risk management than the total elimination evocative of war. As the *National Strategy for Combating Terrorism* acknowledges, 'in this different kind of war, we cannot expect an easy or definitive end to the conflict'.[122] To gauge progress, former CIA chief George Tenet tried a body count approach while President Bush reportedly keeps a scorecard of major terrorist leaders arrested, disrupted or killed. Such an approach is appealing for it provides a concrete measure of success.

This can be misleading, especially since many of those arrested are low-ranking cadres and Al Qaeda is able to replace even top planners like Khalid Sheikh Mohamed. Neither do quantitative measures reflect on dispersed sleeper cells, fundraising skills, morale and the residual ability of Al Qaeda to strike. These are almost impossible to assess precisely. Even those who genuinely believe they are donating to charities might not know they are indirectly supporting Al Qaeda. Given these data problems, Daniel Byman concludes that a more complete and sophisticated method to measuring success is elusive.[123] Nonetheless, less than precise data still beats relying exclusively on a body count approach. Chairman of the JCS Richard Myers warned of 'old think' and that trying to 'quantify what we're doing today in terms of previous conventional wars' was a huge mistake. Rumsfeld further noted that the Afghan campaign was a significantly different situation where success will no longer be defined by tonnage of bombs dropped.[124] Clearly new thinking is required and this is provided by risk management criteria of non-events.

What would victory look like with new thinking? The only visible battle-field victory was ridding Kabul of Taliban and Al Qaeda, yet this produced no prospect of closure. There were no grandiose victory parades. The Taliban collapse produced relief rather than rejoicing in Western capitals. Otherwise much was ambiguous. Mullah Omar and Bin Laden remained at large; most Taliban fighters simply disappeared. Struggling to define victory, Rumsfeld vowed to hunt terrorists until Americans could go about daily routines 'without fear and relative freedom'.[125] When such a stage is attained is impossible to define clearly. Attorney General John Ashcroft in November 2001 suggested one interesting measure of victory: that America had been triumphant in the opening phase of the war on terrorism simply because two periods of extreme peril had passed without another attack.[126] As predicted, such are the non-events and negative indicators of victory in this war. The absence of another terrorist spectacular on US soil so far, even during the Iraq war, was thus touted as success.

Why were such minimalist outcomes defined as victory? The key benchmark of successful risk management here is simply avoiding harm: we want to prevent the worst, rather than attain something good, despite Bush's constant ritual invocation of 'freedom' in his speeches. The war on terror seemed less about what we stand *for*, than what we seek to *avoid*. We 'reduce vulnerabilities' and 'minimise impacts'. As Condoleezza Rice observed, 'most fundamentally, 9/11 crystallised our vulnerability'.[127] The language used has been overwhelmingly negative: 'prevent', 'disrupt', 'deny', 'avoid', 'degrade', 'suppress'. By focusing on avoidable harm, the risk management approach fosters a negative if not dystopian outlook, for the rhetorical war on terrorism is like the war on drugs, 'unwinnable'. Indeed, 100 per cent success in counter-terrorism is not realistic given the myriad risks modern societies face.[128] Bush to his credit has recognised this: 'I don't think you can win it (the war on terror). But you can create conditions so that those who use terror are less acceptable in parts of the world'.[129]

What can be done is to make it more difficult for terrorists to operate by reshaping conditions and environments as suggested earlier. The least bad outcome was accepted as victory. Donald Rumsfeld accepts that is not everyone's 'preferred outcome' but it beats nothing. The goal negatively defined is simply to make sure the terrorists do not win.[130] In September 2002, responding to suggestions that the war in Afghanistan had not been too successful lately, Rumsfeld again defined success in terms of non-events: not finding large numbers of Taliban indicated success, not failure. Success meant dispersing them, leaving only ragtag remnants.[131] This focus on non-visible outcomes differs from a traditional 'events approach' to terrorism, which measures the number of terrorist incidents that occur to indicate whether terrorism is increasing or not. But measurement cannot be precise because fluctuations could be for various reasons: more precautions, disruption or simply because terrorists need more time to prepare a spectacular.[132] Instead, as suggested by the test framework, we seem to be moving towards a 'non-events' approach in which any incident that does *not* occur is regarded as a success. Paul Wolfowitz for one rightly measured victory 'by what does not happen as opposed to what does happen.'[133]

President Bush's address to the Joint Session of Congress on 20 September 2001 made clear that actions would include dramatic strikes as well as covert operations, 'secret even in success'. Not everything that was going on would be shown on TV. Yet visible results have been assumed to be the context of modern war, especially since the Gulf War. The difficulty of measuring success in Afghanistan was exemplified by calls for the coalition to produce numbers of enemy dead in Operation *Anaconda*. UK Defence Secretary Hoon responded that success should not be defined in these terms but rather in terms of the ability to deter terrorists and disrupt their supporting activities.[134] We now have an emerging concept of war where success is defined not by defeating the enemy militarily. Instead success will be low-key, unpublicised, sometimes even unknown, disrupting and quashing of networks.

Events from Afghanistan suggest that counter-terrorism is about 'managing risks, not confronting certainties'.[135] Non-events, like every single day that goes by without a terrorist outrage, can be considered a triumph of risk management. Success must be defined in terms of 'reducing both probability and consequences of further attack.'[136] John Ashcroft noted the potential of another attack was very real but that potential could be reduced by being vigilant.[137]Colin Powell accordingly defined success negatively. It may never mean no terrorist events ever. It may simply mean bringing terrorism under control and making life far more difficult for terrorist organisations.[138] This is typical risk management language recognising and accepting limits.

Yet, encouraged by the terminology of 'war', the prevalent strand of thinking about counter-terrorism is an erroneous tendency towards absolute solutions and the quick eradication of terrorism.[139] In contrast, Europe's long struggle with terrorism views the problem as intrinsic to modern life. It seeks to manage and reduce the problem rather than to solve it.[140] Stephen Flynn notes that a European 'risk management approach' basically assumes invulnerability is unrealistic.[141] In contrast, the idea of a 'war' on terrorism implies that it will end some day, whereas at the time of writing the Afghan campaign shows no signs of conclusion. In fairness, US policy-makers have urged lower expectations. As Bush noted in his weekly radio address of 16 February 2003, 'there is no such thing as perfect security' against elusive killers. Bush reiterated this point again after the July 2005 London bombings. This echoes Madeleine Albright's acknowledgement in August 1998 that missile strikes were 'not perfect insurance'.[142] The National Strategy for Homeland Security admits that eliminating all risks is not practical or possible.[143] Its author Tom Ridge resigned himself to the fact that an absolutely secure environment was impossible and we had to accept that.[144] There is a clear recognition of limits and that no perfect solutions exist. Terrorism should soon seem, like crime, to be an everyday problem, and we can only at best manage the risks.

An open-ended process: tackling the Hydra effect

War as risk management, it is theorised, leads to open-ended operations to continually manage new risks or resurgent old ones. There seemed plenty of evidence for this in Afghanistan. Tony Blair urged patience and digging in for the long haul as the customary public wobble emerged early in the campaign with no visible successes. Bush's warning against expecting 'an instant gratification war' is significant for the finishing line is not easily apparent when managing risks entails constant monitoring, taking repeated action if necessary. Operation *Anaconda* in March 2002 reminded the world that the conflict was not over yet. We have seen numerous operations since. The endgame is far from clear. Geoff Hoon described the deployment of Royal Marine Commandos to Afghanistan in March 2002 as 'open-ended'. Al Qaeda attempts to regroup will be met by what Bush called a 'sustained, tireless, relentless campaign' for as long as it takes.[145] Only in May 2003, almost 16 months after the fall of the Taliban, was there a declared end to major combat but sporadic skirmishes persist. The vague criteria for measuring progress — disrupting terror networks and keeping them running – leaves open the possibility that more action will follow assessments that terrorists once again are posing significant risks.

By October 2002, CIA Director Tenet warned in Congressional testimony that despite a year's efforts Al Qaeda was 'reconstituted' with more attacks in the pipeline, posing almost as serious a risk as 2001. The UN reported in December 2002 that Al Qaeda recruitment and finances remained robust.[146] In May 2003, the International Institute for Strategic Studies' *Strategic Survey 2002/2003* proclaimed that Al Qaeda 'remains more insidious and just as dangerous'. The Afghan campaign and other efforts only made it even harder to identify and thwart as it evolved. Countless others remained in the wings to replace killed or captured operatives. The process was 'self-perpetuating'.[147]

The Afghan campaign suggests risk management lessons. In risk management, it is essential constantly to assess the effectiveness of measures taken: a cyclical and ongoing process, rather than a linear progression. Policy should not be gauged in terms of definitive goals but by way of an ongoing process of risk management. Perhaps we should see the war on terrorism in light of other interminable, unwinnable rhetorical wars (for example, on drugs) where a similar lack of clarity and the 'hydra effect' predominate.[148] With American forces deployed from Georgia to the Philippines and Iraq, calls were made both in Congress and the media for the Bush Administration to clearly define new missions, state how long they will last and clarify objectives.[149] However, counter-terrorism should not be too obsessed with the flavour of the moment or specific timeframes, for there are always others about to appear and ready to replace Bin Laden – the so-called Hydra effect. President Bush rightly counselled patience in a 'task that does not end'.[150]

There is no clear endgame because of the constant need to disrupt terrorist cells and deny them safe havens. This point was not lost on Clinton who back in 1998 already pitted the US in a 'long, ongoing struggle' with terrorism.[151] Noted terrorism expert Walter Lacqueur suggested that perhaps there will be no discernible end to the war on terrorism in the twenty-first century.[152] Tony Blair too realised there was no 'finite point'. Coping with Al Qaeda, warned Tom Ridge, would be a 'permanent condition'.[153] This sounds more like risk management's open-ended nature than war, which presumes at least a defined end point. While 9/11 fuelled new determination to end terrorism, history does not suggest optimism. History tells us that terror groups can be eliminated and terrorism rendered less significant, but terrorists always invent new methods.[154]

Allied maritime patrols in the Mediterranean have only forced terrorists to use overland routes through North Africa. Apparent successes in Afghanistan dispersed Al Qaeda to lawless regions of Yemen, Somalia, Pakistan's tribal areas and even South-East Asia, the so-called Second Front. There are concerns that Al Qaeda is establishing new infrastructure in Lebanon's Bekaa Valley with Hezbollah. This suggested a 'boomerang effect' where initial action to manage risks created more risks as a result. Paradoxically, due to the success of the Afghan campaign, scattered remnants and a more splintered decentralised command structure driven underground might also make it harder to monitor. There are also concerns about relatively simple attacks by 'Lone Wolves' broadly sympathetic to Al Qaeda but not part of it, or cells that plan without guidance. Thus, information about high-level leaders may turn out to be less important than before 9/11. The risk simply evolved rather than disappeared. Indeed, Al Qaeda had a 'remarkably protean nature', constantly adapting.[155]

This is the key conundrum facing counter-terrorism – as military operations, improved security and intelligence cooperation reshape its operating environment, Al Qaeda constantly adapts and assumes more refined forms. Indeed Bruce Hoffman suggests Al Qaeda's greatest feat has been its 'makeover' since 2001. From a somewhat lumbering bureaucratic outfit physically based in Afghanistan, it became more of an idea or concept; a less tangible 'virtual' transnational movement incorporating far-flung loose-knit like-minded organisations working autonomously for the common goal. In this sense Al Qaeda paradoxically benefited from losing its Afghan lair in exchange for greater logistical and operational flexibility with no physical infrastructure to defend.[156] Its loosely affiliated franchises or associates include the Jemaah Islamiyaa (JI) – perpetrators of the October 2002 Bali bombings – and the Salafia Jihadia – the alleged masterminds behind the May 2003 Casablanca bombing. This new breed of terrorists are inspired by Al Qaeda but do not belong specifically to it nor do they directly follow Bin Laden's orders. The JI is an example of how Al Qaeda has exploited and co-opted local grievances into its broader Islamist agenda.[157] Clearly the menace is far from over and open-ended risk management is in a good position to appreciate that.

RISK MANAGEMENT ALL OVER AGAIN

Many commentators have seen the Afghan campaign breaking new grounds in warfare and this was certainly true in some respects. However, this book has adopted a contrary viewpoint: to assess instead continuities with previous campaigns over Kosovo in terms of risk management. Indeed given the similar operational indicators uncovered, it might even be accurate to suggest the Afghan campaign was 'Kosovo redux' not in its original derogatory sense but in terms of the two operations sharing the same basic premise of risk management. Despite conceptual difficulties related to 'war' terminology, what was clearer was the extent to which specific aspects of the Afghan campaign served to manage systemic risks. Employing 'war' terminology focused attention on military actions against easily identifiable state enemies, attaining clear-cut decisive positive results at the end. None of these were observed in Afghanistan.

Instead it exhibited key features of risk management: the philosophy of 'anticipationism' informed proactive military action against Al Qaeda to prevent further attacks. Decision-makers adopted a 'reflexive' rationality more concerned with forestalling possible adverse consequences that had not yet occurred, although instrumental rationality was also present, focused on achieving specific goals such as the expulsion of the Taliban and Al Qaeda. Even where military action was in some sense retrospective, responding to past attacks, officials like Rumsfeld made clear the locus of action remained protecting the future, not revenge or retribution. Recourse to the precautionary principle however was weaker since America had been attacked first, although there were clear inclinations to assume the worst-case probabilistic scenarios without concrete evidence. Continuous surveillance processes provided information on how the level of risks stood and enabled the taking of preventive action where possible. In reshaping the environment, evidence suggested that the counter-terrorism goals indeed became the denial of opportunities for terrorists to plan rather than to fight concrete enemies in a conventional military sense. Bin Laden, while demonised, was predictably sidelined in favour of disrupting the environment he operated within. The Bush Administration presented its reconstruction efforts as crucial to reducing the risks of terrorism. This provided further indication of risk management's utilitarian moral calculus sitting uncomfortably alongside talk of spreading democracy. Eventually, low-intensity conflict in Afghanistan seemed to be the forgotten brother of the Iraq war. Operations became routinised, as terrorism slowly became seen as a risk to be lived with and managed.

The war became an open-ended endeavour against Hydra-headed enemies where results are not clearly visible. The traditional manner of understanding terrorism and terrorists by analysing organisational definitions and attributes is now outmoded, given the continued mutations and evolution of Al Qaeda.[158] Trends also seemed to be pointing towards a non-events approach replacing the previous events-based approach as the benchmark for measuring progress. Managing the 'boomerang effect' meant more risks were actually generated in the dialectical process of war as risk management. Al Qaeda became even more dangerous after its extreme makeover with the loss of its Afghan sanctuary. In sum, a risk management approach is able satisfactorily to explain these specific aspects of the Afghan campaign and the war on terrorism. The next big question is whether risk management could also address the issue of Saddam Hussein and Iraq, which appeared next on top of Washington's 'to do' list.

6

WAR ON IRAQ
Textbook risk management or flawed strategy?

CONTINUITY AND CHANGE

In 2003, regime change in Iraq under the Bush Doctrine of pre-emption arguably broke new ground in war and strategy. The Bush team was particularly mindful about distinguishing itself from Clinton by its disdain for 'containment, partial solutions and messy compromises'.[1] Yet unbeknownst to most, the Bush White House justified war in 'reflexive' terms mirroring those of the Clinton national security team in the late 1990s. Legal arguments put forth in February 2003 also bore eerie resemblance to those of December 1998.[2] Washington had in effect been warring with Baghdad on and off throughout the 1990s, especially since 1998 with the quickly forgotten 'preventive' *Desert Fox* campaign, followed by a little-noticed open-ended struggle over no-fly zones, which morphed seamlessly into regime change. Any semblance of continuity crumbled underneath the rush to criticise Bush's unilateralism. Yet, the criticisms (oil, personal revenge) were 'unhelpfully vitriolic' and unconvincing. There was superficial understanding of motivations, papering over continuities in US foreign policy.[3]

In a similar vein, this final case study assesses the extent to which use of force towards Iraq from December 1998 to February 2005 exhibited continuities in terms of risk management. It does not claim that Washington's case is especially persuasive or justified nor does it pretend to offer a definitive interpretation. Rather it asks whether war is possibly addressed through highlighting the presence of risk concepts. Events are assessed thematically, not chronologically. The same framework of structured questions applied to earlier case studies is repeated, with the aim of pinpointing and engaging specific aspects of the Iraq war through the lens of risk management.

The nature of security concerns over Iraq and their core components – globalised systemic risks or imminent threats – providing impetus for action need first to be carefully appraised. Official rationales for war can then be sieved through for evidence of 'reflexive' rationality guiding future-oriented anticipatory action and resort to the precautionary principle. Surveillance operations over Iraq serve as additional instruments of risk management as did utilitarian use of force through 'routine' operations to reshape the environment. Finally, through the prism of risk management, policy can more appropriately be evaluated in minimalist terms of non-events and avoiding adverse outcomes, rather than perfect solutions. Rather than the linear goals often associated with war, one can discern instead an ongoing cyclical process and a 'boomerang effect'.

A BRIEF HISTORY

In August 1990, UN Security Council Resolution (UNSCR) 661 imposed comprehensive economic sanctions on Iraq after its invasion of Kuwait. These were to remain in place until UNSCR 687 of April 1991 was complied with, the certification that Baghdad had destroyed all its weapons of mass destruction (WMD). The International Atomic Energy Agency and UN Special Commission (UNSCOM) were charged with monitoring and implementing these provisions. However, Iraq repeatedly obstructed inspectors until their expulsion in 1998. Consequently, Britain and America launched a 70-hour air campaign Operation *Desert Fox* in December 1998 to 'degrade' Iraqi WMD facilities. UNSCOM was replaced by the UN Monitoring, Verification and Inspection Commission (UNMOVIC), which returned for short-lived inspections from November 2002 to March 2003. On 20 March 2003, the United States launched Operation *Iraqi Freedom* with a 'decapitation' strike intended to kill Saddam Hussein. Shortly afterwards, coalition ground forces surged into Iraq and, despite resistance from irregular fedayeen, entered Baghdad on 9 April 2003.

The no-fly zones in northern Iraq above the 36th parallel (Operation *Northern Watch*) and southern Iraq below the 33rd parallel (Operation *Southern Watch*) were set up by America, Britain and France somewhat haphazardly after the 1991 Gulf War to protect Shi'ites in the south and Kurds in the north from reprisals after their failed uprisings. The zones were not explicitly UN authorised although the coalition cites UNSCR 688 of 5 April 1991, which deemed Iraqi repression a 'threat to international peace and security'. This resolution was not passed under Chapter VII mandates. It eventually became clear that these zones served not only humanitarian purposes, but also to keep Saddam 'in his box'. After the end of *Desert Fox*, low-key but active sorties continued in no-fly zones against Iraqi air defence targets, which increasingly accosted coalition warplanes. Air strikes had been carried out for policing no-fly zones as well as punishing Iraqi non-compliance with disarmament provisions. Comprehensive containment involved multiple tools of statecraft: economic sanctions, diplomacy and coalition building, intelligence gathering, supporting opposition movements and military force.[4] These are not necessarily exclusive, but the balance between them shifted over time. Military actions are our focus, with the acknowledgement that multiple tools were also involved. Confronting Iraq evolved from a multilateral UN operation into a more bilateral one involving Washington, supported to a lesser extent by London.

Two phases are discernible here for our purposes: the late Clinton/early Bush Administration and post-9/11. Oil smuggling, sanctions fatigue, humanitarian concerns and fragmented Iraqi opposition groups made no-fly zones and military action the de facto US policy by 1999. Initially there was no significant policy change, which the incoming Bush administration promised, apart from 'smart' sanctions. Early tough talk about regime change was notable by its absence. Even Deputy Defence Secretary Paul Wolfowitz, the Administration's resident hawk, admitted there was no plan in the works: 'I haven't seen it yet'.[5] The Bush Administration gradually found itself taking the same line on Iraq as that of Clinton – a policy previously derided by Bush and his top aides.[6] In December 2000, Secretary of State-designate Colin Powell seemed to endorse continuity by stating that America would continue to contain Saddam, and then confront him, if required. Bush defended air strikes in February 2001 as 'part of a strategy, and until that strategy is changed, we will continue to enforce them.'[7]

Nonetheless, these statements left room for change. Prior to 9/11, both Administrations viewed Iraq largely in terms of proliferation risks and regional stability. Terrorism was a separate concern. Indeed, Iraq was seen more as a long-term threat requiring the building of missile defences. After 9/11, the two issues became intertwined rightly or wrongly, and not without precedent either. By the late 1980s America's 'rogue doctrine' had already linked proliferation and terrorism concerns to Third World states quite apart from their previous status as Soviet surrogates.[8] After despatching the Taliban, President Bush unveiled his next priority: preventing terrorists acquiring WMD. Rogue states were slated as the most probable sources of such weapons. Although Washington emphasised Saddam's brutal regime, refusal to disarm and spreading democracy as more concrete issues, the possibility of him reacquiring WMD or passing them to terrorists most animated policy-makers. Bush shifted from Clinton's policy of 'containment plus' (short-term containment through 'smart' sanctions, air strikes and aiding the opposition; overthrow in the long term) to overt regime change. The Bush Administration seemed more motivated by a desire to confront threats head-on rather than simply to manage them.[9] This posed significant conceptual challenges for risk management. Viewing Iraq as part of the broader war on terror also created analytical difficulties. It introduced new variables; previous risks from Iraq could no longer be judged on their own basis.

Various factors account for this policy shift. These are discussed only in brief. The collapse of inspections, sanctions and containment's moral costs was one possible reason for British involvement.[10] September 11 reinforced existing cognitive perceptions and strengthened the hand of hawks like

Paul Wolfowitz. Policy-makers drew analogies such as the need to act preventively. Iraq became 'part of the insecurity we now feel' argued Condoleezza Rice.[11] In his testimony to the Butler report in 2004, Tony Blair also noted that 9/11 changed his mindset with regard to rogue states acquiring WMD. That Iraq, an impoverished state wracked by sanctions for a decade, should cause concern appeared linked to this insecurity felt back in the UK and US rather than to any new concrete evidence. Furthermore, difficulties involved in destroying Iraqi WMD by air alone were considerable: Baghdad concealed its systems underground after Israel's Osirak raid destroyed its above-ground reactors, and knew American tactics well. The role of intellectuals in the Project for a New American Century such as William Kristol should, however, not be overstated. The 'pre-emptive' strike was the logical consequence of a way of thinking, especially post-9/11. It is also important to note subtle differences between London and Washington. Blair was careful to stress WMD and disarmament, not regime change or Al Qaeda links to the same extent Washington did.

CONCEPTUAL ISSUES

Iraq posed interesting and significant questions for understanding a category of war that defied conventional criteria. As Eliot Cohen observed in late 2002, 'the Gulf War did not end in February 1991. For a decade now, we've been fighting this low-level war without calling it such.'[12] In December 1998, Britain and America had already attracted condemnation for using force against Iraq without explicit UN authorisation. Especially since 1998, British and American jets routinely forayed into Iraq, unleashing precision-guided munitions and getting shot at in return. War, broadly construed, described such sustained combat operations.

Yet then-Secretary of State Albright insisted, despite using military force, 'we are not talking about a war'.[13] Furthermore, between December 1998 and the end of the Clinton era, *Southern Watch* aircraft reported coming under fire some 670 times. More than 5000 combat sorties were flown from December 1998 to August 1999 in Operation *Northern Watch* alone. An inconclusive war of attrition was in progress, 'unique in the annals of air combat'.[14] This operation lacked the guidance of the Powell doctrine, which held that military campaigns should have clear goals. Many bemoaned the lack of a consistent Iraq policy without 'guiding purpose or rationale'.[15] This conclusion appears rather harsh if the operation is judged by the open-ended nature of risk management.

In the run-up to regime change, the low-grade war over no-fly zones was ratcheted up to 'shape' the battlefield involving even B-1 strategic bombers, degrading Iraq air-defences and Ababil-100 surface-to-surface missiles. Later, it emerged that this actually involved a plan called *Southern Focus* striking the fibre-optic networks Baghdad used for communications, radars and other key military installations. Coalition forces were thus able to launch ground offensives without extensive air strikes as 606 bombs had already been dropped on 391 selected targets.[16] There was no clear distinction between outbreak of war or continuation of hostilities from no-fly zones. Michael Walzer noted that Washington was already fighting a 'little war' despite all the UN shenanigans for authority to fight a 'big war'.[17] Risk management could provide perspectives to understand the preceding 'little war' and subsequent 'big war'.

By March 2003, Anglo-American resort to war again without UN approval created serious diplomatic rifts, despite policy-makers being more forthright about using the term 'war'. This was also the first time Washington had launched full-scale preventive war and appeared to herald momentous change in the international system. The lack of a so-called smoking gun especially concerned many analysts who feared 'sexed up' dossiers about Iraqi WMD programmes exaggerating the 'imminent' threat.

Despite widespread conspiracy theories, regime change in 2003 was largely *not* motivated by traditional markers such as economic or geopolitical advantages or even moral ones like democracy, revenge or justice for Saddam's victims. Instead, it seemed a 'safety-first' approach based on risk – of Saddam linking up with Al Qaeda or acquiring WMD – was the most compelling answer.[18] Even with the very visible success of capturing Baghdad in April 2003, there was no traditional end game such as surrender ceremonies. These features can be addressed through risk management.

For all the hype over a shock and awe campaign in 2003 utilising network-centric 'effects-based' warfare shrinking sensor-to-shooter times, age-old adages still endured in the fog of war. Describing unanticipated resistance from Iraqi militias, US Army V Corps General William Wallace commented, 'this enemy is a bit different from what we war-gamed'. The dangers of mirror imaging still persisted. Clearly, some continuity in war remained, including similarities with previous wars. Military action against Iraq over the years, mirroring trends in Kosovo and Afghanistan, distinguished government structures (so-called 'regime targets') from society. On 16 April 2003 President Bush enthused at St Louis that through creative strategies and advanced technology, America was redefining war. Strategists will doubtless note the precision targeting and 'every possible care' emphasised by politicians to avoid harming civilians (even dropping laser-guided concrete blocks to minimise shrapnel risks) during *Desert Fox*, no-fly zones operations and *Iraqi Freedom*. Concerns over risks to airmen patrolling no-fly zones also meant tactics evolved from a 'reactive to a pre-emptive approach' of pre-planned strike packages to reduce chances of an Allied plane downed over Iraq.[19] British spokesmen argued that we had to 'manage the risk to our aircrew'.[20]

Such intriguing aspects of tactical risk management should be left to others. Here we are more concerned with continuities from previous wars over Kosovo and Afghanistan in terms of managing systemic risks from Iraq, although tactical risks clearly constrained operations. Analysts have done impressive work evaluating policy toward Iraq since 1991 but none adopt a broad risk management approach.[21] These focused on specifics such as fine-tuning sanctions policy, helping opposition groups, and targeting pillars of the regime such as the Special Republican Guard. The legality of war also preoccupied analysts.[22]

Globalisation and systemic risks: terrorism and proliferation

Iraq exhibited ample systemic risks as the impetus for management action. Risk is inherently subjective and constructed. Iraq constituted a perfect case study for constructivism. EU foreign policy chief Javier Solana observed that fundamentally 'there are different perceptions of risk on both sides', between America and 'old' Europe.[23] Once again, this study is not about explaining different risk perceptions or policy-making. Instead it is more concerned with understanding a chosen strategy rather than factors behind *how* that strategy was chosen. After all there is an exploding array of books examining the inner workings of decision-making on Iraq.[24]

Risk here was used largely as a descriptive term referring to a potentially dangerous state of events or situation. These included proliferation, clandestine WMD programmes, cross-border aggression or alleged links to terrorists. The idea of a rogue state posing proliferation risks was exacerbated with the end of communism. Constraints on WMD materials are much looser than during the Cold War. The 'global trade' in WMD, warned the 2002 US *National Security Strategy*, has become a danger to all nations of the world.[25] Similar concerns were raised throughout Clinton's security documents. Both Presidents Bush and Clinton feared 'plutonium merchants' conniving with 'unbalanced dictators'. During the Clinton era, there were also suggestions that Iraq masterminded the first World Trade Center bombing in 1993. Relying on now infamous crude forged documents, Bush claimed that Iraq sought uranium from Niger. UNSCOM also discovered covert transactions between Iraq and 500 companies from more than 40 countries between 1993 and 1998. These allegedly sought out weapons components such as aluminium tubes. Like Clinton, Bush also worried that in today's open world, Saddam could deliver a WMD with a modified L-39 trainer/UAV or short-range cruise missile smuggled off the US coast on a container ship, or a 'suitcase nuke'. These probabilistic globalisation-linked scenarios of catastrophic consequences were certainly not unique to the Bush Administration. This implied 'anticipatory horizon-scanning' of the strategic landscape for any possible security risks. However, the experience of Iraqi aggression in the first Gulf War and – rightly or wrongly – that of

9/11 also led to a desire to avoid repetition of similar dramatic catastrophic 'tombstone-style' risks. As suggested, these two aspects of risks cannot be clearly isolated.

Throughout the 1990s to 2003, the relative priority of risks shifted from regional stability and proliferation, to increasing concern about terrorist links, WMD and regime change.[26] Policy should be seen not so much as a static coherent whole but as an aggregation of actions evolving over time, sometimes haphazardly, sometimes purposefully. As Anthony Cordesman noted, 'simple and consistent policy on paper is desirable but can rapidly fail under the pressure of events'.[27] Likewise, the strategies implemented were hardly static, responding to changes in strategic context.

Clinton's policy towards Iraq was initially geared towards at least a reduction of WMD, limitation of proliferation, and regional security. The maximal goal, sometimes espoused, sometimes eschewed throughout the late 1990s was the removal of Saddam. Considering the difficulties throughout the 1990s involved in removing Saddam and the aftermath, it made sense to simply manage him as best as possible.[28] Lacking a viable policy, support of Arab partners and Security Council mandate, Clinton preferred to keep him isolated and militarily weak. Washington adopted the minimalist option of Saddam in power over a fragmented Iraq causing regional instability. Containment through sanctions, inspections, no-fly zones and bombing was the risk management strategy adopted.

Having said that, it was under Bill Clinton that regime change and the Iraq Liberation Act became US policy in 1998 as sanctions faltered, inspections ended and the 1991 anti-Saddam coalition frayed. Richard Haass, head of Policy Planning at Powell's State Department, argued in 1998 that confronting an Iraq armed with WMD would be far more dangerous, especially if it supplied weapons to terrorists. Purely relying on reactive US retaliation would be inadequate.[29] Such a scenario would receive more attention post-9/11. Nonetheless, invasion was not seriously contemplated before 9/11.

September 11 marked a sea change in public opinion making invasion more plausible. Advocates of containment now supported regime change in 2003 because of the collapse of sanctions and the unpredictability of Saddam's reaction to deterrence. For Kenneth Pollack, the risk was not so much a Baghdad-Al Qaeda alliance but Saddam's reckless decision-making and his crossing the nuclear threshold.[30] There was also a risk to US credibility if regime change were not implemented. Others, however, disagreed that Saddam was irrational and undeterrable.[31] Sceptics argued that Bush needed an easy victory because Al Qaeda was more complicated. To realists such as Stephen Walt, lumping the two together may also have obfuscated and undermined international cooperation on terrorism, just as Washington initially misread the Communist bloc as a monolithic entity.

But to President Bush, Al Qaeda and Saddam Hussein are indistinguishable, 'they're both risks. The danger is that they work in concert'.[32] Rumsfeld observed that 9/11 changed everything. It highlighted the appreciation of vulnerability – 'the risks the US faces from terrorist networks and terrorist states armed with weapons of mass destruction'.[33] In his testimony to the Butler report, Tony Blair too alluded to the impact of 9/11 on his mindset with regard to WMD. Clinton's National Security Adviser Sandy Berger weighed in, 'A nuclear-armed Hussein sometime in this decade is a risk we cannot ignore', while Jack Straw warned Saddam 'posed an intense risk'.[34] The language of risk is clearly apparent, but did policy-makers in 2003 confuse risk with threat in their interchangeable loose usage of terms, as forewarned in Chapter Three? After all there is strong evidence that Washington misconstrued Iraq as an extension of global terrorism and failed to discriminate between different types of dangers just as it did with the supposedly monolithic communist bloc.[35]

Risk or threat?

Risk and threat occupy different positions on a conceptual spectrum of dangers.[36] This issue merits some analysis especially in 2002—03 where regime change can be construed as 'threat elimination' aggressively resolving problems, implying a powerful shift away from 'risk management'. The drastic impatient means employed implied the risk had somehow solidified into an imminent threat, but this did not appear to be so. According to Bush, we should not wait for dangers to 'fully materialize' but instead take the initiative to prevent their emergence.[37] Blair too suggested it made more sense to take action against a 'gathering threat or danger' before it materialised.[38] Colin Powell signalled in March 2001 that Saddam was not yet in a position to 'present a full-fledge threat' and this certainly had not changed by 2003.[39] These statements suggested that the vague danger remained a risk requiring proactive management to forestall it becoming a fully formed threat, rather than an imminent one. More recent analyses indeed suggest that Blair's choice for war was not based on an imminent threat, nor did Blair claim so. The real cause was fear of the danger growing in future.[40] However, Washington did seem on occasion to believe the threat was clearer.

To be sure, the language of threat was also clearly employed. Bush declared at his news conference on 6 March 2003 just before war, that 'Saddam Hussein and his weapons are a direct threat'. In September 2002, Secretary Rumsfeld detailed to Congress the dangers in terms of 'intentions and capabilities' and concluded Saddam posed an 'inevitable threat'.[41] However, these two components, which normally form the basis of classical 'net assessment' of 'threat', proved inadequate in conceptualising the dangers from Iraq. Kenneth Pollack, contradicting Rumsfeld's assessment, believed it would be some time before Saddam was an 'irredeemable danger'. This was due to both capabilities and intentions.[42] Top US military officials believed in summer 2002, based on intelligence about Iraqi WMD capabilities, that Saddam posed 'no immediate threat'.[43] Paul Pillar further concluded that Iraqi terrorism was constrained more by intentions than capabilities.[44] Saddam has shown little inclination to use terrorism against the US since a botched assassination attempt on former President Bush in 1993. Even the CIA was unsure what Saddam's intentions were regarding Al Qaeda. Bin Laden apparently met Iraqi intelligence (Mukhabarat) officials in Khartoum in 1996. Despite sharing a common enemy, top Al Qaeda planners in custody revealed that Bin Laden rejected an alliance.

Washington's case for regime change is strong based on Saddam's history of aggression and WMD use. However flaws rested with assuming Saddam's future intentions – that he would develop WMD and slip one to terrorists to attack America and its allies. But Saddam could simply have been seeking his own deterrent in a dangerous region.[45] Perhaps the fear was that Washington itself might be deterred by a nuclear-armed Iraq. If Saddam's foremost concern was regime survival, he could theoretically be deterred, unlike stateless terrorists. This, however, assumed 'mirror imaging' that Hussein shared Washington's rationality and would not miscalculate. Intentions and capabilities thus did not quite reflect our concerns over Iraq.

Perhaps it might be more illuminating to highlight risk components in the equation: consequences or probabilities rather than classical 'net assessment' of threats. After all, the basic premise for war was that some time in the future there could be a link between Iraqi WMD and Islamic terrorism. Worst-case analysis was now propelled to the top of the agenda.[46] Post-9/11 America's concern with mass-casualty terrorism led it to 'focus on consequences rather than probabilities'. To Bush's mind the mere possibility of Iraq using WMD or passing them to terrorists justified pre-emptive or preventive force.[47] Although the ideological gap between Hussein and Al Qaeda suggested such transfer was unlikely, the possibility could not be discounted.[48] Saddam could supply WMD to his Palestinian proxies, if not Al Qaeda. It is also extremely difficult to trace biological attacks, as the October 2001 anthrax mailings showed. Indeed, the 'bulk of informed opinion coalesced not around probabilities but consequences'. If cooperation with Al Qaeda occurred, no matter how small the chance, the risk to America would be intolerable.[49] The issue was not Iraqi capabilities or Al Qaeda's intentions but the speculative scenario of the possibility of a link between the two creating the Perfect Storm.[50]

This type of risk assessment seemed more relevant to the debate. Anxiety thrived on the tension between our knowledge and ignorance of risks like Iraqi links to terrorists. Policy-makers seemed more concerned with possibilities, than with correctly assessing intentions. Tony Blair accepted that the association between rogue nations seeking WMD and terrorism was 'loose' but emphasised the *possibility* of the two coming together'.[51] In the post-war furore over WMD, it emerged that the US Defence Intelligence Agency in September 2002 without concrete information reported that 'Iraq *probably* possesses chemical agents in chemical munitions and stockpiles'.[52] Increasingly we are going to war on such probabilities and possibilities.

Risk-oriented thinking allows us to comprehend the focus on probabilities and catastrophic *consequences*. America's new security doctrine is now couched in terms of risk scenarios rather than an actual concrete and specific threat. Condoleezza Rice talked on CNN in September 2002 of 'a mushroom cloud', without providing specifics on how this might occur. The 2002 *National Security Strategy* emphasised 'the magnitude of potential harm' that could be caused by WMD.[53] Clinton similarly justified *Desert Fox* by guaranteeing that once Saddam had an 'arsenal of devastating destruction' he would use it.[54] Focusing on consequences and probabilities situated us within the risk discourse during the Clinton and Bush Administrations. However, as will be shown, Washington in 2003 employed impatient means of elimination. The lack of post-war evidence and ontological uncertainty suggested that elevating the risks to an imminent threat was somewhat premature, although to be fair most intelligence agencies did believe Saddam held some stocks of chemical and biological WMD. Perhaps to make the war sound more like one of necessity than the choice it actually was (and thus more acceptable to public opinion and international law), the intelligence and the risks were presented as an imminent threat rather than the potential dangers actually posed.[55]

By October 2004, Rumsfeld belatedly conceded there was no 'hard' evidence of Iraqi-Al Qaeda ties. The Iraq Survey Group (ISG) also concluded Baghdad posed no imminent threat in terms of intentions and capabilities. It had no significant WMD capabilities despite Saddam's intention to re-arm once sanctions were lifted. The inadequacies of the threat concept relating to Iraq were aptly summed up by former ISG chief David Kay, 'intent but no capability does not equal imminent threat'.[56] Instead war was based on probabilistic speculation and fear of catastrophic consequences.

RISK MANAGEMENT IN ACTION

Active anticipation and reflexive rationality

The West did not yet face a fully developed threat from Baghdad but possible security risks. If these were not addressed immediately, it was not clear harm would definitely occur for much uncertainty existed. Yet, not acting was seen as more risky. Washington and London saw themselves as potential victims of some hypothesised future harm from Saddam. The idea of risk gave them the choice of taking preventive avoidance measures by adopting a 'reflexive' rationality. Risk here is not only a descriptive term but also a normative one implying the desirability of avoidance action. It also formed part of a strategic calculation.

In 2003, the fear of potential victimhood (in the sense of being a victim again) drove Bush's 'never again' mindset after 9/11. At Camp David with Tony Blair in early February 2003, Bush noted that America's strategic vision had shifted dramatically after 9/11. The uppermost obligation was now to 'protect the American people from further harm'. Addressing the nation just before war, he declared that 'instead of drifting along toward tragedy, we will set a course toward safety'.[57] Safety was to be found in adopting proactive 'reflexive' rationality.

The weighing up of counter-factual and alternative courses of action that can shape the future, so prevalent in contemporary society, has jumped into security planners' notebooks. Officials espoused active anticipation, occasionally even without specific cause-effect relationships. To Paul Wolfowitz, 'the fundamental question is how to weigh the risks of action against the risks of inaction'. Ultimately this meant trying to estimate what will happen in the future along different courses we might take.[58] This indicated a 'reflexive' rationality focused on averting possible adverse consequences that had not yet occurred. It certainly did not imply an imminent threat existed where no choice existed. Invading Iraq itself carried high risks such as significant American and civilian casualties, WMD attacks, terrorist strikes, a fractured Iraq, regional instability and higher oil prices; not to mention the long-term consequences for international institutions and law. Wolfowitz's boss Donald Rumsfeld, however, reminded us that the penalty for inaction was another 9/11.[59]

This could arguably be seen as a 'reactive' response to past events like 9/11. But the key point here is not so much backward-looking concepts like justice or retribution; rather, the locus of action was in the future, to prevent repetition of similar harm. Indeed, Rumsfeld even suggested that the issue at hand did not hinge on any previous Iraqi link to 9/11. It was not vengeance, retribution or retaliation – 'it is whether the Iraqi regime poses a growing danger' in future.[60] Active anticipation of future outcomes was the key.

While such statements could come from any politician considering policy options, the 'reflexive' rationality discernible in Washington emphasised the graver risks of not acting while others focused on the risk of acting. It predictably opted for proactive risk management. Both Vice President Cheney and Secretary Rumsfeld concluded that 'the risks of inaction are far greater than the risks of action'.[61] Blair contended that failing to address the risk of WMD passing to terrorists would be to do too little, too late.[62] President Bush rationalised at some length that, 'the risk of doing nothing, the risk that somehow inaction will make the world safer is not a risk I'm willing to take ... I think of the risks, and calculated the costs of inaction versus the cost of action'. [63] This emphasised not so much instrumental calculation of Iraqi capabilities, as reflexive consideration of alternative negative futures that had yet to manifest but had to be averted nonetheless.

This sort of 'reflexive' proactive reasoning is by no means limited to the Bush Administration or 2003. In December 1998, Tony Blair justified air strikes on Iraq by arguing that the risks then were nothing compared to the risks if Saddam's WMD programmes were not halted.[64] Blair was less concerned about instrumentally achieving some present goals but more about 'reflexively' averting possible adverse consequences in the future. The locus of reasoning was the future. There is additionally more continuity between the Clinton and Bush Administrations on Iraq than normally acknowledged. Clinton's statement on *Desert Fox* reflected the same 'reflexive' calculus Bush was to adopt in 2003: 'the costs of action must be weighed against the price of inaction.' Failing to act would only mean a greater menace in future.[65] The underlying proactive premise on risk was identical. The difference was the increased sense of urgency after 9/11.

To prevent or pre-empt?

Among the case studies, Iraq incurred greatest controversy on whether it was 'pre-emptive' or 'preventive'. This merits some discussion. Legally speaking, Bush's pre-emptive doctrine could qualify as anticipatory self-defence. However, the danger from Iraq was neither specific nor proven to be imminent: conditions under which anticipatory self-defence could be invoked.[66] Pre-emption under Just War doctrine as developed by its foremost proponent Michael Walzer was justifiable only if there was serious intent to harm, active preparations making that intent a real danger, and a situation under which doing nothing greatly increased the danger. The potential harm must also be of the gravest nature: loss of territorial integrity or political independence. The mid-nineteenth century *Caroline* case – where British forces pre-emptively sank an American ship helping Canadian rebels – and the resulting diplomatic correspondence outlined the criteria accepted since then for anticipatory action: the 'necessity' must be 'instant, overwhelming, leaving no choice of means and no moment of deliberation'. Iraq posed no such specific urgent threat. Instead, Saddam posed potential risks based on possible unsubstantiated Al Qaeda links. The Bush Doctrine was perhaps preventive rather than pre-emptive.

The Pentagon defines 'preventive war' as 'initiated in the belief that military conflict, while not imminent, is inevitable and that delay would involve great risk'. In contrast, 'pre-emption' depends on 'incontrovertible evidence' of an imminent attack.[67] If Iraq was pre-emptive, the evidence was hardly watertight. Secondly, the definition of 'imminence' has shifted. Condoleezza Rice argued that extremists and new technology require 'new thinking'.[68] While pre-emption was previously predicated on visible mobilisation for attack, the concept of imminent threat had to be modified when terrorists can use WMD without any warning. In this way, Washington actually produced a sophisticated legal basis for the legitimacy of its argument by noting international law recognises that states need not suffer an attack before taking action against imminent attack.[69] Indeed, international law and the UN charter were not created to deal with elusive dangers like terrorism or WMD but more conventional ones from states and regular armies, which require obvious mobilisation to commit aggression.[70]

Pre-emptive war has some legal sanction; not so, preventive war. Israel pre-emptively struck first in 1967 with Arab troops clearly massing on its borders. Christopher Greenwood, however, observed that the Israeli raid in 1981 on Iraq's Osirak reactor was widely condemned not because it had no right of anticipatory self-defence but because 'the risk was too distant, too far in the future'.[71] It was preventive, not pre-emptive. Washington has a record of preventive actions against Iraq: *Desert Storm* targeted WMD facilities unrelated to liberating Kuwait; and *Desert Fox*. Lawrence Freedman argued that prevention was a more accurate moniker than pre-emption. Prevention confronts factors likely to contribute to a threat before it has become imminent. Pre-emption is a more desperate strategy employed in the midst of crises.[72] Without convincing evidence of a Baghdad–Al Qaeda strategic alliance or that Iraqi aggression was imminent, Freedman concluded that the rationale for *Iraqi Freedom* was preventive. Reconsidering the concept of 'imminence' as the National Security Strategy suggests, thus required recognising that prevention, not pre-emption is the key here. Francois Heisbourg agreed that the 'semantics' – the synonymous use of pre-emption and prevention – required careful examination because they blur essential distinctions in international law.[73] Preventive actions generally, and especially *Desert Fox*, qualify as proactive risk management strategies geared toward ambiguous risks rather than compelling or imminent threats.

Desert Fox first created similar unease about a controversial doctrine of preventive war against 'abstract Iraqi threats' stretching anticipatory self-defence and imminence to breaking point.[74] Many critics berated the unauthorised enforcement of the Security Council's 'will' and Anglo-American auto-determination of a material breach of Iraqi obligations. Marc Weller concluded that legalism could not explain such actions. Perhaps proactive risk management can. Concern about the future was present in the declared purposes of air strikes. Clinton stated that the aim was to prevent reconstitution of Saddam's WMD and his ability to threaten his neighbours in the future. Madeleine Albright noted the difficulties of communicating and comprehending the dangers because 'it is a threat of the future rather than a present threat, or present act' such as aggression.[75]

While traditional approaches to counter-proliferation involved diplomatic and political measures, Washington even during the Clinton era was considering military measures against emerging WMD arsenals.[76] Operation *Desert Fox* demonstrated this. Furthermore, self-defence includes a right to move against WMD programmes with high potential danger to the United States, 'while it is still feasible to do so.'[77] Once a rogue like North Korea acquires WMD, effective action against it may be untenable. Iraq is comparatively more manageable. At this stage, the proactive justifications behind preventive military actions from *Desert Fox* to the more controversial Bush Doctrine still chimed with outcomes distilled from the test framework.

War and the precautionary principle

To US strategic thinkers, 9/11 confirmed that the rules of the game had changed, with much more uncertainty, erosion of deterrence and incalculable risks in possible links between Iraq and Al Qaeda. The unthinkable had to become thinkable and acted upon. The precautionary principle suggests itself to such situations. This over-caution already existed before Bush came to power. In 2000, State Department spokesman Jamie Rubin stated that US policy on sanctions was 'prepared to err on the side of caution', so as not to let any dual-use material leak through.[78] As Congressional drafters supporting the Iraq Liberation Act wrote to President Clinton in August 1999, international security could not wait until evidence emerged that Saddam had developed weapons of mass destruction and then responding. That after all was the rationale behind *Desert Fox*. The point was that we could not afford to wait for conclusive evidence before taking military action.[79] The question of evidence and over-caution clearly animated the *Desert Fox* campaign, though not to the same extent as *Iraqi Freedom*.

By 2003 the precautionary language of environmental discourse had seeped more prominently into strategy. 'Unknown unknowns', a concept espoused by Robin Grove-White (leading British advocate of the precautionary principle on environmental change), described lurking risks that we might know nothing of. This concept, *ad verbum*, featured prominently in Donald Rumsfeld's ruminations on Iraqi complicity with terrorists.[80] Rumsfeld described 'known unknowns ... things we now know we don't know' and 'unknown unknowns: things we don't know we don't know' – a classic distinction prevalent in the risk discourse where precautionary strategies are taken to reduce and anticipate dangers. Speaking like a risk management guru on the precautionary principle, Rumsfeld argued that 'absolute proof cannot be a precondition for action' and that 'absence of evidence is not evidence of absence', while emphasising the catastrophic consequences of WMD attack.[81] The end game boiled down to this dictum.

Almost enshrining the precautionary principle in the process, the 2002 *National Security Strategy* categorically stated that, where the danger is grave, there is a need for 'anticipatory actions even if uncertainty remains as to time and place of the enemy's attack'.[82]

As both sides of the Atlantic expressed unease about the lack of evidence, Rumsfeld derided sceptics for living in the past and 'still thinking in pre-9/11 terms'. It would be too late once we see a smoking gun. A gun 'smokes *after* it is fired.'[83] The point was to stop it *before* it was triggered. Precautionary risk management strategies lower the requirement for conditions of proof. They involve risk potentials characterised by relatively high degrees of uncertainty about the probability of occurrence and extent of damage. 'We don't know' appeared to be the consensus answer at Congressional hearings to ascertain the urgency of threat. As Anthony Cordesman testified, there will not be a clear smoking gun. Quipped Senator Bob Graham, 'the central reality is uncertainty'. [84] The British Government's first dossier also hardly provided any killer facts.[85]

Yet this uncertainty drove regime change. Bush described Saddam Hussein as 'an enemy until proven otherwise'.[86] The Commander-in-Chief displayed extreme precaution about Iraq: 'we have every reason to assume the worst, and we have an urgent duty to prevent the worst from occurring'.[87] Such over-vigilance bore the classic hallmarks of a precautionary principle and concern about omission (being blamed for not taking precautionary action). Richard Perle summed up cogently, 'we cannot know for sure, but on which side would it be better to err?'[88] Given this what-if mentality, it is unsurprising then that war on Iraq was fought 'in the subjunctive – based on a string of *ifs*.'[89] *If* Saddam has usable WMD, *if* he uses UAVs to launch an attack on Washington, or as Bush put it, 'secretly and without fingerprints, he could provide one of his hidden weapons to terrorists or help them develop their own'. This sort of thinking matched that of precautionary risk management strategies at this point. However, Washington also sought to move against Iraq now partly because of analogies drawn with 9/11 and the desire to avoid similar harm. This is indicative of 'tombstone' style approaches to risk rather than a purely 'precautionary approach'. As suggested before, these cannot be strictly segregated. Nonetheless, the 'precautionary' aspect has gained most attention.

Post-war searches of top suspected WMD sites drew blanks and the war appeared to be based on 'false positives'. The level of risk turned out to be less serious or urgent than originally thought. Hans Blix, the chief UN inspector, already suspected that WMD did not exist one month into the return of inspectors to Iraq in late 2002.[90] The intelligence and evidence was hardly the 'slam dunk' that CIA chief Tenet previously claimed it was. This implied perhaps no need for such drastic regime change. The very same precautionary sentiments voiced by Washington could have translated into political will for more inspections and expanded no-fly zones. Like the Kosovo campaign earlier, there were post-war inquiries into whether governments exaggerated the dangers to justify war. In July 2004 the US Senate Select Committee on Intelligence concluded that earlier intelligence claims were 'either overstated or not supported by underlying information'.[91] The Butler Inquiry in the UK noted that Iraq's WMD activities were not of more immediate or pressing concern than other countries. Private companies were contracted to help the WMD hunt by the Iraq Survey Group (ISG). The secretive Task Force 20 comprising the shadowy Grey Fox military unit proved equally unsuccessful. The search was formally terminated by February 2005; nothing was found despite trawling through Iraq for more than a year. Former ISG head David Kay resigned in January 2004 convinced that 'we were all wrong'.[92]

Surveillance

Surveillance is the vehicle of risk management, for investigating how things stand and a contributor to action in the face of uncertainty about future consequences. Iraq is a prime example for 'monitoring power'. It involved formal inspections and surveillance operations.[93] This was carried out either through covert or military-technical means such as satellites, U-2 spy planes and no-fly zones. A continuous monitoring and review process gauged the level of risk and effectiveness of management measures taken.

The ethos of constant monitoring is aptly encapsulated by naming no-fly zones as Operations *Northern Watch* and *Southern Watch*. Since 1991, the United States averaged over 34,000 sorties per year supporting the zones. These were enforced for more than ten years. Indeed, monitoring can occasionally be more important than the actual no-fly aspect. The majority of *Southern Watch* aircraft were not strike planes but surveillance assets.[94] According to Rumsfeld, no-fly zones helped 'keep good awareness' of Saddam's activities.[95] In June 1998, the Security Council was given U-2 overflight photographs of sites where Iraq claimed no activity was ongoing. Satellite surveillance also helped uncover nuclear programmes, gauging their progress and tracking movement of components. The Director of the National Reconnaissance Office argued that without satellites America would know much less and 'these programs would be more dangerous than they are today'.[96]

Surveillance served not just retrospective knowing of wrongdoing but also as a basis for action in advance of possible offences. Where military action is demanded as a result of monitoring to avert future harm, this is implemented if necessary. During Operation *Desert Fox*, this was reflected in Tony Blair's official statement: 'If we have serious evidence from our intensive surveillance, that his capability is being rebuilt, we will be ready to take further military action.'[97] Clinton had stressed earlier that the US would 'carefully monitor' and if necessary strike at the first sign of Saddam rebuilding his WMD.[98] Bush similarly argued before 9/11: 'we're going to watch very carefully' and if Saddam were caught out, action would follow.[99] The concern with monitoring Iraq continued for a while after 9/11 before regime change. The Pentagon, observed Rumsfeld, had been 'attentive ... for at least more than a decade now'.[100] There is clear evidence of a long-term monitoring ethos toward Baghdad, together with the warning that action could follow assessments that the risk was again of concern.

With weapons inspectors withdrawn in 1998, US satellites were central to monitoring Iraq, supplemented by commercial providers like Ikonos. In August 1999, US satellites imaged reconstruction of the Al-Kindi missile facility damaged in *Desert Fox* eight months earlier. Infrared satellites detected test flights of short-range Al-Samoud missiles. Lacrosse radar imaging satellites monitored Iraqi weapons storage sites. In March 2002, Washington provided the Security Council with satellite photos of modified Iraqi trucks allegedly mounting missile launchers. In August 2002, satellites detected Iraqi trucks moving material from weapons facilities. Satellites are non-intrusive, provide wider spatial resolutions covering broader swathes of territory, and are less vulnerable to Iraqi fire, which has downed Predator surveillance UAVs. The dangers lie in misinterpretation of images and limited overflight times. They can best supplement inspectors on the ground, not replace inspections totally.[101]

Inspections are another way to monitor risks and indeed even generated the information necessary for management action through air strikes. Commentators agreed it was preferable to have UNSCOM at the price of abandoning sanctions rather than the other way round. It would be foolish to leave Saddam's arsenal unmonitored.[102] However, Saddam consistently resisted, using all sorts of deception, camouflage and denial, ultimately expelling the inspectors.[103] In March 1999, a UN panel advocated that 'reinforced monitoring and verification' systems were necessary to prevent reconstitution of Iraqi WMD programmes.[104] Inspectors returned in late 2002 but failed to uncover any 'smoking gun'. Although regime change in 2003 ended monitoring, it appeared that the inspections process before it ended in 1998 generated the most reliable information for intelligence agencies and for targeting during *Desert Fox*. Such surveillance operations now helped in the waging of war. Having no inspectors amounted to 'losing your GPS guidance'.[105] Analysts were reduced to groping for fragmentary information such as alleged Iraqi interest in uranium from Niger. A more patient surveillance regime could have worked to manage Iraq. Expanding the existing low-grade air war over no-fly zones coupled with robust inspections suited a subtler concept of war as risk management.

THE UTILITARIAN 'LESS THAN HEROIC' STRATEGIES OF RISK MANAGEMENT

Routine war

In criminology, crime is seen as an everyday risk to be managed, a routine part of life. Operations against Iraq reflected this to a certain extent. As with recent wars over Kosovo and Afghanistan, war against Iraq from late 1998 to 2003 hardly affected Western societies or engaged passions for a noble goal despite Bush's touting of democracy. Instead it fuelled a different type of passion: protests. Before regime change, war became routine in two senses: it was largely instrumental rather than existential, and almost a surreal everyday occurrence as risk management theory prescribes. As Luttwak points out, the fact that Baghdad hardly reacted to *Desert Fox* constituted more technical challenges for coalition forces directing ordnance to targets, rather than real combat.[106] The utilitarian approach to the operation was encapsulated in then Central Command chief General Zinni describing it as a 'degrade and diminish' tasking. These bombings were quickly forgotten, as was the subsequent air war over no-fly zones.

For reasons previously described, no-fly zones became by default the 'cornerstone of containment' after *Desert Fox*.[107] The concept emerged as a new dimension of containment and US air power. Yet there seems to be superficial understanding of their purpose, which received scant academic attention.[108] Cat-and-mouse tussles with Iraqi gunners from late 1998 hardly merited any space in newspaper columns. Yet coalition fliers were firing, and being fired at, on an almost daily basis, by most accounts a definition of war. Repetitive air strikes became so commonplace that hardly anyone kept count. Good risk management should be routinely integrated into general activity, and Clinton appeared to have succeeded. The no-fly zones became a forgotten war. The Clinton Administration announced almost daily air strikes in a low-key manner, making Iraq seem like an everyday risk to be managed, as predicted by the test framework. By February 2001, the continuity in bombing missions over Iraq reached such a stage as to be described by President Bush as 'routine'.[109] US naval presence in the Gulf too became commonplace over the years. There is clear 'routinisation' of what previously would be considered crisis response.[110] War appeared to have morphed into utilitarian, patient 'housekeeping' tasks to keep Saddam in order. Bombing no-fly zones after *Desert Fox* was not directed at Iraqi ability to rebuild WMD, nor was it explicitly linked to anything else. It became part of a routine of general management of Iraq, a 'policing' action straddling the boundaries of war rather than traditional concepts of warfare such as decisive battles. Indeed, it was within the context of no-fly zones that the concept of 'policing' became increasingly prominent. 'Policing' action is after all a routine activity occasionally elided into force to manage conditions of risk indefinitely rather than seek grand narratives and clear goals.[111]

While regime change was clearly out of the ordinary and went against the 'routine' grain of risk management, it suggests useful lessons. Before 2003, while other major powers disapproved of the intermittent coalition bombings, no acrimonious major split on the Security Council or between NATO allies was produced, in contrast to that engendered by regime change. Indeed, other powers such as Russia and China in late 2002 were even willing to cooperate on getting weapons inspectors back despite the ongoing no-fly zone bombings. This strengthened the risk management process as a result, albeit only with the less palatable alternative of regime change in play.[112] Low-key 'routine' war might well be the acceptable optimum level of force for risk management if the risks in question require military action but are not urgent, as Iraq now turns out to be in hindsight. Taking on the appearance of an everyday occurrence, it does not cross the threshold of 'maximalist' force, which other allies and powers might find unacceptable. Germany and France even suggested an expansion of no-fly zones over the whole of Iraq together with inspections as an alternative to regime change: an implicit endorsement of their value as a risk management tool. Continuing with what had after all been an ongoing routine air war, together with surveillance and inspections might well have managed the risks. This type of protracted low-level 'war' over no-fly zones with low media interest, 'virtual public consent' and no casualties appeared most sustainable.[113]

Personifying risks

Risk management should not seek to reform particular individuals or bring justice to them, but simply manage the risks they pose. In the case of Iraq, focusing on Saddam the individual – the so-called 'biology' approach[114] – drove many aspects of US policy. The Clinton Administration's Assistant Secretary of State for Near Eastern Affairs Edward Walker asserted in March 2000 that Iraq under Saddam 'cannot be rehabilitated or reintegrated' into the international community.[115]

Despite demonising Saddam, however, in February 1998, Defence Secretary Cohen and Madeleine Albright declared that Washington was 'not seeking to topple Saddam, not destroy his country', but to 'contain him'.[116] Cohen later reiterated that the goal of *Desert Fox* was to degrade WMD facilities, and not to undermine the regime[117] – a view echoed by both Tony Blair and Bill Clinton. The message seemed to be that Saddam was a problem and had done many bad things but we could only manage him. To be sure, containment was also linked confusingly to his removal. Clinton insisted that sanctions would persist as long as Saddam was around.[118] This ambiguity served to bolster the anti-Saddam coalition as well as satisfy domestic constituents baying for his demise. Some argue that Clinton erroneously sought to contain Iraq and WMD rather than focus on 'evil' Saddam himself.

Yet, mirroring recent trends in criminology, utilitarian risk management policies trumped moral concerns about justice for 'evil' Saddam gassing the Kurds. Despite the mounting civilian toll of sanctions, Albright infamously declared the cost was worth it as long as Saddam was contained. Demonising Saddam largely helped bolster support for policies to manage rather than remove him. The overwhelming practical focus of policy before September 2001 was risk management tools – air power, no-fly zones and revised 'smart' sanctions.[119]

After 9/11, the 'evil' tag all too often described America's nemeses like Bin Laden. Saddam Hussein too was described by Condoleezza Rice as an 'evil man' who was not 'reformable'.[120] Here again was an individual deemed to pose risks but continued management rather than elimination was suggested in some quarters. Jessica Matthews contended that the Bush Administration's newly energised efforts to oust Saddam were misplaced: 'the number one problem' should remain the risk of Saddam acquiring WMD, rather than Hussein himself.[121] The Carnegie Endowment in September 2002 thus suggested 'coercive inspections' accompanied by UN-approved airmobile and armoured cavalry forces with air support and J-Stars surveillance planes, supporting go-anywhere, any time inspectors. France and Germany also suggested expanding no-fly zones to cover the whole of Iraq. This approach is more appropriate to risk management than impatient regime change focused on one man. Non-proliferation goals also carry more legitimacy, and can assist, not undermine long-term cooperation in fighting terrorism. However, many believed the only option was regime change: even with UN inspectors in the 1990s, many programmes remained hidden until the 1995 defection of Hussein Kamal, Saddam's son-in-law.

In a tactical shift to reinsert inspectors in autumn 2002, even 'regime change' was redefined, further complicating analysis. Powell suggested that Iraq deserved a better leader, but the main concern was WMD: 'all we're interested in is getting rid of these weapons. Then you have a different kind of regime no matter who's in Baghdad'.[122] Bush hinted that as long as Saddam disarmed and distanced himself from terrorists, that would 'signal the regime has changed'.[123] Whether Bush really meant what he said is impossible to tell.

On the eve of war, Bush was even willing to let 'evil' Saddam go into exile – hardly the right moral move, but a correct one from the utilitarian risk management perspective. US officials sought to downplay Saddam to avoid tricky questions similar to those about Bin Laden's fate. Secretary Powell claimed that it was irrelevant whether Saddam was found or not.[124] However by personifying the issue to the extent it did rhetorically – and with two 'decapitation' attempts and later a bounty for his eventual capture in

December 2003, the Bush Administration after 9/11 clearly targeted the Iraqi leader rather than managed him.

Reshaping the environment

On 10 March 2003, *Financial Times* editor Philip Stephens reflected a common view that the US previously policed the world. Now it sought to remould it in its image. Wolfowitz suggested that the invasion's strategic reordering of the region was a major consequence.[125] Democratic Iraq, so went the argument, would trigger a so-called 'demonstration effect' through 'shock and awe' to rein in or remove regimes that breed terror through repression. The Bush Administration actually could have something of a Middle East vision. This meant using American power to 'reshape the Middle East' by removing Hussein and promoting gradual reforms in moderate Arab states.[126] Whether this grand strategy is workable is another matter. Eliot Cohen is dismissive that Washington had the vision 'to be grand conceptualisers'.[127] A more utilitarian understanding of 'reshaping' to simply reduce opportunities for harm could provide alternative answers.

Before 2003, given the difficulties of removing Saddam, 'reshaping the environment' shaped the milieu within which the actors operated, simply reducing opportunities for offending and risks of harm occurring. Containment and no-fly zones clearly constrained his freedom of action rather than removing him outright. Sanctions, inspectors and routine bombing pressured Iraq to divert resources to smuggling and hiding; thus making reconstitution of WMD more difficult. UNSCOM also placed remote monitoring sensors at suspect sites. Operation *Desert Fox*, which was justified largely as reinforcing containment, aimed to 'make it more difficult' for Iraq to use WMD against its neighbours.[128] This 'made it less likely' that we will face these dangers in future'.[129] No-fly zones, argued Clinton, served a similar function in making it more difficult for Saddam to repress his own people militarily or attack neighbours, although arguably classical deterrence could have served the same purpose.[130] Rather than militarily defeating an enemy, war in this sense now seemed geared towards reducing an enemy's chances and opportunities to offend in future. The combined effects of inspections, *Desert Fox* and no-fly zones reshaped Saddam's strategic environment, mitigating the likelihood and opportunities for unwanted outcomes to occur.

There was some evidence that the Bush Administration too sought denial of opportunities for Saddam to cause harm, this time with terrorists after 9/11 as the risks evolved. Colin Powell's Davos speech on 26 January 2003 warned that delay only means 'more *chance* for this dictator' to do all sorts of nasty things. If Washington's goal was to prevent terrorists acquiring WMD – Bush had identified rogue states as their 'most likely source' – regime change arguably reduced their chances despite post-war looting.

Indeed Foreign Secretary Jack Straw suggested that one reason for military action was to deny Baghdad any possible opportunities to develop other terrorist networks to attack the West.[131] General Myers similarly suggested that operations in Iraq were denying terrorists the chance to get their hands on WMD.[132] In this sense, the war was more about 'reshaping the environment' to reduce opportunities for harm than traditional conquest. Bush, however, also seemed intent on eliminating Hussein almost like a personal vendetta, running counter to risk management prescriptions. Washington's haste furthermore meant the departure of inspectors who could have continually reduced opportunities for Iraq to develop WMD.

Nation-tending

Bush has repeatedly stated that Washington will not turn tail and leave Iraq prematurely. Contrary to pre-9/11 Bush scepticism, it undertook an ambitious nation-building programme apparently to change societies and governments. Yet post-war reconstruction had little grand design and, according to Simon Chesterman, the Administration was desperately trying to make its exit not look too much like a frantic dash.[133] Nation-building responsibilities were justified to domestic public opinion as part of the war on terror. This translated into highlighting military goals over political and moral concerns in Iraq. More importantly, Senator Richard Lugar, chairing the Senate Foreign Relations Committee, warned that 'to leave (Iraq), as we usually do, is to leave ... an incubator for terrorism' just like Afghanistan was.[134] Concern with reconstruction revolved not just around America's obligation to democracy, but also the fear that lawlessness would provide terror sanctuaries, the old nation-tending argument.

Notwithstanding Bush's vision of post-war Iraq as beacon of democracy, the motive force for war was fear about a Saddam-Al Qaeda alliance or prospect of nuclear-armed Iraq. Most people believed Bush was not concerned about 'repairing the world'. America exuded not optimism but fear despite talk of spreading democracy.[135] This opinion seemed vindicated as the post-war goal, declared Tommy Franks, was to avoid creating another safe haven for terrorism and WMD proliferation.[136] In this view, rehabilitating Iraq appeared necessary only to the extent of reducing post-war risks, much like nation-tending Afghanistan. Rather than America's mission, Bush emphasised he had no 'empire to extend or utopia to establish'.[137] He seemed more intent on preventing further attacks on America and adopting a safety-first mentality. Subsequent accelerations of timetables for transfer of authority to Iraqis were less a reflection of progress than a need to show achievements.[138]

To be fair Bush's Washington adopted a dualistic approach to Iraq, seeing both opportunities and risks. It exhibited a minimalist 'safety-first' ethos while espousing more positive notions of spreading liberal democracy.

While these need not necessarily be mutually exclusive, war was driven largely by fear of possible Saddam-Al Qaeda links or a nuclear-armed Iraq. Furthermore in reconstructing Iraq, lofty themes of democratisation might well be replaced by more basic issues like peace, stability and territorial integrity.[139] The results of a demonstration effect to promote democracy are mixed. Palestinian elections preceded relatively successful Iraqi elections in late January 2005, giving a slight boost to hitherto sluggish support in US opinion polls. In Egypt, President Mubarak too moved towards multi-candidate presidential elections for the first time. Yet stability is still elusive in Iraq. The first round seems to have gone to inflamed Muslim fundamentalism, anti-American sentiments and Arab nationalism rather than democracy, although this could well change.[140]

DEFINING SUCCESS

Non-events and the minimalist criterion for success

Theoretically, seeking only non-events like avoiding harm, this definition of success should correspondingly be reflected in war as a risk management strategy. Lambasting policy before 9/11 for failing simply because Saddam remained in power was a red herring; the more appropriate minimalist benchmark was managing risks. We still like to think that wars end neatly with formal surrenders. Unfortunately this did not happen during the no-fly zone air war, *Desert Fox* or *Iraqi Freedom.*

It is undoubtedly important to assess policy in terms of national security as well as its humanitarian implications. The harm to civilians cannot be discounted. Critics pointed to Saddam's survival but the more important thing was keeping him contained, slowly eroding his WMD capabilities and maintaining sanctions and inspections if possible. Evaluation in positivist terms of 'solving the problem' furnishes an incomplete picture.[141] Minimalist risk management is different from policy geared towards clearly defined goals or higher expectations. By focusing on avoidable harm, it emphasised preventing negative outcomes like the reconstitution of WMD, rather than positively eliminating problems.

John Hillen lamented that containment 'is inconclusive, having not yielded even the glimmer of a solution to the Iraq problem over the past eight years'.[142] The penchant for complete solutions – also reflected in opinion polls during *Desert Fox*, which thought force was only a temporary measure – is counter-productive when sometimes managing problems is the only plausible option, especially in the international environment before 9/11, which could not countenance regime change. Attacking Iraqi WMD facilities could not solve the problem, but could reduce its magnitude.[143]

Senior officials, to their credit, admitted that it was impossible to eliminate all WMD, which was why they used the word 'degrade'. Albright rightly emphasised that there was no 'silver bullet'.[144] We now have a concept of war where patience is a virtue and a risk management approach helps appreciate modest partial success not defined in terms of instant perfect solutions.

Edward Luttwak might have approved, having lamented that the 1991 *Desert Storm* air campaign shifted prematurely to supporting the ground offensive due to a misplaced Clausewitzian emphasis on urgency and decisive battles, leaving Iraqi WMD facilities untouched. As a result, 'strategic precision air attack, slow but effective in cumulative results, could not fulfil its true potential.'[145] This slow cumulative form of combat and partial results was certainly mirrored in *Desert Fox* and the no-fly zones. Furthermore, policing operations over no-fly zones were not designed to resolve underlying issues or win decisively, but simply to make the situation tolerable by reducing risks.[146]

Policies had actually been to some extent 'a qualified success'.[147] Despite Iraqi evasion and cheating, UNSCOM reportedly destroyed 817 of Iraq's 819 Scud missiles, chemical weapons, and together with sanctions generally made it more difficult for reconstitution. A December 2001 National Intelligence Estimate concluded that a combination of air strikes, IAEA and UNSCOM inspections significantly retarded the Iraqi WMD programme.[148] More recent evidence suggested that reconstitution was hampered also for lack of a suitable delivery platform.[149]

As we have seen, risk management is about preventing and avoiding negative outcomes. Success is thus measured in non-events. Inevitably, this complicates outcome specification, for non-events obviously are not as clearcut as removing Saddam. In August 1999, a bipartisan Congressional group wrote to President Clinton, lamenting 'continued drift in US policy toward Iraq'.[150] Anthony Cordesman opined after *Desert Fox*, 'we have not set out what we're doing beyond degrade, we haven't defined what success is.'[151] However, clearly defined success cannot be reconciled with risk management. This was active military containment, which did not necessarily look like full-scale war.

A more 'minimalist' yardstick of managing risks might replace the stark margin between success and failure. Indeed, in February 1998, the Clinton Administration backed away from coercing Saddam to accept inspectors unconditionally. Instead, the bar was set even lower: to simply reduce Iraqi WMD capacity and generally constrain Iraqi action, leaving Washington to decide when 'success' had come about.[152] It is hard to establish a clear marker as a result. Clinton repeatedly argued that sanctions had denied Saddam $120 billion that would *otherwise* have gone into WMD programmes: a non-event. Although maximal goals like Saddam's ouster were not met until April 2003, at least minimal ones and non-events like preventing Iraqi WMD reconstitution were. The best that can be achieved in managing risks is that no harm results. Saddam had not invaded his neighbours for more than a decade. This was progress from a regime that had done so almost every year since 1979. Policy should be judged not in terms of 'perfect solutions' but rather in terms of how a particular risk is managed.

Unsure of its convictions or even the goal, public relief, rather than the rejoicing normally associated with victory, accompanied US troops into Baghdad as the now customary 'public wobble' evaporated. Even after achieving the 'perfect solution' of deposing Saddam, the war also created the biggest non-event in recent times. Indeed, at the time of writing, the Iraq Survey Group had terminated the hunt for WMD. In fact, the failure to find WMD appeared to vindicate the patient risk management approach adopted over the years. It had apparently produced the desired non-event by constraining the full reconstitution of Iraqi WMD programmes. If so, then there was perhaps no need for impatient invasion.

An ongoing, cyclical process

On 3 March 1991, President George H. W. Bush reported to Congress that 'aggression is defeated, the war is over'. However, a month before, Bush intimated to his diary: 'it hasn't been a clean end; there is no battleship *Missouri* surrender'.[153] Bush's laments indicate how some policy-makers prefer idealised notions of war such as a 'clean end' and historical analogies to past wars when in fact war has moved on into the risk management sphere. Events from late 1998 certainly eluded easy closure, since war as risk management leads to operations of indefinite duration to continually manage new risks or resurgent old ones. Risks cannot be totally eliminated. The finishing line is not easily apparent in cyclical risk management processes, which are ongoing and non-linear. This defied conventional appraisal of definitive end goals as the measure of policy success or conclusion of wars. The vague criteria for measuring progress in *Desert Fox* – 'degrading and diminishing' – also left open the possibility that more action would follow assessments that Baghdad once again could cause harm. Cabinet officials Albright, Berger and Cohen declared that US commitment to use force against Iraq was 'open-ended'.[154] Tony Blair warned that if increased Iraqi WMD activity were detected, military action would result again.

However, bombing created more risks in the sense that international consensus for inspections was now irrevocably undermined: the postulated 'boomerang effect'. Iraq paradoxically became freer after *Desert Fox* to continue its WMD efforts without having to divert resources to hiding from inspectors, and portrayed itself as victim of superpower bullying. The alleged use of UNSCOM information to generate targets also greatly discredited the international arms control system as a cover for US espionage, undermining international cooperation. *Desert Fox* thus created 'one of the worst possible outcomes': a discredited monitoring agency unable to re-enter Iraq, low-intensity undeclared air war, a further divided Security Council and the continuation of sanctions with huge humanitarian impact.[155]

Since the announced end of the 70-hour *Desert Fox* campaign, low profile but robust sorties continued over the no-fly zones against air defence assets that hardly seemed linked to *Desert Fox*'s goals of degrading WMD facilities or contributed positively to resolving the crisis. It is also not certain that policy-makers knew exactly what the goals were. Some still insisted it demonstrated commitment to enforcing inspections, which by that time were already dead in the water. Greatest unease was expressed over the intermittent bombing of no-fly zones, derided as pointless with no end in sight.[156] Critics argued this was not 'conclusively linked to an end game in Iraq'.[157] More nuanced recent analyses suggest no-fly zones run the risk of 'perpetual patrol' if simultaneous activity for resolving the crisis is not undertaken and policy objectives and exit strategies are unclear. This leaves the enemy leader untouched, thus not addressing the 'origin of the problem'. Furthermore they had been found wanting in compelling Saddam to cooperate.[158] The risk management perspective would offer different insights. It suggests patient open-ended commitment and ambiguous results such as avoiding harm, not specifying in advance decisive instant solutions. Operations over no-fly zones appeared consigned to a fate of 'perpetual policing', which seeks in fact to 'avoid decisive battle' of the Clausewitzian mould. Rather than a clear-cut political goal in mind or compelling Saddam to cooperate, it seemed instead to manage a condition of risks that might affect security interests.[159] This dispensed with the artificial setting of maximalist goals of problem-resolution in an intractable situation such as Iraq when the more realistic aim should be risk management. Expectations could then be managed and results judged more appropriately.

By April 2003 regime change seemed to draw the finishing line decisively in the sand. However, just as there was a 'rolling' start to the war, there was a 'rolling victory'.[160] There was no neat tidy end. US generals lolled around in Saddam's palaces, clearly a symbol of victory. Yet there were no vanquished to sign formal capitulation documents, which for much of the modern era had defined the conclusion of wars. Two months after Bush declared the end of major combat in May 2003, the US ground commander in Iraq admitted 'we're still at war'. Almost two years later, US forces were still engaged in numerous sweeps to eliminate insurgents that had inflicted increasing US casualties. Disappointment and puzzlement greeted these operations as public opinion is driven by clean ends and Bush's proclamation appeared to provide that.

Furthermore, as President Bush declared on the carrier *Lincoln* on 1 May 2003, 'the battle of Iraq is one victory in a war on terror ... and still goes on'. If war was about the risk of terrorists acquiring WMD, that risk was certainly not eliminated. Reports suggested WMD were smuggled to Syria or other groups in Iraq. The post-war chaos led IAEA chief Mohamed El Baradei to warn that looting of WMD installations especially at Tuwaitha could mean WMD falling into terrorist hands. Former weapons inspector Terry Taylor worried that looting increased the original proliferation risk, a view shared by Britain's Joint Intelligence Committee.[161] Out-of-work scientists might also work with other rogue states or terrorist groups. The world was not much safer than before. Invasion could also create a backlash, such as the May 2003 bombings in Riyadh and Casablanca, and the March 2004 Madrid train blasts. Furthermore, CIA chief Porter Goss's February 2005 testimony to Congress confirmed that Islamic extremists are indeed exploiting the conflict not only to aid recruitment but also to cut their teeth in operations for future use.[162] America essentially created a terrorist problem and breeding ground in Iraq where there was none before.[163] Rather than conclusively solving the problem through regime change, new risks were created through the 'boomerang effect'. This is certainly suggestive of the inconclusive nature of risk management.

ALL RISK MANAGEMENT ROADS LEAD TO AND FROM BAGHDAD?

From the evidence presented here, risk management provided an explanation for specific aspects of recent 'wars' over Iraq. Previously distinct sets of proliferation and stability risks posed by Baghdad during the late Clinton/early Bush period became interlinked after 9/11 with terrorism and created significant analytical difficulties for this study. Nonetheless, these dangers were understood primarily through risk components rather than threat components. Policy-makers were more concerned with risk features yet plumped for threat elimination instead.

While largely dissimilar in strategic context and eventual results, military actions from 1998 until 2003 nonetheless shared key features of risk management worth highlighting. It was anticipatory in nature, concerned with probabilistic thinking in terms of counter-factuals and proactively preventing unwanted futures. Indeed, the language and 'reflexive' rationality adopted by both administrations were strikingly similar, whether justifying *Desert Fox* or *Iraqi Freedom*. This bore further similarities to official rationale for air strikes against Kosovo in 1999 and Blair's on Afghanistan in 2001. Contributing to anticipatory actions, aerial and satellite surveillance and inspections provided information on the level of risks Iraq posed, until the Bush Administration tired of the process. The precautionary principle, with emerging precursors in the late Clinton years, was applied to the letter especially after 9/11. Rumsfeld sounded in particular like the archetypal risk manager. Bush, like Clinton, saw war in this sense as a utilitarian tool to avert future harm, although the former to be sure espoused also positive visions of democracy and freedom. Post-war reconstruction was confused, and while nation-building was indeed undertaken, mirrored nation-tending's utilitarian concerns about terrorist sanctuaries. Before 9/11, Saddam was managed by reshaping the environment through inspections, sanctions, no-fly zones and bombing. This simply reduced his opportunities to cause harm, despite ostracising him as 'evil'. Even regime change, argued US officials, was conceivably designed to reduce opportunities for terrorists to acquire WMD or sanctuary from Iraq.

In evaluating risk management, it should be seen as a 'minimalist' ongoing process of avoiding harm, not attaining positivist end goals. Thus, non-events before 9/11 such as caging Saddam and limiting his WMD programmes could be considered a 'success'. The much-criticised open-ended nature of policing no-fly zones could receive fewer brickbats if understood as a non-linear routine process of management. Even with regime change, some outcomes were non-events indicative of an existing risk rather than a fully formed threat. Indeed, failure to find WMD by February 2005 vindicated the patient risk management approach over the years: creating a 'non-event' in which preventing the reconstitution of WMD was apparently successful. There was even evidence of the 'boomerang effect' as regime change, instead of permanently solving the problem, only created new sets of risks with missing WMD materials and increased Al Qaeda recruitment.

Before 9/11, the Bush Administration in fact 'ended up affirming the basic course set by Democrats' on no-fly zones.[164] Containment, rather than regime change was the de facto policy despite rumblings to the contrary. What was an almost textbook risk management strategy in the late Clinton/early Bush years however turned into threat elimination by 2003 under the impact of 9/11 and the drawing together of analogous but not necessarily similar sets of risks. This revealed serious flaws in risk management. Policy-makers became too impatient and escalated towards the other end of the ladder: threat elimination. Problematically, risk perceptions diverged even among close allies. Acting on the precautionary principle and worst-case scenarios without rigorous assessment in retrospect appeared unnecessary. Linking the security risks Iraq posed with Al Qaeda was unwarranted in hindsight.

Yet, the language, rationale and negative ethos of *Iraqi Freedom* certainly bore classic hallmarks of risk management, even more so than *Desert Fox* or the no-fly zones operations. Warning of the 'risks of inaction', President Bush sought to 'prevent the worst' (the exact phrase Beck used to describe the negative mindset of Risk Society) while certainly making the right noises about precautionary actions – all intrinsic components of a risk management package. After all, Bush's emphasising the Iraq issue at the UN, backed by military force, had already produced the return of inspectors for the first time in four years with even France and Germany suggesting an expansion of no-fly zones. However, the impatient means selected – combined arms ground invasion and regime change – were not suited for managing risks, reflecting once again the need for a more subtle concept of war. A more patient risk management war-form – inspections, continuous surveillance and occasional military force where necessary, routinely policing no-fly zones to 'reshape the environment', appreciating partial results – like that practised before 9/11 and even arguably, in the months before regime change, could thus have been more appropriate than full-scale threat-elimination. After all, no one seemed to notice the 'small war' already going on with Iraq.

7

THE RISE AND FALL OF WAR
AS RISK MANAGEMENT?

HISTORICISM AND WAR

How to end but with where we began: candidate Bush's speculation while on the 2000 campaign trail about elusive dangers 'out there' somewhere circling vulture-like, waiting to inflict catastrophic harm in an age of globalisation. For students of war and strategy in this context, what springs to mind is Clausewitz's time-honoured maxim that each war is a product of the specific societies and cultures that fight it. It reflects the ideas, emotions and conditions of particular historical periods. The French Revolutionary wars demonstrated how war had become the business of the people and citizens infused with concepts of liberty and nation dominant at that time. For Risk Societies of the West operating within the framework of globalised insecurity, ideas of 'risk management' certainly lend themselves readily to understanding conflict and strategy as the international system reoriented away from military 'threats' towards concerns about 'security risks'. This has posed further challenges to idealised understandings of war involving a response to well-defined threats, and a desire for clearly defined outcomes to end proceedings.

Risk management instead involves ambiguous risks where success is defined as much by less visible non-events as by what can be seen. Classical 'net assessment' or specific threat-based approaches thus cannot readily explain specific aspects of recent wars where the enemy's military capability hardly posed serious challenges, and intentions were underemphasised, misread or simply unknown. Cumulative evidence presented here suggests that risk-based scenarios composed of probabilities and consequences provide by all accounts a convincing interpretation of the recourse to war. Such an approach largely persisted through the change in US administrations in 2001 – the Bush White House even accentuated some aspects of risk management in justifying war. While Clinton talked up proactive policies, the Bush team practically enshrined the precautionary principle into strategy and security policy, especially with regard to terrorism and Iraq.

This study has emphasised and uncovered continuity where one might realistically expect discontinuity.

Many compelling theses on the transformation of war and international security have been suggested over the past decade. It was certainly not the intention here to dislodge any of them from the pantheon of works deserving of study and respect. Rather the goal has been to contribute to them. Neither has any effort been made to deny that subjective perceptions of policy-makers or bureaucratic infighting had an influence on policy outcomes, and there are many existing analyses of such decision-making processes. This book has instead adopted a broader investigative angle and sought to highlight the presence of recurrent patterns in warfare across different recent cases that were consistent with risk management strategies. By also emphasising the theoretical benefits international relations can derive from an interdisciplinary approach, hopefully it has served to stimulate more debate and research on this hitherto neglected, yet increasingly significant, dimension of risk management in strategy, conflict and international relations.

In this light, the validity of the main hypotheses advanced and key summary findings will be re-evaluated through a structured cross-comparison of case study results. Some concerns were left unresolved, some admittedly problematic but none of which fatally undermined the hypotheses as a whole. Promising research avenues that have not been explored here will also be pointed out in order to build on what has already been attempted. As always, cautionary policy-relevant lessons then should and can be drawn from the findings. This draws to a close a theoretical enterprise that began with a perceived need to reconceptualise war in response to real-world events that had unsettled accepted wisdom. Finally developments in early 2005 demand a reappraisal of how the renewed ideological zeal of the re-elected Bush Administration for grand narratives and spreading democracy might plausibly foretell the possible demise of the minimalist model of war as risk management. No paradigms are eternally valid – perhaps risk management's time was up with the ostensible shift toward re-emphasising ideological issues. This could prove as unsettling, for both allies and enemies, as the previous overriding concern about safety and risks. On the other hand an argument could be made that spreading democracy and war as risk management are simply two sides of the same coin, both concerned with and designed ultimately to reduce international security risks. If these two ostensibly antithetical approaches can somehow be fashioned into coherent and sustainable policies – and evidence points to the contrary for various reasons – Bush might well have plugged the gaping hole in the heart of risk management: that it is predicated mainly on fear and utilitarian concerns and presents no rousing visions.

A STEP IN THE RIGHT DIRECTION?

Emphasising and highlighting the elements of risk management in war, this study has helped explain specific emerging aspects of contemporary warfare such as the recourse to proactive policies and the need to appreciate modest partial results. Utilising an interdisciplinary analytical framework derived from overarching principles and strategies of risk management practised in sociology and criminology, these aspects of war could be seen in a different light with greater explanatory power. The broad findings indicated that while empirical evidence surveyed in the case studies validated theoretical predictions to varying degrees, these reflected in the main operational indicators of war as risk management. The two main hypotheses presented in Chapter One can now be re-evaluated in light of the evidence examined. These interlinked hypotheses were:

i   Under specific circumstances and parameters, Britain and America's recent wars in Kosovo, Afghanistan and Iraq bore telltale indicators of risk management in terms of impetus for action; modes of implementation; and criteria for evaluating success.
ii Contemporary wars exhibit risk management features rather than 'classical' notions of war.

The findings will now be discussed and assessed in detail.

Impetus

In combination with an increasingly probabilistic culture focused on managing risk scenarios, the main impetus for military actions was systemic risks aggravated by globalisation, such as free flow of people and materials across porous borders, and the demise of Cold War constraints. Such risks included ethnic cleansing, transnational terrorism and WMD proliferation. This implied quite a significant departure from historical concerns with Great Power rivalry, balance of power and arms races. Previous chapters highlighted the difficulties of conceptualising dangers purely in terms of threat components. This is not to claim that intentions and capabilities were completely irrelevant. Rather, this is a logical consequence of a post-Cold War world and the nature of specific security challenges where classic 'net assessment' in actuarial terms of counting military hardware is no longer as applicable: a fact acknowledged by the US *National Strategy for Combating Terrorism*.

In none of the case studies did opponents pose serious and imminent survival threats in terms of military capabilities, not even Al Qaeda's impressive organisational abilities. Iraq, in particular, posed risks that did not warrant its premature elevation to an imminent threat requiring regime change.

Intentions of adversaries, while still important, were misread or underemphasised in favour of risk components – probabilistic worst-case scenarios and catastrophic consequences. This often involved a combination of 'anticipatory horizon-scanning' of the strategic landscape for any possible security risks, and a desire to avoid repetition of 'tombstone-style' risks ever happening again.

Implementation and justifications

The proactive language of risk used in justifying wars from Kosovo to Iraq was broadly similar. Policy-makers in question, whether Bill Clinton, Tony Blair or George W. Bush, employed the same catch-all phrase for action, repeated verbatim in all cases surveyed: 'the risks of inaction outweigh the risks of action'. Probabilistic future-oriented reflexive rationality in terms of averting adverse scenarios that had not yet occurred was practised as theorised.

There was evidence of a shift from previous reactive approaches to more proactive stances. NATO signalled its transformation into a proactive alliance over Kosovo; counter-terrorism in Afghanistan became proactive; while preventive military action was launched against Iraq as early as December 1998. This fostered an approach seeking more to 'prevent' or 'avoid', rather than to attain 'heroic' noble goals often associated with war. Britain and America acted to avert 'potential victimhood' of some hypothesised future harm, to avoid becoming victimised again by Milosevic, Bin Laden or Hussein.

Rather than the definitive 'smoking gun' many presume should trigger recourse to war in responsive mode, Iraq in 2003 represented the clearest indicator of the precautionary principle proactively applied to strategy and war: in Rumsfeld's famous words, 'absolute proof cannot be a precondition for action' and his use of the classic 'unknown unknowns' concept. The Kosovo campaign in 1999 also exhibited some indications of the principle as both NGOs and NATO were inclined to overestimate the worst. However evidence of ethnic cleansing was certainly more concrete than Baghdad's links to Al Qaeda. As for the Afghan campaign in 2001, it was hardly precautionary in nature since the US had been attacked first on that fateful September day. Nonetheless, Government dossiers in the UK acknowledged they offered less than evidentiary proof while officials stressed the need in future for taking precautionary actions under the domain of uncertainty. Iraq and Kosovo both represented 'false positives' as precautionary actions taken on systemic risks, which ultimately proved less serious than thought.

Continuous surveillance served as the vehicle of risk management, providing information necessary to anticipate and act on risks. For more than a decade over Iraq, the most notable instances were the appropriately named long-term surveillance Operations *Northern Watch* and *Southern*

Watch, which elided easily into military actions from 1998 to 2003. Problematically for this aspect of risk management, regime change ended any further surveillance. Kosovo was monitored by a precursor air surveillance mission before *Allied Force* and continuously since for possible risk factors. Satellite and other aerial surveillance provided much useful information on terrorist movements and infrastructure in Afghanistan and other potential havens elsewhere, aiding in air strikes. Officials stressed that surveillance helped to reduce the terrorist dangers.

War as risk management employed utilitarian 'less than heroic' strategies designed simply to reduce systemic risks. These included the 'routine' use of force, 'reshaping the environment' and 'nation-tending'. In contrast to the existential struggles defining twentieth century Great Power conflicts, war to manage risks became routine in a few respects – it was largely passionless, instrumental and even had a familiar ring to it. This was especially noted in the low-key daily skirmishes over Iraqi no-fly zones, which went largely unnoticed. Regime change certainly aroused many people but only to oppose, not support it. Kosovo – to Bacevich, a 'routine' all too familiar air war – also hardly engaged Western publics watching safely and emotionally detached in their living rooms. Ethnic cleansing too seemed a commonplace security risk in the 1990s, repeatedly managed according to the same template of air power. Similarly in Afghanistan and the US homeland, terrorism seemed slowly but surely almost like another everyday risk to be managed such as crime. Counter-terrorism operations in Afghanistan eventually became low-intensity and 'routinised', just like counter-drug patrols in the Caribbean.

The strategy of 'reshaping the environment' served simply to reduce systemic risks by managing conditions of instability and turbulence to reduce opportunities for harm, rather than the more observable criteria used to gauge past wars, such as destroying enemy hardware. Most evident in Afghanistan, this meant shrinking zones of sanctuary and generally creating a less permissive environment for terrorists without being able to provide clear verifiable evidence of success such as body counts, which some have called for, or even visibly identifiable enemies to target. The Kosovo campaign ultimately managed the risks in question by denying Milosevic freedom of action in the region, although militarily speaking the campaign was relatively unsuccessful in terms of 'tank-plinking'. Coalition no-fly zones operations before regime change generally constrained Baghdad's ability to cause harm despite generating no noticeable military triumphs. Regime change in 2003 could be construed as reducing opportunities for terrorists to gain WMD or a safe haven from Iraq, although its aftermath was to create a veritable terrorist magnet instead.

Related to 'reshaping' environments was the idea of 'nation-tending', most obvious in Afghanistan. Washington's overriding goal there seemed to be to reduce risks by making it inhospitable to terrorists rather than properly rehabilitating the country. Regime change in Iraq certainly seemed to imply Bush had now embraced nation-building, but this was not simply about social work or the ideological narratives of democracy. It was presented also as part of the broader war on terror and reducing risks. Although risks remain, Kosovo experienced relatively successful stabilisation due to several factors: the war and rebuilding was more multinational in nature, America was willing to subcontract reconstruction to the UN and EU. Kosovo suggests that perhaps the most appropriate form of multilateral nation-tending would be reducing the footprint of individual powers and managing risks in the process, without actually solving underlying problems. This not only lent more legitimacy, but also helped in stability operations, notwithstanding the difficulties of coalition warfare and war by committee.

Risks were personified in all cases: Milosevic in Kosovo, Hussein in Iraq, Bin Laden in Afghanistan. However, as with parallel developments in criminology, the emphasis appeared to be on reducing opportunities for their offending rather than on bringing these 'errant' individuals to justice. Despite his subsequent arrest and trial, Milosevic remained in power until October 2000, tolerated as long as he posed no serious risks. Kosovo proved the best example of this. Capturing Bin Laden would strike a mortal blow to Al Qaeda but military operations became more focused on disrupting terrorists rather than capturing the 'evil one' as Bush had initially promised. Prevention rather than revenge or justice was the core utilitarian concern. As long as the risks posed by Baghdad were tolerable, and since there were no other feasible options, Saddam was kept throughout the 1990s in his 'box' rather than removed despite his 'evil' tag. Regime change in April 2003 constituted the strongest counter-argument that personifying risks now meant elimination, not management. Yet the Bush Administration's redefinition of regime change in October 2002 suggested, no matter how implausible or far-fetched in retrospect, that it could conceivably live with a disarmed Saddam regime posing fewer risks as long as it had no WMD in its possession or terrorist ties.

Outcome evaluation

Non-events and vague suggestions about simply avoiding harm were, as predicted, key criteria for success rather than unambiguous 'perfect solutions' and the formal treaty ceremonies commonly identified with war endings. Patience, acceptance of limits and partial results were required. This minimalist definition was especially relevant to Afghanistan. Success was measured in terms of what does not happen (terrorist incidents) rather than what does. The Kosovo campaign ended with the ambiguous 'mother of all compromises' and regional instability was largely averted: another non-event. Successfully managing Iraq before regime change was also negatively defined: preventing Saddam committing aggression or reconstituting

WMD. Even while regime change visibly departed from the minimalist script of risk management, key outcomes were non-events: where were Iraq's WMD? By March 2005, the formal termination of the WMD hunt and the failure to find a fully reconstituted WMD programme in fact vindicated the patient risk management processes undertaken over the years producing the desired non-event after all.

The 'boomerang effect' too suggested risk management was dialectical and cyclical without the clearly defined endpoints implied by linear concepts of war and threat elimination. This affects outcome evaluation, as risks cannot be completely eradicated. They often evolve, and can only be reduced and constantly managed. While risk of regional instability was eventually reduced in Kosovo, more risks were initially created through accelerated expulsions and these still remain to be managed continuously six years after K-FOR entered Pristina. Attempts to root out terrorists in Afghanistan only dispersed the networks underground and elsewhere, paradoxically making them more difficult to track in a campaign without a finite end. Al Qaeda emerged with a stronger organisational structure in the process. The decade-long open-ended 'police actions' over Iraqi no-fly zones exemplified the unremitting yet ill-defined nature of risk management. *Desert Fox* created more risks, undermining UNSCOM inspections while Saddam was ironically freer to pursue WMD programmes. Even an ostensible threat-elimination operation to solve the problem conclusively – regime change in 2003 – only spawned new risks. Terrorists could acquire WMD in the post-war chaos, gaining new breeding grounds too.

The analytical framework used to explore these results discussed above reflected the widely held notion that strategic studies is essentially eclectic in nature, receptive to ideas and concepts from other social sciences. Furthermore, new developments in theory and the world meant that novel approaches were necessary. The framework adopted was not in any way reified. Instead, it merely served as a useful mode of investigating systematically what seemed obscure or tenuous links not only between case studies but also the disciplines of international relations, sociology and criminology.

FURTHER RESEARCH AVENUES

In this section I suggest how the risk management concepts presented earlier could be enhanced or modified. The process of risk management is multi-faceted and complex with so many related concepts and strategies that it is impossible to utilise all of them without sacrificing quality for quantity. The intention here is to help address some gaps in the analytical prism adopted in preceding case studies, as well as to demonstrate its wider validity. The template of risk management employed in this study has been limited to directly reducing risks through anticipatory military means, for instance the reshaping of environments. It inevitably downplayed other risk management methods such as 'risk distribution'. Risk after all also presents market opportunities.[1] Nowhere has this been more notable than in the subcontracting of high-risk situations like de-mining to private military contractors or regional crises delegated to regional allies to manage.

Risk distribution

Distributing risks and ideas of 'New Prudentialism' have emerged as a rather distinct corollary of state responses to managing security risks. 'New Prudentialism' progressively removes responsibility for risk protection from state agencies and places it in the hands of individuals or community-based groups where feasible. The concept of risk is consequently privatised and entrepreneurial.[2] Risks are increasingly distributed by states where possible to 'risk-fighting businesses' such as US-based RONCO Consulting, which specialises in de-mining, and expert NGO de-miners.

For example, after the first Gulf War, Kuwait marked the beginning of the privatisation and commercialisation of de-mining. Private firms such as CMS Environmental Inc. and Explosive Ordnance World Services were responsible for clearing the American sector of liberated Kuwait. This itself was a dangerous venture as 84 contract de-miners were killed, more than the number of American soldiers killed in combat by enemy fire.[3] The Australian government similarly structures its aid to Mozambique's de-mining organisations such that Australian de-miners do not actually clear mines. Risks are totally undertaken by locals.[4] There is an important distinction between contract de-mining companies and NGO humanitarian de-miners such as British-based HALO Trust and Norwegian People's Aid. The latter are generally more respected. HALO Trust is the first NGO to have humanitarian de-mining as its primary mission.

America's 'Demining 2010 Initiative' has the explicit aim of developing public-private partnerships. In Kosovo, there was a good mix of NGO and contract de-miners. These ranged from NGOs like HALO Trust to private companies such as RONCO Consulting, International De-mining Alliance of Canada Inc. and European Landmine Solutions Ltd.[5] Donor government agencies like USAID paid the bills for de-miners who bid for humanitarian de-mining contracts. This distributes risks away from service personnel, by outsourcing to private contractors and NGOs.[6] After the Afghan campaign in early 2002, RONCO again won a five-year contract from the State Department to defuse unexploded US cluster bombs and landmines, especially from the main US airbase at Bagram and the southern city Kandahar. The NGOs Save the Children and HALO Trust also received funding from the State Department for de-mining. In fact, humanitarian de-mining is the single largest industry in Afghanistan with over 4500 de-miners, indigenous employees and support staff.[7] Afghanistan also has the world's largest de-mining programme, given more impetus by recent events and the concern for risk distribution.

Apart from helping to manage tactical risks like landmines, the concept of risk distribution appears to be cropping up in compiling how-to manuals on managing troubled regions and systemic risks around the world. The East Timor intervention in 1999 was one example where the Clinton Administration 'subcontracted' the managing of a problematic situation to a willing partner (Australia) by providing it logistical and intelligence support. Elsewhere, the Africa Crisis Response Initiative is an effort to improve peacekeeping capabilities of select African nations, to lessen the risks and burdens imposed on US forces in the region's problems.[8] The US private military company (PMC) Military Professional Resources Incorporated's role in training Croatian forces for Operation *Storm* in 1995 meant it 'effectively acted as a mechanism of US policy in the Balkans at less cost and lower political risk than that incurred if the US military were directly involved.'[9]

In Latin America, with Congressional limits on official American participation in Colombia's drug wars, another PMC subcontractor DynCorp working on Pentagon contracts employed mostly ex-Special Forces personnel to fly surveillance missions monitoring poppy production and eradication. These involved occasional heavy firefights with FARC (Revolutionary Armed Forces of Colombia) guerrillas especially since DynCorp helicopter gun-ships often ride shotgun for crop-dusting aircraft.[10] US actions in Colombia tread dangerously the thin line between counter-narcotics and counter-insurgency in its war on drugs. Human Rights Watch complained that 'deniability is the name of the game' and 'We're outsourcing the war in a way that is not accountable.'[11] The rise of Private Military Companies is generating increasing attention from international relations academics and policy-makers, and the notion of risk distribution suggests a potentially fruitful research angle to explaining resurgence of this phenomenon and its particular appeal to governments in a risk age.[12]

IMPLICATIONS AND LESSONS

This book demonstrated that war as an ever-changing phenomenon has manifested itself in ways largely consistent with key operational indicators of risk management. What has hopefully emerged from this study is that an understanding of contemporary warfare derived from conventional models, such as visible successes after decisive battles culminating neatly in surrender procedures, is misleading. Preconceived idealised notions do not do justice to war, which Clausewitz aptly called a 'true chameleon', and furthermore made it difficult to properly appreciate its new guise. Risk management operates from a rather different template and offers fresh insights. The risk management concepts recently emerging in wider social sciences can thus be usefully employed to help clarify our understanding of recurrent trends in contemporary warfare. Another implication of the interpretation of war as risk management is re-emphasising the need for a deeper understanding of the wider strategic and societal context of war, not just a narrow focus on technology and the RMA. The overall picture is unmistakable: war seen as risk management is informed by broader changes in the international system and domestic societies in an age of globalisation.

Furthermore, recent wars have been disavowed by leading Realists such as Henry Kissinger and Stephen Walt, mindful of the need for war only against clearly defined threats. The results presented here suggest a re-evaluation of the predominant concept of 'net assessment' of threats as currently practised in military and security manuals might be in order. Classical net assessment by itself is insufficient for a more complete understanding of a global Risk Society and peculiar strategic circumstances of the twenty-first century. The main outlines of this set of circumstances were previously outlined: the end of the Cold War; American pre-eminence without existential material threats on a scale posed by the Soviet Union; an interdependent world of globalisation and looser constraints on states, people and material moving across porous borders; and failed states endangering security rather than powerful conquering ones. It is however not only within this specific historical context that the concept of war as risk management recommends itself. It would also have to be feasible in the first place. In the cases studied here, this condition was satisfied. In others such as North Korea, this was unfulfilled.

The evidence presented here indicated that core justifications resorted to by both the Clinton and Bush Administrations in explaining wars reflected a negative, minimalist and dystopian ethos. The crucial issue in all cases was that both Presidents Clinton and Bush, and Prime Minister Blair sought largely to prevent the worst, while admittedly also espousing more positive visions of spreading democracy or human rights. The general theoretical background was described as follows:

i   Risk Society in the West understands misfortune and harm in terms of avoidable risks rather than magic, fate or God.
ii   General disillusionment with notions of 'progress' and greater recognition of limits, a negative dystopian ethos focused on avoiding harm.
iii Concern with managing risks, a forward-looking probabilistic mindset focused on 'reflexively' averting extreme improbabilities in a future that is only more or less probable.

Risk, wrote *Washington Post* columnist Robert Samuelson, was the 'defining characteristic of our era'. This claim is illuminating not only in the domestic context he described (terrorist warnings, accounting scandals and Washington snipers) but also the international security domain as shown in this book. Risk management has become the central organising principle as this study has demonstrated. One of the chief criticisms of the few international relations researchers who have attempted to employ theories derived from Ulrich Beck's *Risk Society* is their weak distinction of the differences between concepts of 'threat' and 'risk'. This is certainly an important methodological problem and it is hoped sufficient attention has been paid to this issue. Additionally, by clarifying the 'risk-threat' distinction, this adds to attaining a conceptual grasp of the increasingly important strategic issue of systemic risks. With the publication of Francis Fukuyama's recent book *Our Post-Human Future* , the 'post' prefix seemed to blanket almost everything in contemporary international relations: from post-human, post-Cold War to post-Westphalia and post-modern. Yet this study demonstrated also the increasing prevalence of the 'pre' prefix from 'pre-crime' in popular culture (Tom Cruise's *Minority Report* is one notable example), to 'systematic pre-detection' in surveillance studies, to 'pre-emptive' surgery against high-risk cancers. The 'pre' prefix certainly encapsulates the proactive essence of wars as risk management.

Inevitably, there will be those who argue that in a world of international anarchy, talk of risks is simply an updated definition of a Hobbesian world of dangers and perils. Studying it is a pointless exercise, which would yield no useful or original insights. This study has clearly stated its assumptions in Chapter One: that it is time-bound and pertinent only to specific historical circumstances. It speaks only to this particular period of time where the notion of risk has become predominant in mindsets and society. Life is not exactly nasty, brutish and short. Instead, it is increasingly comfortable, as problems of weight-loss have replaced those of hunger. We seek additionally to manage and prevent security risks to our way of life, and not just accept undesirable outcomes as fated or God's will, as the world of Hobbes was inclined to. The way we conceptualise dangers and perils is greatly different. Furthermore, the notion of 'managing risks' evokes painful memories of a 'managerial' or 'calibrated' approach to war long derided since the Vietnam War. Two points should be made here. First, the time periods and strategic contexts are hugely dissimilar. Second, Vietnam was seen as part of the overarching communist threat and thus infused with some elements of an existential struggle. Risk management on the other hand, lacks such grand purposes and is largely utilitarian.

Nor is it totally accurate to suggest that an 'imperial' mindset informed the wars in question. At the time of writing the previously unfashionable and politically incorrect discourse of 'empire' has been resurrected as a legitimate tool of analysis.[13] Analysts from both left and right now referred to 'American empire' as the 'dominant narrative' of the twenty-first century.[14] However, America, noted Niall Ferguson, was an 'empire that dare not speak its name'. It was in denial, and lacked an 'imperial' ethos or metaphysical narratives; its military primed for high-intensity warfare, not patient colonial-style nation-building. Furthermore its imperial ambivalence derives from democratic traditions, anti-colonial origins and isolationist tendencies.[15] To many, the toppling of Saddam Hussein's statue in Baghdad on 9 April 2003 signified the moment when the American Republic finally became an empire, just like ancient Rome did. In the heat of the moment, hubris occasionally overcame more reasoned analyses of recent evidence presented here that could have suggested otherwise. Donald Rumsfeld correctly insisted to Al-Jazeera that 'we don't do empire'. In fact, analysts suggest we don't even 'do conquest' anymore as an imaginable legitimate war aim.[16] What America *does* do is risk management, with its minimalist ethos seeking to reshape environments and 'prevent the worst' in Bush's own words.

Overall, enough conceptual consistency in the patterns of recent wars survived the change in administration in Washington in 2001 to justify the collective labelling of these wars as 'risk management'. This was most evident in the 'reflexive' recourse to proactive war of an anticipatory nature, justifications given and non-events defined as success on minimalist terms. Although evidence does suggest that regime change in Iraq was really more about threat elimination, especially in the impatient and maximalist manner of ground invasion, the impetus, ethos and outcomes behind it closely parallel those of risk management. Indeed, the 'non-events' and 'hollow' victory in the afterglow of regime change strongly suggested ironically that risk management had been successful in the years before Saddam's ouster.

On a theoretical level, case studies demonstrated the need for a dynamic interdisciplinary approach, with international relations engaged in a constant dialogue with theoretical developments elsewhere in the social sciences, to address new theoretical challenges and the impact of real-world developments. As far as the author is aware, this book is the first such inter-disciplinary piece systematically and specifically focused on war as risk management, as its contribution to the field. It underlined how new under-standings of war can be arrived at through the exploration of risk and risk management strategies previously employed mainly in the disciplines of criminology and sociology. For instance, the notion of 'reshaping the envi-ronment', a crime control mechanism to reduce the risks of offending, has clear parallels in the idea of 'shaping the international environment' first touted in strategy documents of the late Clinton years. These documents clearly suggested that Washington would take a more proactive approach, although the element of using force was initially largely absent. It was only towards the end of the Clinton era that it recognised that military action over Kosovo constituted one such example of 'shaping' to reduce systemic risks. The concept of 'shaping' has since been employed in the Bush Administration's February 2003 strategy to combat terrorism, with its full implications of using force to reduce risks by attacking terrorist sanctuaries in Afghanistan and elsewhere. This lent further weight to the contention that risk management strategies such as 'reshaping the environment' employed in policing and crime control can be usefully applied to the study of war.

Policy lessons

The purpose of analysis undertaken here is certainly not to claim that everything about recent wars could or should be conceptualised through the prism of risk management. The focus on implementing risk management has meant that certain aspects of these wars – the role of subjective perceptions, decision-making theories such as Prospect Theory, hidden agendas, etc. – were not addressed in depth. Yet there remain certain useful lessons to be derived in future attempts to understand and, if possible, avoid precautionary wars based on 'false positives'.

The issue of perceptions has been raised often in explaining war. From the case studies examined, policy-makers appeared to draw analogies from various different sets of risks, most popular of which were historical ones. In Kosovo, the analogy drawn was that of Hitler and appeasement and then Srebrenica and the failure to act. In Iraq, the analogy drawn was again that of Hitler and of course 9/11. However, these analogies, while no doubt serving to portray politicians as learned students of history, served no practical purpose in terms of proper appreciation of the nature of risks involved. Though Milosevic and Hussein were brutal dictators, they were, as Kissinger memorably noted, mere regional thugs. They were certainly not a Hitler with the capability to shift the balance of power fundamentally. NATO further misread the intentions of Milosevic and how he would respond to military force, in its focus on worst-case scenarios for Kosovo. We need reasoned arguments based on more concrete evidence rather than continuously imagining worst-case scenarios, especially over Iraq.

However, there is no sure way of getting around this problem as risks fundamentally involve perceptions and, as the Copenhagen School will agree, politicians have the innate ability to 'securitise' issues through language and shaping the agenda. Policy-makers, when presented with dissenting intelligence information, can shape it to suit their cognitive preferences. This was all too apparent in the post-war controversy over 'sexed up' dossiers in Britain, and the infamous 16-word sentence in President Bush's January 2003 State of the Union speech claiming Iraq had sought uranium from Niger without concrete intelligence backing. Still, perhaps the starkest warning one can have for politicians is that a society already deficient in trusting political institutions will become even more cynical when presented with the apparent 'false positives' that seemed at the time of writing to have propelled regime change in Iraq. A related cautionary lesson is the emphasis on worst-case scenarios and the impatience policy-makers had on occasion in dealing with the issue. Low-probability high-impact scenarios such as 'dirty bomb' attacks can divert resources from more probable low-impact events like truck bombings. Impatience as a result of inflating the risk into an 'imminent threat' meant other possible means of risk management were sidelined. Many still maintain that air power, weapons inspections and patient containment could have reduced the risks associated with Saddam Hussein's Iraq without regime change and the costs in blood and treasure on both sides. More importantly, if policy-makers can grasp the complex nature of elusive systemic risks they face, which require patient management rather than relatively straightforward threat elimination, they could then manage unrealistic public expectations of clearly decisive outcomes and end points.

The dangers of endless 'risk scenarios' and acting in purely precautionary fashion should give us food for thought. The Kosovo and Afghan campaigns were to a limited extent, precautionary. But it is most significantly the post-war difficulties in Iraq, especially the failure to find WMD, that highlight important issues about intelligence. This is especially significant when the intelligence was presumed to be in CIA Director Tenet's infamous words a 'slam dunk'. The quality of intelligence is crucial if it is to properly inform the execution of the pre-emptive doctrine in an efficient and expeditious manner. However, the Iraq war was at base not an intelligence-driven crisis caused by dramatic new information.[17] Lawrence Freedman, like many other reasoned analysts, thinks it was more likely a result of 9/11 changing how we conceptualise and pre-empt security risks before they solidify. A focus on worst-case probabilistic scenarios and trying to avert them was the most natural reaction of a Risk Society. The invasion of Iraq and its aftermath is a clear downside of this mindset and the precautionary principle acting on false positives. As a result, higher, not lower, standards of proof and evidence will be demanded than those dished out by the US and UK in 2002–03. This might well sound the death knell of the precautionary principle in international security yet there are real and significant terrorist dangers, which require precisely such action where the occasion and intelligence merits it. This will be increasingly difficult to sell to ever-more sceptical public opinion in the UK and US.

Yet precaution is precisely what reflexive 'risk calculus' prescribes, taken to its logical conclusion. Herein lies the biggest obstacle for the continued viability of war as risk management: how to reconcile the need for proactive policies to reduce risks with the requirement for not only reliable proof but also visible results. Historical evidence also counsels caution when it comes to gauging the progress of risk management policies. The *process* of Cold War containment eventually obscured the *objective* of changing Soviet concepts of international relations. In Vietnam, as Kissinger famously remarked, 'we would not have recognised victory … because we did not know what our objectives were.'[18] Waging war as risk management incurs similar dangers since the objective of success is defined by vague criteria of 'preventing harm' without clear end-points. Thus the question to broach is: do recent trends towards precautionary war say anything about its future and is it possible to achieve more precise risk assessments on an inherently elusive issue greatly complicated by globalisation processes? The answer could have significant ramifications for war and international relations in a globalised risk age.

Summing up

The three main contributions of this book relate to the concerns raised in Chapter One:

i   It contributes a new perspective to understanding specific aspects of contemporary wars.
ii It reinforces the benefits and importance of an interdisciplinary approach to international relations in understanding the current strategic situation of ill-defined systemic risks.
iii It provides fresh and satisfactory explanations of certain features of military campaigns that have challenged long-established thinking in the minds of policy-makers and the public, adding to the 'transformation of war' debate.

This project took three case studies of wars in Kosovo, Afghanistan and Iraq and used an analytical framework to systematically map and assess the presence of cross-cutting risk management patterns in these wars. These largely chimed with empirical evidence at least in impetus and outcomes, although evidence indicated that implementation was not as patient or minimalist as predicted in Iraq by 2003. Yet, the aftermath of regime change with the failure to find compelling Al Qaeda links or fully reconstituted WMD actually warranted the previous, more patient risk management approach to war. That said, the case studies presented here also helped develop the notion of war as risk management, refining the concept in the process.

Four years after the 9/11 attacks, and despite countless claims that 'everything has changed', such suggestions are premature at least in the regularities and patterns of warfare uncovered here. Rather than signalling a complete sea change, evidence from the case studies presented here suggested that 9/11 only consolidated what had previously been an emerging trend: war as a tool to manage systemic risks in terms of impetus, implementation and justification, and outcome evaluation. Continuity was as important as discontinuity. Globalisation and interdependence have not heralded the end of war, as some claim. Instead, war has been redefined as a result of the globalisation of risks and their management. The revamped war-form is proactive, 'reflexive' and minimalist in nature.

RISK MANAGEMENT'S LAST HURRAH?

More recently, however, developments in the US threaten to unravel the reconfiguration of war as a risk management strategy. The rhetoric coming out of Washington has been stridently and overtly theological and ideological. A re-elected President Bush appears to be sketching the outlines of a grand vision of spreading democracy and transforming the world to a greater extent than he ever did before. Such 'heroic' projects run instinctively counter to the minimalist safety-first ethos of risk management. However these developments might not necessarily be irreconcilable if war is seen as simply one half of a two-pronged strategy to combat terrorism. With heightened awareness of the risks America and the world faced after 9/11, the watershed 2002 National Security Strategy (NSS) specified two key planks in fighting terrorism: ideas about spreading democracy and stability as good security policy in a globalised world, and pre-emptive strikes. Risk management concepts in this book have so far been closely linked to the latter, while the former in recent months (March 2005) has been getting substantially more attention, at least rhetorically speaking. The term 'pre-emptive' seems to have gone under the radar somewhat, perhaps as a result of the manifest failure of that term as applied to Iraq. Taken together with the discrediting of the precautionary principle in the deserts of Iraq, this might suggest a relative shift towards the ideological segment of the NSS focused on democracy and freedom as opposed to the minimalist risk management tone that has largely dominated the past few years. The pendulum could well swing back again.

President Bush's second inauguration speech on January 2005 touted democracy and freedom as antidotes to the problem of 'tyranny' by ending repression and political frustration, thereby reducing terrorism as a result. Critics fear this could entail greater eagerness to militarily subject problematic states to an extreme makeover, akin to what has been done in Afghanistan and Iraq. Predictably dubbed 'Wilsonianism in boots' as early as 2002,[19] the US Army now seems to be the driving engine for democratic transformation, displacing previous emphases on the democratising impact of economic development. Once problem states are reformed from tyranny into democratic systems, theoretically speaking they should no longer pose risks. Iran, Syria and North Korea have taken turns filling the neo-con target sights, although full-scale invasion does not seem feasible in the short-term militarily, economically or politically.

This more positive moral view of changing the world for the better could thus be in a real sense about risk management, since the goal is ultimately to reduce the risks we face by sculpting the political set-up of other countries. As Tony Blair put it, 'in the war against terrorism, the moralists and realists are partners, not antagonists'.[20] The snag for the United States is that, to Muslims around the world, America's legitimate security interests dictating continued occupation of Iraq could be blotted out by increasingly theological religious Administration rhetoric on spreading democracy and freedom.[21] Moralistic preaching could in fact be making the situation more complicated for realists. The end result of pronouncements tinged with religious tones will help stoke pre-existing fires of hatred for the modern-day Crusaders, which Al Qaeda has been quick to exploit.

Bush's sweeping vision for transformation of the world might furthermore not be tenable for various more secular reasons. For starters the American domestic polity has so far been prone to 'wobbles' and doubts when it comes to waging wars and might not be willing to sustain this new agenda. US domestic politics stands famously accused by Niall Ferguson of having an 'attention deficit', when the task could last for decades. Additionally the Federal budget deficit is at record levels. The Administration and the people have no stomach for higher taxes, military drafts or any other bitter pills to buttress continued open-ended campaigns overseas.[22] Public opinion has turned against the meat grinder that the occupation of Iraq has turned out to be, with quite significant numbers thinking the cost too high in economic, moral terms as well as lives. America can resurrect Iraq if it is willing to bear the burdens and go the full distance, but the price seems too high for the American people are hardly eager beavers when it comes to rebuilding efforts there and elsewhere.[23] The Bush Administration has also rediscovered multilateralism and the UN to endorse a multilateral force in Iraq. In recent tangles with Iran and Syria, the President has stressed the international community's role, although this could very easily change again. In sum, there is 'no stable grand vision of order' into which other states, notably the major European powers, could buy.[24] G. Ikenberry laments that the neo-con/Bush blueprint pales in comparison to that offered by Roosevelt of a more prosperous, secure world after the rigours of conflict had been endured. Instead it is overwhelmingly focused on confronting the immediate scourge of terrorism. It inspires far more fear than hope, despite purporting to advance high-sounding values.

Yet claims that military occupation serves righteous goals have long been used – from the age of empires bringing civilisation to the 'natives', to spreading democracy and freedom today. It is in truth utterly unrealistic to expect states to behave in a completely altruistic manner. Chris Brown rightly suggests that we should discard so-called 'pop realism'; the assumption that once self-interests are involved, morals and ethics have no place whatsoever.[25] States in fact often act on a combination of interests. In the age of empires, this involved self-proclaimed noble colonial missions together with economic interests and great power competition. During the Cold War, it was fighting godless communism and superpower competition. In an age of risks and globalisation, spreading democracy not only served moral goals but also security concerns about repressive states as well. The question was which of this set of interests was being emphasised at any one time; the balance might well shift to and fro. Furthermore, nation-building projects in Afghanistan and Iraq have been presented both as part of the war on terror as well as part of the broader ideological project of spreading democracy. The so-called 'nation-building is the best defence' school of thought popular after 9/11 indeed recommends that America take on such tasks as a matter of national security.[26] However, the main 'strategic problem' with this prescription is its sustainability and the need to ensure resources are not needlessly drained from tackling the main challenge from the Al Qaeda network.[27] The Bush Administration's recent nation-building projects are currently driven by national security interests and exigencies of the domestic political agenda rather than requirements of the nation/state being constructed.[28] This was not just social work for the sake of doing something good and spreading democracy.

'The world's most powerful nation often appeared also to be the most frightened'.[29] Sometimes it seems America spawns far more fear and paranoia with its endless worst-case scenarios than it does democracy and optimism, understandably so after 9/11. And if there is one lesson to take away from here, it is that fear and anxiety on a wide plethora of probabilistic scenarios spread very easily and quickly indeed in an age of globalisation. Unfortunately these spread much faster than democracy. Bush's America went to war on Iraq largely based on such risks and fears, with democracy significantly lower down the list. It ended up having to justify war in terms of democracy and freedom with the failure to find WMD. As Bob Woodward recounts in his insider account of decision-making in the Bush White House, the WMD issue was highlighted among a range of possible concerns because it 'had legs' in the run-up to war.[30] Ironically democracy and the human rights record of Saddam Hussein were deemed much less 'leggy'.

Yet liberty and freedom are now the new overused buzzwords in Washington and London. That being the case, it is still unclear how governments will sell future wars to their publics: in terms of spreading democracy or managing security risks? If the gut instinct of Risk Societies is anything to go by, and nothing seems to have changed fundamentally, the language of risk might retain the upper hand, although memories of Iraq are still painfully raw given the divisive nature of ambiguous risks. The shifting dynamics in Washington between spreading democracy and risk management could constitute the new axis upon which the shape of international relations, conflict and strategy will revolve for the foreseeable future in an era of globalised risks. This state of unstable flux will in turn likely determine the face of warfare, whether we have minimalist safety-first wars or grand military adventures under the banner of democracy to transform the world, or more likely, schizophrenic shades of both. After all, the Bush Administration has displayed an uncanny knack for coming across as both extremely fearful and self-assured at the same time.

NOTES

1 THE RECONFIGURING OF WAR

1 Frank Bruni, 'The 2000 Campaign: the syntax', *New York Times*, 23 January 2000.
2 Michael Clarke, 'War in the new international order', *International Affairs*, Vol. 77 No. 3, July 2001, p. 663.
3 Jeffrey Record, 'Collapsed countries, casualty dread and the new American way of war', *Parameters*, Vol. XXXII No. 2, Summer 2002, pp. 4–23. Also Andrew Bacevich and Eliot Cohen (eds), *War Over Kosovo: Politics and Strategy in a Global Age*, New York: Columbia University Press, 2001.
4 Sia Spiliopoulou Akermark, 'Storms, foxes and nebulous legal arguments: twelve years of force against Iraq, 1991–2003', *International Comparative Law Quarterly*, Vol. 54, January 2005, p. 231.
5 Robert Kagan, 'A higher realism', *Washington Post*, 23 January 2005.
6 M. Boyle, 'Utopianism and the Bush foreign policy', *Cambridge Review of International Affairs*, Vol. 17 No. 1, April 2004.
7 Simon Clarke and Paul Hoggett, 'The Empire of Fear: The American political psyche and the culture of paranoia', *Psychodynamic Practice*, Vol. 10 No. 1, February 2004.
8 See John Gaddis, 'A grand strategy of transformation', *Foreign Policy*, Issue 133, Nov/Dec 2002.
9 Remarks at 20th Anniversary of the National Endowment for Democracy, Washington D.C., 6 November 2003.
10 George W. Bush, Inaugural Address, 20 January 2005.
11 'Department of Defence (DoD) News Briefing – Secretary Rumsfeld', 20 September 2001.
12 Testimony before the Senate Armed Services Committee, 15 April 1999.
13 Stephen Walt, 'Rational choice and international security' in Michael E. Brown, Owen R. Cote Jr, Sean Lynn-Jones and Steven E. Miller (eds), *Rational Choice and Security Studies: Stephen Walt and his critics*, Cambridge, MA: MIT Press, 2000, pp. 8–9. Precision means identifying boundaries and assumptions to avoid misapplying theory in unsuitable circumstances. Logically consistent theories have conclusions that flow logically from initial premises. Originality means theory should help researchers see familiar phenomena in a new way and tells us things we did not originally know. It imposes order on phenomena previously hard to understand and addresses conceptual or empirical problems that earlier theories could not adequately explain. Empirical validity determines usefulness of a theory by comparing it against appropriate evidence.

14 See John Mueller, *Retreat from Doomsday: the obsolescence of major war*, New York: Basic Books, 1991; Michael Mandelbaum, 'Is major war obsolete?', *Survival*, Vol. 40 No. 4, Winter 1998–9.

15 See text of the lectures published in John Keegan, *War and our World*, London: Hutchinson, 1998, p. 72. Many definitions of war exist which I do not address in detail. Hedley Bull's *The Anarchical Society* (London: MacMillan, 1977) defined war as organised violence by political units against each other for a political purpose. Raymond Aron's *Peace and War* (London: Weidenfeld and Nicholson, 1966, trans. from the French) defined 'perfect' war as between two states recognising each other but there are of course many forms of war. Clausewitz's famous definition of course is that war is a controlled, rational political act: 'War is not only an act of policy, but a true political instrument, a continuation of political discourse, carried out with other means'. Karl Von Clausewitz, *On War*, translated and edited by Michael Howard and Peter Paret, Princeton: Princeton University Press, 1976, p. 75.

16 John Mueller, *The Remnants of War*, Ithaca: Cornell University Press, 2004.

17 Colin McInnes, *Spectator Sport War*, London: Lynne Rienner Publishers, 2002.

18 Christopher Coker, *Humane Warfare*, London: Routledge, 2001, p. 4.

19 Christopher Coker, *Waging War Without Warriors: the Changing Culture of Military Conflict*, London: Lynne Rienner Publishers, 2002, pp. 7, 12, 34; Martin Van Creveld, *The Transformation of War*, New York: Free Press, 1991.

20 See Philip K. Lawrence, *Modernity and War*, Basingstoke: Macmillan, 1997, pp. 13–14, 19; also Hans Joas, *War and Modernity*, Cambridge: Polity Press, 2003.

21 See David Brooks, 'A modest little war', *The Atlantic Monthly*, February 2002.

22 Mueller, *The Remnants of War*.

23 See Mary Kaldor, *New and Old Wars*, Cambridge: Polity Press, 1999 and David Keen, *The Economic Functions of Civil Wars*, Adelphi Paper 320, 1998 Oxford: IISS.

24 Jeremy Black, *War in the New Century*, London: Continuum, 2001, p. 3. Also see Colin S. Gray, *The Sheriff: America's Defence of the New World Order*, Lexington, KY: University of Kentucky Press, 2004.

25 Lawrence Freedman, 'Prevention, not pre-emption', *Washington Quarterly*, Vol. 26 No. 2, Spring 2003, p. 111.

26 Anthony Cordesman, *Lessons and Non-Lessons of the Kosovo Air War*, Washington DC: Centre for Strategic and International Studies, July 1999 Executive Summary, p. 9.

27 Wesley Clark, *Waging Modern War*, New York: Public Affairs, 2001, pp. xxiii, 418, 423.

28 Colin McInnes, 'A different kind of war? September 11 and the United States' Afghan war', *Review of International Studies*, Vol. 29 No. 2, April 2003, p. 178.

29 Lawrence Freedman, 'War in Iraq: Selling the threat', *Survival*, Vol. 46 No. 2, Summer 2004, p. 7.

30 However the 1950–3 Korean War for example has technically not ended after 50 years, being in a state of 'temporary' armistice. It also involved no victors or vanquished. Nonetheless, the point remains that most perceptions of war revolve around surrender ceremonies like those ending World War Two separating victors and defeated. See an analysis of these notions of war in Christopher Coker, 'How wars end', *Millennium*, Vol. 26 No. 3, 1997, pp. 615–29.

31 Giles Andreani, 'The war on terror: Good cause, wrong concept', *Survival*, Vol. 46 No. 4, Winter 2004–05, p. 35.

32 See Williamson Murray, 'Clausewitz out, computer in', *National Interest*, Issue 48, Summer 1997.

33 Alan Beyerchen, 'Clausewitz, nonlinearity and the unpredictability of war', *International Security*, Vol. 17 No. 3, Winter 1992–3, p. 71.

34 Melissa Applegate, *Preparing for Asymmetry: as seen through the lens of Joint Vision 2020*, US Army War College Strategic Studies Institute, Sep 2001.

35 Andrew Erdmann, 'The US presumption of quick costless wars', *Orbis*, Vol. 43 Issue 3, Summer 1999. Lack of a coherent viable strategy and leadership from civilian and military elites were the real cause of the collapse of public will in Vietnam and Somalia.

36 Edward Luttwak, 'Toward post-heroic warfare', *Foreign Affairs*, May/June 1995, Vol. 74 No. 3, pp. 116–20.

37 Andrew Bacevich, *American Empire*, Cambridge, MA: Harvard University Press, 2002, pp. 148, 154–5, 166.

38 James W. Gibson, *The Perfect War: Technowar in Vietnam*, New York: Atlantic Monthly Press, 2000, p. 97.

39 See M. Evans and K. Lunn (eds), *War and Memory*, Leamington: Berg, 1999.

40 See Martin Shaw, 'A regressive crystallisation of global state power: Theorising a response to the "war against terrorism"', *www.theglobalsite.ac.uk* (accessed 23 May 2003), 2001.

41 Kalevi Holsti, *Peace and War: Armed Conflicts and International Order 1648–1989*, Cambridge: Cambridge University Press, 1991, p. 272.

42 Creveld, *The Transformation of War*, pp. 2, 71.

43 Luttwak, 'Toward post-heroic warfare', is among the more prominent discussions of risk-averse warfare using long-range precision air power. The moral and ethical implications of sanitising wars where violence is out of sight are explored in James Der Derian's *Virtuous War: Mapping the military-industrial-media-entertainment network*, Boulder, CO: Westview Press, 2001, and Michael Ignatieff's *Virtual War: Kosovo and Beyond*, London: Chatto and Windus, 2000.

44 Quoted in Dana Priest, 'A Four Star Foreign Policy? US Commanders wield rising clout, autonomy', *Washington Post*, 28 September 2000.

45 Clausewitz, *On War*, pp. 586–93.

46 Jeremy Black, *Why Wars Happen*, London: Reaktion Books, 1998, p. 87.

47 Mats Berdal and Spyros Economides (eds), *Strategic Thinking: an Introduction and Farewell*, London: Lynne Rienner, 2002, pp. 172–77.

48 Alvin and Heidi Toffler, *War and Anti-war: Making sense of today's global chaos*, London: Warner Books, 1995.

49 Chris Hables Gray, *Post-modern War: the New Politics of Conflict*, New York: Guilford Press, 1997, p. 149. A similar view is expressed in Philip K. Lawrence, *Modernity and War*, Basingstoke: Macmillan, 1997, Chapter 3.

50 'Rediscovering Risk', *Washington Post*, 23 October 2002.

51 Colin S. Gray, *Modern Strategy*, New York: Oxford University Press, 1999, p. 1.

52 Applegate, op. cit., p. 8.

53 UK Ministry of Defence, *Strategic Defence Review*, July 1998, Cm 3999, paras 40 and 54, and Chapter 1 'A Strategic Approach to Defence'.

54 'Rumspeak', *The Economist*, 04 December 2003.

55 Colin S. Gray, *Strategic Studies and Public Policy*, Lexington, Kentucky: University Press of Kentucky, 1982, p. 184.

56 Ulrich Beck, *World Risk Society*, Cambridge: Polity Press, 1999, p. 8; Ulrich Beck, 'The terrorist threat: World Risk Society revisited', *Theory, Culture and Society*, Vol. 19 No. 4, August 2002, pp. 39–56.

57 Hans Joas, *War and Modernity*, Cambridge: Polity Press, 2003, p. 177.

58 Christopher Dandeker, 'New times and new patterns of civil-military relations', in Jurgen Kuhlman and Jean Callaghan (eds), *Military and Society in 21st Century Europe: A comparative analysis*, Hamburg: Lit Verlag, 2000, p. 30.

59 Celeste Wallander and Robert Keohane, 'Risk, threat, and security institutions' in Helga Haftendorn, Robert Keohane and Celeste Wallander, *Imperfect Unions: Security institutions over time and space*, New York: Oxford University Press, 1999, p. 25.
60 Joas, *War and Modernity*, p. 171.
61 A brief sample of sociological and criminological works include Les Johnston, *Policing Britain: Risk, Security and Governance*, Harlow: Longman, 2000; Pat O'Malley (ed.), *Crime and the Risk Society*, Aldershot: Dartmouth Publishing, 1998; Ulrich Beck, *Risk Society: Towards a New Modernity*, Cambridge: Polity Press, 1992.
62 Mikkel Vedby Rasmussen, 'It sounds like a riddle: Security studies, the war on terror and risk', *Millennium*, Vol. 33 No. 2, March 2004, p. 381.
63 Mikkel Vedby Rasmussen, 'Reflexive security: NATO and International Risk Society', *Millennium*, Vol. 30 No. 2, 2001, pp. 285–310; Johan Eriksson (ed.), *Threat Politics: New Perspectives on Security, Risk and Crisis Management*, Aldershot: Ashgate Publishing, 2001; also Gearoid O'Tuathail, 'Understanding Critical Geopolitics: Geopolitics and Risk Society', *Journal of Strategic Studies*, Vol. 22 No. 2/3, June/Sep 1999, pp. 107–24.
64 Jacob Bercovitch and Patrick Regan, 'Managing Risks in international Relations', in Gerald Schneider and Patricia Weitsman (eds), *Enforcing Cooperation: Risky States and Intergovernmental Management of Conflict*, Basingstoke: Macmillan, 1997, p. 187.
65 See a critique of Beck's works in Joas, *War and Modernity*, Chapter 10 'War and the Risk Society', Cambridge: Polity Press, 2003.
66 For a compelling defence of Realism, see for instance Colin Gray, 'World Politics as usual after September 11: Realism vindicated', in Ken Booth and Tim Dunne (eds), *Worlds in Collision: Terror and the future of global order*, Basingstoke: Palgrave Macmillan, 2002.
67 McInnes, 'A different kind of war? September 11 and the United States' Afghan war', p. 165.
68 A similar line of thought is revealed in Tony Blair's musings. When asked why focus on Saddam but not Robert Mugabe or the Burmese junta, the PM replied: 'Yes let's get rid of them all. I don't because I can't but when you can you should'. Of course the risks from Iraq were greater but the feasibility factor remains. See Peter Stothard's *Thirty Days: Tony Blair and the Test of History*, New York: Harper Collins, 2003.
69 See John Baylis and James J. Wirtz, 'Introduction' in *Strategy in the Contemporary World: An Introduction to Strategic Studies*, New York: Oxford University Press, 2002.
70 Chris Brown, Chapter 12 'Conclusion: New Agendas', *Understanding International Relations*, (2nd edn), Basingstoke: Palgrave, 2001.
71 See Barbara Adam, Ulrich Beck and Joost Van Loon (eds), *The Risk Society and Beyond*, London: Sage Publications, 2000.
72 Eriksson, 'Conclusion', in Eriksson (ed.), *Threat Politics*, pp. 224–5.
73 Clausewitz takes a similar view. See Beyerchen, 'Clausewitz, nonlinearity and the unpredictability of war', p. 90.

2 THE DAWN OF A RISK AGE

1 See for example America's latest *Quadrennial Defence Review*, Washington DC: Department of Defence, September 2001.
2 Robert Johnson, *Improbable Dangers: US Conceptions of Threat in the Cold War and After*, New York: St Martin's Press, 1994, p. 2.

3 See Lawrence Freedman, 'War in Iraq: selling the threat', *Survival*, Vol. 46 No. 2, Summer 2004, p. 7.

4 Mats Berdal and Spyros Economides (eds), *Strategic Thinking: an Introduction and Farewell*, pp. 54, 168.

5 John Lewis Gaddis, *Strategies of Containment: A Critical Appraisal of Postwar American National Security Policy*, New York: Oxford University Press, 1982, Preface viii (italics added).

6 See Garthoff, *A Journey through the Cold War*, p. 15.

7 Recently declassified US documents support this view. See William Burr and Jeffrey T. Richelson, 'Whether to "strangle the baby in the cradle": The United States and the Chinese nuclear program 1960–64', *International Security*, Vol. 25 No. 3, Winter 2000/01, pp. 54–99.

8 Grenada and Panama were relatively small-scale campaigns that occurred in America's own backyard. Recent wars in Afghanistan and Iraq are a different matter altogether in terms of force structure, power projection capabilities and firepower deployed.

9 Michael E. O'Hanlon, 'The Bush Doctrine: strike first', *San Diego Union-Tribune*, 14 July 2002.

10 See Richard Ned Lebow and Janice Gross Stein's *We all lost the Cold War*, Princeton: Princeton University Press, 1993.

11 Emily Goldman and Larry Berman, 'Engaging the world: first impressions of the Clinton foreign policy legacy' in Colin Campbell and Bert Rockman (eds), *The Clinton Legacy*, New York: Chatham House Publishers, 2000, p. 252.

12 Quoted in Johnson, *Improbable Dangers*, p. 47.

13 See Carl Conetta and Charles Knight, 'Inventing Threats', *Bulletin of the Atomic Scientists*, Vol. 53 No. 2, March/April 1998.

14 Remarks by President Clinton and others at NATO/Russia Founding Act signing ceremony, Paris, France, 27 May 1997.

15 Raymond Garthoff, *A Journey through the Cold War*, Washington DC: Brookings Institution Press, 2001, p. 15.

16 Zaki Laidi, *A World Without Meaning: Crisis of Meaning in International Politics*, London: Routledge, 1998, p. 109.

17 Laidi, *A World Without Meaning*.

18 Quotes cited in Ben MacIntyre, 'Bush fights the good fight with a righteous quotation', *The Times*, 8 Mar 2003.

19 Stephen Biddle, 'The new way of war', Review Article, *Foreign Affairs*, Vol. 81 No. 3, May/June 2002.

20 Francis Fukuyama, 'History is still going our way', *Wall Street Journal*, 5 Oct 2001.

21 Mary Douglas, *Risk and Blame: essays in cultural theory*, London: Routledge, 1992, pp. 14, 24.

22 Dana Allin and Steven Simon, 'America's Predicament', *Survival*, Vol. 46 No. 4, Winter 2004–05, p. 9.

23 'New poll finds Bush priorities are out of step with Americans', *New York Times*, 3 March 2005.

24 Brooks, 'A modest little war'.

25 Brooks, 'A modest little war'. While it is suggested that America's wars of risk management are modest in scope, 1930s America also fought modest 'small wars' in Latin America. These were however within an overarching framework of noble goals, and as War Secretary Elihu Root earlier suggested in 1912, 'obligations ... of the highest character'. Quoted in Robert Tucker and David Hendrickson, *The Imperial Temptation: The New World Order and America's Purpose*, New York: Council on Foreign Relations, 1992, p. 149.

26 See Gorm Rye Olsen, 'Europe and Africa's Failed States: from development to containment', Paper presented to conference on The global constitution of failed states: the consequences of a new imperialism?, University of Sussex, 18–20 April 2001; also Paul Rogers, *Losing Control: Global security in the 21st century*, London: Pluto Press, 2000, p. 60.

27 Robert Cooper, *The Post Modern State and World Order*, London: Demos, 2000, p. 41; and his *The Breaking of Nations: Order and Chaos in the 21st Century*, Cambridge: Polity Press, 2003.

28 See for instance the debate involving John Mearsheimer, Barry Posen and Eliot Cohen, 'Reassessing net assessment', *International Security*, Vol. 13 No. 4, Spring 1989, pp. 129–79.

29 Garthoff, *A Journey through the Cold War*, p. 391.

30 Mikkel Vedby Rasmussen, *9–11: Globalisation, Security and World Order*, DUPI Working Paper 2002/2, Copenhagen: Danish Institute of International Affairs, 2002, p. 11.

31 Prepared Statement for the House and Senate Armed Services Committees: 'Building a military for the 21st century', 3–4 October 2001.

32 Anthony Giddens, *Modernity and Self-identity: Self and society in the late modern age*, Cambridge: Polity Press, 1991, pp. 35–69.

33 Ulrich Beck, *World Risk Society*, Cambridge: Polity Press, 1999, p. 133.

34 Mikkel V. Rasmussen, 'Reflexive security: NATO and International Risk Society', *Millennium*, Vol. 30 No. 2, 2001, p. 285.

35 The Alliance's Strategic Concept agreed by the Heads of State and Government participating in the meeting of the North Atlantic Council, Rome, 8 November 1991.

36 Michael Ignatieff, *Virtual War*, London: Chatto & Windus, 2000, pp. 162–3.

37 Andrew Bacevich, *American Empire*, Cambridge, MA: Harvard University Press, 2002, p. 203.

38 *National Security Strategy of the United States of America*, Washington DC: The White House, September 2002, Chapter I.

39 Cited in Jim Garone, 'DoD Balancing Risks, Missions', *Armed Forces Information Service News Articles*, 08 Aug 2001.

40 See James Der Derian, 'Global events, national security and virtual theory', *Millennium*, Vol. 30 No. 3, December 2001, p. 680.

41 *Annual Report to the President and the Congress*, Washington DC: DoD, 15 Aug 2002, Chapter 1.

42 Prepared Statement for the House and Senate Armed Services Committees: 'Building a military for the 21st century', 3–4 October 2001.

43 Ole Waever, *Security: A Conceptual History for International Relations*, Paper Presented at ISA Annual meeting, 24–27 March 2002.

44 See *Report of the Quadrennial Defence Review*, Washington DC: The White House, May 1997, Section X (italics added).

45 *The National Security Strategy of the United States of America*, Washington DC: The White House, 20 Sep 2002, Chapter V. Secretary of State Colin Powell later clarified that pre-emption was simply an existing tool of statecraft that had been elevated after 9/11, rather than a new doctrine displacing all other existing tools such as containment or deterrence.

46 Ashton B. Carter and William J. Perry, *Preventive Defence: A New Security Strategy for America*, Washington DC: Brookings Institution Press, 1999, p. 8.

47 John Steinbrunner, *Principles of Global Security*, Washington DC: Brookings Institution Press, 2000, p. 195.

48 Remarks by Secretary of Defence Les Aspin at the National Academy of Sciences Committee on International Security and Arms Control, 7 December 1993.

49 See Martin Kettle, 'US strategy on nuclear war', *Guardian (UK)*, 9 Dec 1997.

50 Lawrence Freedman, 'The Revolution in Strategic Affairs', *Adelphi Paper 318*, Oxford: OUP for the IISS, 1998.

51 See James J. Wirtz, 'Counterproliferation, conventional counterforce and nuclear war', *Journal of Strategic Studies*, Vol. 23 No. 1, March 2000, p. 7.

52 See Francois Heisbourg, 'A Work in Progress: the Bush Doctrine and its consequences', *Washington Quarterly*, Vol. 26 No. 2, Spring 2003. Also see a short description in Richard Haass, *Intervention: the use of American military force in the post-Cold War world*, Washington DC: Brookings Institution Press, 1999, p. 51.

53 Quoted in Andrew Bacevich, 'Do-goodism gone bad: the lesson of the USS *Cole*', *National Review*, 20 November 2000.

54 Chapter 1: The Defence Strategy and the National Security Strategy, *Annual Defence Report to Congress and the President*, Washington DC: DoD, 1998.

55 Bacevich, *American Empire*, p. 242.

56 Peter Riddell, 'America must share its imperial burden', *The Times*, 24 April 2003.

57 Geoff Hoon, *The Strategic Defence Review: A new chapter*, London: MoD, July 2002, Introduction.

58 Lynn E. Davis's *Security Implications of Globalisation*, Santa Monica, CA: RAND, 2003 for example highlights terrorism, ethnic cleansing, WMD proliferation, and infectious diseases.

59 Thomas Friedman, 'A Manifesto for the Fast world', *New York Times Magazine*, 28 March 1999, p. 42.

60 Prime Minister's Speech, Doctrine of the International Community, Economic Club of Chicago, 24 April 1999.

61 Rogers, *Losing Control: Global Security in the 21st Century*, p. 60.

62 *A National Security Strategy for a New Century*, Washington DC: The White House, December 1999, Chapter I, p. 1.

63 David Mutimer, 'Reconstituting security? The practices of proliferation control', *European Journal of International Relations*, Vol. 4 No. 1, March 1998, pp. 99–129.

64 Cabinet Office Strategy Unit report, *Risk*, London, November 2002 *http://www.strategy.gov.uk/2002/risk/risk/report/report/summary/summary.htm#bk 001* (accessed 10 May 2003).

65 Hugh Dyer, 'Environmental security and international relations: the case for enclosure', *Review of International Studies*, Vol. 27 No. 3, July 2001, pp. 441–3.

66 *National Security Strategy of the United States of America*, Washington DC: The White House, September 2002, Introduction. This document brought to the centre the focus on failed states that was first discussed in security documents of the late Clinton years.

67 Ulrich Beck, *Risk Society: Towards a new modernity*, London: Sage Publications, 1992 (trans. Mark Ritter).

68 Earlier works on international relations could include Ulrich Beck, *Democracy without enemies*, Cambridge: Polity Press, 1998 where he also discussed the lack of a grand consensus creating ambivalence and doubt without ever-present enemies. However this work was less geared towards international relations than his later writings.

69 Beck, *World Risk Society*, p. 3.

70 Ulrich Beck, *What is Globalisation?*, trans. Patrick Camiller, Cambridge: Polity Press, 2000, p. 40.

71 Beck, *World Risk Society*, p. 14.

72 Ulrich Beck, 'The World Risk Society Revisited: the terrorist threat?', LSE Public Lecture, London 14 February 2002; 'Terror and solidarity' in Mark Leonard (ed.), *Re-ordering the World*, London: The Foreign Policy Centre, 2002.

73 See Pat O'Malley, 'Introduction', in Pat O'Malley (ed.), *Crime and the Risk Society*, Aldershot: Dartmouth Publishing, 1998.

74 Jane Franklin, 'Introduction' in Jane Franklin (ed.), *The Politics of Risk Society*, Cambridge: Polity Press, 1998, p. 1.

75 Cabinet Office Strategy Unit, *Risk: improving government's capacity to handle risk and uncertainty*.

76 Ulrich Beck, 'Risk Society and the Provident State' in Scott Lash, Bronislaw Szerszynski and Brian Wynne (eds), *Risk, Environment and Modernity*, London: Sage, 1996, p. 31.

77 Ulrich Beck, 'Politics of Risk Society', in Franklin (ed.), *The Politics of Risk Society*, p. 12.

78 Martin Woolacott, 'The Politics of Prevention,' in Franklin (ed.), *The Politics of Risk Society*, p. 122.

79 Beck, *World Risk Society*, pp. 2–3, 69.

80 See Anthony Giddens and Christopher Pearson, '*Conversations with Anthony Giddens*', Cambridge: Polity Press, 1998, p. 115; also Giddens, *Modernity and Self-identity*, p. 20.

81 See Ulrich Beck, *The Reinvention of Politics*, Cambridge: Polity Press, 1997, pp. 23, 28.

82 For the differences between means-end rationality and reflexive rationality, see Rasmussen, 'Reflexive Security', pp. 288, 290.

83 Niklas Luhmann, *Risk: A Sociological Theory*, New York: Aldine de Gruyter, 1993, trans. Rhodes Barrett, Introduction, pp. viii–ix.

84 Ulrich Beck, *Risk Society: Towards a New Modernity*, Cambridge: Polity Press, 1992, p. 19.

85 Beck, *Risk Society: Towards a New Modernity*, p. 76.

86 Frank Furedi, *The Culture of Fear*, London: Cassell, 1997, p. 29.

87 Douglas, *Risk and Blame: essays in cultural theory*, pp. 14, 24.

88 Beck, *Risk Society: Towards a new modernity*, pp. 22, 33, 73.

89 See Woolacott in Franklin, (ed.), *The Politics of Risk Society*, p. 121.

90 Beck, *World Risk Society*, p. 50.

91 Lupton, *Risk*, pp. 124–144.

92 Lupton, *Risk*, p. 106.

93 Furedi, *The Culture of Fear*, 1998, pp. 8, 20.

94 Beck, *Risk Society*, p. 49.

95 David Lyon, *Surveillance Society: Monitoring Everyday Life*, Buckingham: Open University Press, 2001, p. 49.

96 Zygmunt Bauman, *Times Higher Education Supplement*, London, 13 Nov 1992, p. 25.

97 See Giddens, *Modernity and Self-identity*, p. 3.

98 Zygmunt Bauman, *Post-modern Ethics*, Oxford: Blackwell, 1993, p. 225.

99 Mick Hume, 'Are they heroes or victims? We're tying ourselves in knots with yellow ribbon', *The Times*, 31 March 2003.

100 Christopher Lasch, *The Minimal Self: Psychic Survival in Troubled Times*, London: Norton, 1984, Preface; and Christopher Lasch, *Culture of Narcissism: American Life in an Age of Diminishing Expectations*, London: Abacus Press, 1980, p. 72.

101 Ericson and Haggerty, *Policing the Risk Society*.

102 Ulrich Beck, 'The fight for a cosmopolitan future', *New Statesman*, 5 November 2001, p. 33.

103 Ericson and Haggerty, *Policing the Risk Society*, p. 41.
104 Malcolm Feeley and Jonathan Simon, 'Actuarial Justice: the emerging new criminal law' in David Nelken (ed.), *The Futures of Criminology*, London: Sage Publications, 1994, p. 173.
105 Ericson and Haggerty, *Policing the Risk Society*, p. 92.
106 Gordon Hughes, *Understanding Crime Prevention: Social Control, Risk and Late Modernity*, Buckingham: Open University Press, 1998, p. 7.
107 Barbara Hudson, 'Punishment, rights and difference: defending justice in the risk society', in Kevin Stenson and Robert Sullivan (eds), *Crime, Risk and Justice: the Politics of Crime Control in Liberal Democracies*, Cullompton, Devon: Willan Publishing, 2001, p. 144.
108 David Blunkett on BBC Radio 4 'Today' Programme, July 17 2002.
109 Clive Norris and Gary Armstrong, *Maximum Surveillance Society*, Oxford: Berg, 1999, p. 24.
110 Lyon, *Surveillance Society*, Introduction; also see Norris and Armstrong, *Maximum Surveillance Society*, p. 24.
111 David Garland, *The Culture of Control: Crime and Social Order in Contemporary Society*, Oxford: Oxford University Press, 2001, pp. 446–7.
112 Garland, *The Culture of Control*, pp. 446–7.
113 Hughes, *Understanding Crime Prevention*, pp. 60, 63.
114 Pat O'Malley (ed.), *Crime and the Risk Society*, Aldershot: Dartmouth Publishing, 1998, p. 234.
115 Hughes, *Understanding Crime Prevention*, p. 14.
116 Hughes, *Understanding Crime Prevention*, p. 14.
117 Robert Castel, 'From dangerousness to risk', in Burchell, Gordon and Miller (eds), *The Foucault Effect*, pp. 287–8.
118 Les Johnston, *Policing Britain: Risk, Security and Governance*, Essex: Pearson Education Ltd, 2000, pp. 56, 157.
119 See Richard Ericson and Kevin Haggerty, *Policing the Risk Society*, Toronto and Buffalo: University of Buffalo Press, 1997.

3 FORGING THE LINK

1 See an analysis of the various societal actors involved in defining risks in Stuart Allan, Barbara Adam and Cynthia Carter, *Environmental Risks and the Media*, London: Routledge, 2000.
2 See the discussion of Douglas in Deborah Lupton, *Risk*, London: Routledge, 1999, p. 38.
3 Ulrich Beck, *What is Globalisation?*, trans. by Patrick Camiller, Cambridge: Polity Press, 2000, p. 100.
4 See Johan Eriksson (ed.), *Threat Politics: New Perspectives on Security, Risk and Crisis Management*, Aldershot: Ashgate Publishing, 2001; Mikkel Rasmussen, 'Reflexive security: NATO and International Risk Society', *Millennium:Journal of International Studies*, Vol. 30 No. 2, 2001, pp. 285–310.
5 For this view, see Lupton, *Risk*, pp. 59–60.
6 Ulrich Beck, *World Risk Society*, Cambridge: Polity Press, 1999, p. 22.
7 Quoted in Amy Charlene Reed, 'Federal Commission Proposes Risk Management Framework', *RiskWorld News, http://www.riskworlDCom/NEWS/96Q1/nw5aa010.htm*, 13 June 1996 (accessed 27 June 2003).
8 See Barbara Adam and Joost Van Loon, 'Repositioning Risk: the challenge for social theory', in Barbara Adam, Ulrich Beck and Joost Van Loon (eds), *The*

Risk Society and Beyond: Critical Issues for Social Theory, London: Sage Publications, 2000, p. 24.

9 Lupton, *Risk*, p. 3.

10 Mary Douglas, *Risk and Blame: essays in cultural theory*, London: Routledge, 1992, p. 24.

11 'Surgery is best option for high-risk cancers', *The Times*, 28 Sep 2002; also Monica Greco, 'Psychosomatic subjects and the "duty to be well"', *Economy and Society*, Vol. 22 No. 3, pp. 356–70.

12 John Adams, *Risk*, London: UCL Press, 1995, p. 180.

13 W. B. Gallie, 'Essentially contested concepts', in Max Black (ed.), *The Importance of Language*, Englewood Cliffs, NJ: Prentice Hall, 1962, pp. 121–46.

14 Barry Buzan, *People, States and Fear*, (2nd edn), Hemel Hempstead: Harvester, 1991, p. 3.

15 Andreas Klinke and Ortwin Renn, 'Precautionary Principle and discursive strategies: classifying and managing risks', *Journal of Risk Research*, Vol. 4 No. 2, April 2001, p. 159.

16 See Ortwin Renn, 'Three decades of risk research: accomplishments and new challenges', p. 50 and Eugene A. Rosa, 'Metatheoretical foundations for postnormal risk', p. 28 *Journal of Risk Research*, Vol. 1 No. 1, Jan 1998; Frank Furedi, *The Culture of Fear*, London: Cassell, 1998, p. 17.

17 Tim O'Riordan, James Cameron and Andrew Jordan (eds), *Reinterpreting the Precautionary Principle*, London: Cameron May, 2002, p. 77.

18 Douglas, *Risk and Blame: essays in cultural theory*, p. 22.

19 Adams, *Risk*, pp. 26–7.

20 Lupton, *Risk*, pp. 9–10.

21 Royal Society, *Risk: Analysis, perception and management*, London: Royal Society, 1992, pp. 13, 135.

22 John Adams, 'Frameworks for thinking about risk', Paper presented at *Goodenough-Chevening Conference on Risk*, 11 April 2002, Goodenough College, London.

23 Howard Kunreuther and Paul Slovic, 'Science, values and risk', in Howard Kunreuther and Paul Slovic (eds), Challenges in risk assessment and risk management: Special Volume, *The Annals of the American Academy of Political and Social Science*, Vol. 545, May 1995, p. 122.

24 Beck, *World Risk Society*, p. 31.

25 'US Securities and Insurance Industries: Keeping the promise', Hearing of the House Financial Services Committee, 107th Congress, 1st session, 26 Sep 2001.

26 Christopher Hood, Henry Rothstein and Robert Baldwin, *The Government of Risk: Understanding Risk Regulation Regimes*, Oxford: Oxford University Press, 2001, p. 140.

27 See Ulrich Beck, 'The World Risk Society Revisited: the terrorist threat', *LSE Public Lecture*, 14 February 2002, London; Cabinet Office Strategy Unit report *Risk: Improving Government's Capacity to Handle Risk and Uncertainty*, London, November 2002, available at *http://www.strategy.gov.uk/2002/risk/risk/report/report/ summary/summary.htm#bk001* (accessed 10 February 2003).

28 Adams, *Risk*, p. 180; Lupton, *Risk*, pp. 59–60.

29 Beck, *World Risk Society*, p. 55; Ulrich Beck, *Democracy Without Enemies*, trans. Mark Ritter, Cambridge: Polity Press, 1998, pp. 25–6.

30 Eriksson, 'Introduction', p. 9 (italics added) and Lennart Sjoberg, 'Risk perceptions: taking on societal salience', pp. 21–2, in Eriksson (ed.), *Threat Politics*.

31 Rasmussen, 'Reflexive security?', p. 285.

32 Shlomo Griner, 'Living in a World Risk Society: A reply to Mikkel V. Rasmussen', *Millennium*, Vol. 31, No. 1, 2002, p. 157.
33 For further discussions of 'risk' and 'hazard', see Waring and Glendon, *Managing Risk*, pp. 3–4; also Yaacov Vertzberger, *Risk-Taking and Decision-Making: Foreign Military Intervention Decisions*, Stanford: Stanford University Press, 1998, p. 25.
34 Niklas Luhmann, *Risk: A Sociological Theory*, New York: Adline de Gruyter, 1993, trans. Rhodes Barrett, pp. 22, 46.
35 Bertel Heurlin, *The Threat as a Concept in International Politics*, Copenhagen: The Information and Welfare Service of the Danish Defence, 1977, pp. 5, 6.
36 Rasmussen, 'Reflexive Security', p. 289.
37 Francois Ewald, 'Insurance and Risk', in Graham Burchell, Colin Gordon and Peter Miller (eds), *The Foucault Effect*, Chicago: University of Chicago Press, 1991, p. 199.
38 Luhmann, *Risk: A Sociological Theory*, p. 49.
39 Douglas, *Risk and Blame: Essays in Cultural Theory*, p. 39.
40 Adams, *Risk*, Preface, p. ix.
41 Heurlin, *The Threat as a Concept in International Politics*, pp. 16–17, 21.
42 Ashton B. Carter and William J. Perry, *Preventive Defence: A New Security Strategy for America*, Washington DC: Brookings Institution Press, 1999, p. 8.
43 Christopher Hood and David K. C. Jones, *Accident and Design: Contemporary Debates in Risk Management*, London: UCL Press, 1996, p. 10.
44 Iain Wilkinson, *Anxiety in a Risk Society*, London: Routledge, 2001, p. 42.
45 Anthony Giddens, *Modernity and Self-identity*, Cambridge: Polity Press, 1991, pp. 109–43, 181–208.
46 Sigmund Freud, *Beyond the Pleasure Principle*, London: The International Psycho-Analytical Press, 1922, trans. C. J. M Hubback, p. 9.
47 Wilkinson, *Anxiety in a Risk Society*, pp. 20–1.
48 Cabinet Office Strategy Unit, *Risk*.
49 Denis Smith and Steve Tombs, 'Conceptualising issues of risk management within the Risk Society', in Eve Coles, Denis Smith and Steve Tombs (eds), *Risk Management and Society*, Dordrecht, Netherlands: Kluwer Academic Publishers, 2000, p. 1.
50 William T. Stanbury, 'Reforming risk regulation in Canada: the next policy frontier?', in Laura Jones (ed.), *Safe Enough? Managing Risk and Regulation*, Vancouver: Fraser Institute, 2000, p. 197.
51 David Moss, *When All Else Fails: the Government As the Ultimate Risk Manager*, Cambridge, MA: Harvard University Press, 2002, pp. 1–2.
52 Moss, *When All Else Fails*, pp. 9, 13.
53 For good surveys of the concept, see Coles, Smith and Tombs (eds), *Risk Management and Society*, Kluwer Academic Publishers, 2000; also Waring and Glendon, *Managing Risk*.
54 *Quadrennial Defence Review*, Washington DC: DOD, 30 September 2001, pp. 13, 57.
55 See Smith and Tombs, 'Conceptualising issues of risk management within the Risk Society', p. 24; also Waring and Glendon, *Managing Risk*, Introduction; Hood and Jones, *Accident and Design: Contemporary Debates in Risk Management*, p. 7.
56 N. Rose, *Powers of Freedom: Reframing Political Thought*, Cambridge: Cambridge University Press, 1999, p. 237.
57 Hood and Jones, *Accident and Design*, p. 10.
58 *Strategic Trends*, Introduction, London: Ministry of Defence, March 2003.
59 For tombstone-style strategies, see Hood, Rothstein and Baldwin, *The Government of Risk: Understanding Risk Regulation Regimes*, p. 183.

60 See GAO, *Combating Terrorism: Threat and Risk Assessments Can Help Prioritise and Target Program Investments*, Report Number NSIAD-98–74, 09 April 1998, Washington DC.

61 Royal Society, *Risk: Perception, Analysis and Management*, pp. 142–3.

62 A recommendation by the New Zealand Society of Risk Management, *http://www.risksociety.org.nz/dealing.html*, (accessed 22 November 2002).

63 Waring and Glendon, *Managing Risk*, pp. xxii, 5. On the other hand, 'speculative risks', in the entrepreneurial sense of calculating positive risks and returns, involve spectacular gains, or losses. This is associated with economics and finance where risk management normally meant diversification of portfolios.

64 Smith and Tombs, 'Conceptualising issues of risk management within the Risk Society', pp. 25–7, 47; also R. E. Hester and R. M. Harrison (eds), *Risk Assessment and Risk Management*, Cambridge: The Royal Society of Chemistry, 1998, p. 6.

65 A concept suggested by Ulrich Beck, *Risk Society*, trans. Mark Ritter, London: Sage Publications, 1992, p. 37.

66 O'Malley, *Crime and the Risk Society*, p. 109.

67 See for example, Michael V. Deaver, *Disarming Iraq: Monitoring power and resistance*, Westport: Praeger, 2001, p. 5.

68 Royal Society, *Risk: Analysis, Perception and Management*, p. 53.

69 David Lyon, 'Introduction' in David Lyon (ed.), *Surveillance as Social Sorting: Privacy, Risk and Digital Discrimination*, London: Routledge, 2003, p. 8.

70 Michael Crouhy, Dan Galai and Robert Mark, *Risk Management*, New York: McGraw-Hill, 2001, p. 109.

71 David Lyon, *Surveillance Society: Monitoring Everyday Life*, Buckingham: Open University Press, 2001, pp. 2, 47–9; also Christopher Dandeker, *Surveillance, Power and Modernity*, Cambridge: Polity Press, 1990, Preface, p. vii.

72 Ericson and Haggerty, *Policing the Risk Society*, pp. 41, 55–8.

73 David Lyon, 'Surveillance as social sorting: Privacy, risk after September 11', *LSE Public Lecture*, 6 Nov 2002, London.

74 See Lyon, *Surveillance Society*, pp. 89, 104; David Lyon, 'Chapter 1' in Lyon (ed.), *Surveillance as Social Sorting*, pp. 24, 39.

75 Beck, *World Risk Society*, pp. 139–141.

76 Hood and Jones, *Accident and Design*, p. 190.

77 Poul Harremoes, David Ge, Malcolm MacGarvin, Andy Stirling, Jane Keys, Brian Wynne, Sofia Guedes Vaz (eds), *The Precautionary Principle in the 20th Century*, London: Earthscan Publications, 2002, pp. xi, 4–5; O'Riordan, Cameron and Jordan, 'The Evolution of the Precautionary Principle', in O'Riordan, Cameron and Jordan (eds), *Reinterpreting the Precautionary Principle*, p. 9.

78 See John D. Graham, 'A future for the precautionary principle?', *Journal of Risk Research*, Vol. 4 No. 2, April 2001, pp. 109–10; European Commission, *Communication from the Commission on the Precautionary Principle*, Brussels, 2 February 2000, p. 4.

79 O'Riordan, Cameron and Jordan, 'The Evolution of the Precautionary Principle', in O'Riordan, Cameron and Jordan (eds), *Reinterpreting the Precautionary Principle*, p. 27.

80 Klinke and Renn, 'Precautionary Principle and discursive strategies: classifying and managing risks', pp. 162–8.

81 Anthony Giddens cited in Jane Franklin (ed.), *The Politics of Risk Society*, Cambridge: Polity Press, 1998, p. 29.

82 Mark Neal, 'Risk Aversion: the rise of an ideology', in Laura Jones (ed.), *Safe Enough? Managing risk and regulation*, Vancouver: Fraser Institute, 2000, p. 21.

83 Richard J. Zeckhauser and W. Kip Viscusi, 'The Risk Management Dilemma', in Kunreuther and Slovic (ed.), *Challenges in risk assessment and risk management: Special Volume*, p. 150.
84 See Rose McDermott, *Risk-taking in International Politics: Prospect Theory in US Foreign Policy*, Ann Arbor: University of Michigan Press, 1998, p. 9.

4 THE KOSOVO CAMPAIGN

1 David Chandler, *From Kosovo to Kabul: Human Rights and International Intervention*, London: Pluto Press, 2002, pp. 17, 168.
2 Michael Mccgwire, 'Why did we bomb Belgrade?', *International Affairs*, Vol. 76 No. 1, Jan 2000, p. 14; and Adam Roberts, 'NATO's Humanitarian war over Kosovo', *Survival*, Vol. 41 No. 3, Autumn 1999, pp. 102, 108, 120.
3 See Nicholas Wheeler, *Saving Strangers: Humanitarian intervention in international society*, Oxford: Oxford University Press, 2003.
4 Secretary of Defence William S. Cohen and Chairman of the Joint Chiefs of Staff Henry Shelton, 'Joint Statement on the Kosovo After-action Review', presented before the Senate Armed Services Committee, 14 October 1999, *http://www. defenselink.mil/news/Oct1999/b10141999_bt478–99.html* (accessed 16 April 2003).
5 Colin McInnes, 'Fatal attraction? Air Power and the West', in Colin McInnes and Nicholas Wheeler (eds), *Dimensions of Western Military Intervention*, London: Frank Cass, 2002.
6 Ivo H. Daalder and Michael E. O'Hanlon, *Winning Ugly: NATO's War to Save Kosovo*, Washington DC: Brookings Institution Press, 2000, pp. 99, 209.
7 See Paul W. Kahn, 'War and Sacrifice in Kosovo', *Philosophy and Public Policy*, Spring–Summer 1999, *http://www.puaf.umd.edu/IPPP/spring_summer99/ kosovo.htm*; see Christopher Cviic, 'A victory all the same', *Survival*, Vol. 42 No. 2, Summer 2000, p. 174.
8 Andrew Bacevich and Eliot Cohen (eds), *War over Kosovo: Politics and Strategy in a Global Age*, New York: Columbia University Press, 2001, Introduction.
9 Stephen Biddle, ' The new way of war', Review Article, *Foreign Affairs*, Vol. 81 No. 3, May/June 2002, *http://www.foreignaffairs.org/20020501faessay8063/ stephen-biddle/the-new-way-of-war.html* (accessed 23 April 2003).
10 Michael Ignatieff, *Virtual War: Kosovo and Beyond*, London: Chatto & Windus, 2000, pp. 162–3.
11 Timothy Garton Ash, 'Round Table: the global order in the twenty-first century', *Prospect*, August/September 1999, pp. 50–8.
12 Cited in S. Zizek, *The Fragile Absolute: or Why Is the Christian Legacy Worth Fighting For?*, London: Verso, 1999, p. 56.
13 Charles Krauthammer, 'The short unhappy life of humanitarian war', *The National Interest*, Fall 1999, No. 57, p. 6.
14 Wesley K. Clark, *Waging Modern War*, Oxford: Public Affairs, 2001, pp. 166–7.
15 Krauthammer, 'The short unhappy life of humanitarian war', p. 7.
16 Independent International Commission on Kosovo. 'Conclusions', *www.kosovocommision.org* (accessed 16 May 2003); Michael Ignatieff, 'A post-modern war', *Time*, 12 April 1999.
17 Ignatieff, ' A post-modern war', p. 78.
18 Christopher Coker, *Humane Warfare*, London: Routledge, 2001, p. 128.
19 Andrew Bacevich, *American Empire*, Cambridge, MA: Harvard University Press, 2002, p. 196.
20 Howard Caygill, 'Perpetual police? Kosovo and the elision of police and military violence', *European Journal of Social Theory*, Vol. 4 No. 1, February 2001, p. 74.

21 Clark, *Waging Modern War*, p. 11.
22 Press Statement by Dr Javier Solana, Press Release (1999) 040, 23 Mar 1999, Brussels, Belgium.
23 Testimony before the Senate Armed Services Committee, 15 April 1999.
24 Quoted in Roberts, 'NATO's "Humanitarian War" over Kosovo', p. 112.
25 See Benjamin S. Lambeth, *Nato's Air War for Kosovo: A Strategic and Operational Assessment*, Santa Monica, CA: RAND, 2001, p. 51.
26 Lord Robertson, 'The aims of the air campaign' and 'Could it have been done better?' in *Kosovo: One year On*, NATO HQ, Brussels, Belgium, Oct 2000.
27 Cited in Daalder and O'Hanlon, *Winning Ugly: NATO's War to Save Kosovo*, p. 105.
28 Quoted from 'Minutes of evidence' given on 03 February 1999, in the House of Commons Defence Select Committee Report, *The Future of NATO: The Washington Summit*, 31 March 1999, p. 48.
29 Interview with Wesley Clark cited in James Der Derian, *Virtuous War*, Boulder, CO: Westview Press, 2001, p. 192.
30 Ignatieff, *Virtual War: Kosovo and Beyond*, pp. 3, 110.
31 Richard Haass, *Intervention: the Use of American Military Force in the Post-Cold War World*, Washington DC: Brookings Institution, 1999 revised edition, pp. 174–5.
32 Quoted in Donald C. F Daniel, Bradd C. Hayes, Chantal de Jonge Oudraat, *Coercive Inducement and the Containment of International Crises*, Washington DC: United States Institute of Peace, 1999, p. 22.
33 Thomas Schelling, *Strategy of Conflict*, Cambridge, MA: Harvard University Press, 1960, *Arms and Influence*, New Haven, CT: Yale University Press, 1966, pp. 2–3.
34 McInnes, 'Fatal attraction? Air Power and the West', pp. 42–3.
35 Michael Clarke, 'British perceptions' in Mary Buckley and Sally N. Cummings (eds), *Kosovo: Perceptions of War and Its Aftermath*, London: Continuum, 2001, p. 80.
36 House of Commons Defence Committee, Session 1998–9, 'The Future of NATO: the Washington Summit', HC 39, Evidence, p. 147, Q. 375.
37 Stephen P. Aubin, 'Operation Allied Force: War or "coercive diplomacy"?', *Strategic Review*, Vol. XXVII, No. 3, Summer 1999, pp. 5–8.
38 Department of Defence, Report to Congress: Kosovo/Allied Force after-action Report, 31 Jan 2000, Washington DC, p. 6.
39 For example, Charlie Lyon, 'Operation Allied Force: A lesson on strategy, risk, and tactical execution', *Comparative Strategy*, Vol. 20 No. 1, Jan–Mar 2001, pp. 57–75.
40 Clark, *Waging Modern War*, p. 11.
41 See Bruce R. Nardulli et al., *Disjointed War: Military Operations in Kosovo 1999*, Santa Monica, CA: RAND Arroyo Centre, 2002, p. 2.
42 Clark, *Waging Modern War*, pp. 185, 348.
43 Edward Luttwak, *Strategy: the Logic of Peace and War*, Cambridge, MA: Harvard University Press, 2001, pp. 76 and 201.
44 Buckley and Cummings, 'Introduction' in Buckley and Cummings (eds), *Kosovo*, p. 3.
45 See David Auerwald, 'Explaining wars of choice: an integrated decision model of NATO policy in Kosovo', *International Studies Quarterly*, Vol. 48 No. 3, September 2004; Steven B. Redd, 'The influence of advisers and decision strategies on foreign policy choices: President Clinton's decision to use force in Kosovo', *International Studies Perspectives*, Vol. 6 No. 1, February 2005.

46 For this concept, see David McLaughlin (ed.), *Managing Conflict in the Post-Cold War World*, Aspen, CO: The Aspen Institute, 1995, pp. 74–5.

47 Michael Howard, 'Managing Conflict: lessons from the past', in McLaughlin, *Managing Conflict in the Post-Cold War World*, p. 37.

48 Edward Luttwak, Strategy: *The Logic of War and Peace*, (revised and enlarged edition), Cambridge, MA: Harvard University Press, 2001, p. 70.

49 Caygill, 'Perpetual police? Kosovo and the elision of police and military violence', p. 78.

50 Prime Minister's Speech, Doctrine of the International Community, Economic Club of Chicago, 24 April 1999.

51 A National Security Strategy for a New Century, Washington DC: The White House, December 1999, Chapter 1, p. 1.

52 'New World Order', *Le Monde Diplomatique*, June 1999.

53 Remarks by the President to AFSCME Biennial Convention, 23 March 1999.

54 Henry A. Kissinger, 'No US ground forces in Kosovo', *Washington Post*, 22 Febuary 1999, p. A15.

55 Tony Weymouth, 'Why war, why NATO?' in Tony Weymouth and Stanley Henig (eds), *The Kosovo Crisis: The last American war in Europe?*, London: Pearson Education Limited, 2001, p. 1.

56 Daalder and O'Hanlon, *Winning Ugly*, 2000, p. 2.

57 Common Position of 19 March 1998, defined by the Council on the basis of Article J.2 of the Treaty on European Union on restrictive measures against the Federal Republic of Yugoslavia (98/240/CFSP), Brussels; Statement on Kosovo adopted by the members of the Contact Group, Rome 29 April 1998.

58 Roberts, 'NATO's Humanitarian war over Kosovo', pp. 102, 108, 120.

59 House of Commons Debate on Kosovo, 25 March 1999, Hansard, cols. 537–53.

60 Lord Robertson, 'A just and necessary action' in Kosovo: one year on, NATO HQ, Brussels, Belgium, October 2000.

61 Clarke, 'British perceptions' in Buckley and Cummings (eds), *Kosovo: Perceptions of war and its aftermath*, p. 80.

62 Dana H. Allin, *NATO's Balkan Interventions*, Adelphi Paper 347, Oxford: Oxford University Press for the IISS, July 2002, p. 99.

63 Prime Minister's Speech, Doctrine of the International Community, Economic Club of Chicago, 24 April 1999.

64 Danner, ibid., p. 63.

65 Danner, ibid., p. 63.

66 Cited in Mark Danner, 'Endgame in Kosovo' in William J. Buckley (ed.), *Kosovo: Contending Voices on Balkan Interventions*, Grand Rapids, MI: William B. Eerdmans Publishing Company, 2000, p. 63.

67 Danner, 'Endgame in Kosovo', p. 63; also see James Hooper, 'Kosovo: America's Balkan problem', *Current History*, Vol. 98 No. 627, April 1999, p. 159.

68 Statement by the Prime Minister, Tony Blair, in the House Of Commons, 23 March 1999, Hansard (House of Commons Daily Debates), *http://www.publications.parliament.uk/pa/cm199899/cmhansrd/v0990323/debtext/9 0323–06.htm* (accessed 3 May 2003).

69 Mccgwire, 'Why did we bomb Belgrade?', p. 14.

70 Address to the Nation, 24 March 1999, The White House, Washington DC.

71 Henry Kissinger, 'Kosovo and the Vicissitudes of American foreign policy', in Buckley (ed.), *Kosovo: Contending Voices on Balkan Interventions*, p. 268.

72 Figures from Biddle, 'The New way of war?'.

73 See for example Ted Galen Carpenter, 'Bill Clinton, Aggressor', CATO Institute Daily Commentary, 23 March 1999.

74 See Elaine Sciolino and Ethan Bronner, 'How a President, distracted by scandal, entered Balkan war', *New York Times*, 18 April 1999.
75 Remarks by the President on Foreign Policy, San Francisco, California, 26 February 1999.
76 Statement by President Clinton on Kosovo, 24 March 1999, Office of the Press Secretary, White House, Washington DC.
77 Lord Robertson, Secretary General of NATO, Kosovo One Year On, 'Background to the crisis', *http://www.nato.int/kosovo/rep02000/backgrou.htm* (accessed 29 April 2003), 21 March 2000, (italics added).
78 The Alliance's Strategic Concept approved by the Heads of State and Government participating in the meeting of the North Atlantic Council in Washington DC on 23rd and 24th April 1999, available at *http://www.nato.int/docu/pr/1999/p99–065e.htm* (accessed 18 April 2003).
79 Richard Rupp, 'NATO 1949–2000: from collective defence toward collective security', *Journal of Strategic Studies*, Vol. 23 No. 3, September 2000, p. 172.
80 Ted Galen Carpenter, 'Kosovo as an omen: the perils of a new NATO', in Ted Galen Carpenter (ed.), *NATO's Empty Victory*, Washington DC: CATO Institute, 2000, pp. 174–5.
81 Ted Galen Carpenter, 'Relations with Russia and China' in Carpenter (ed.), *NATO's Empty Victory*, p. 78.
82 The Alliance's Strategic Concept approved by the Heads of State and Government participating in the meeting of the North Atlantic Council in Washington DC on 23rd and 24th April 1999, available at *http://www.nato.int/docu/pr/1999/p99–065e.htm* (accessed 1 May 2003); also see David Yost, *NATO Transformed: the Alliance's new roles in international security*, Washington DC: United States Institute of Peace, 1998, p. 80.
83 The Alliance's Strategic Concept, available at *http://www.nato.int/docu/pr/1999/p99–065e.htm* (accessed 5 April 2003).
84 'Preparing NATO for the 21st Century: Keynote address' by Dr Javier Solana, Maritime Symposium, Lisbon, Portugal, 4 September 1998.
85 Statement by President Clinton on Kosovo, Office of the Press Ssecretary, The White House, Washington DC, 24 March 1999.
86 Statement by the Prime Minister, Tony Blair, in the House Of Commons, 23 March 1999, Hansard (House of Commons Daily Debates), *http:// www.publi-cations.parliament.uk/pa/cm199899/cmhansrd/v0990323/debtext/90323–06.htm* (accessed 7 April 2003).
87 The idea of 'victimhood' was played out in fact on all sides of the conflict. The Kosovar Albanians portrayed themselves as victims of Milosevic to attract NATO intervention, while Belgrade made itself out to be the victim of NATO bullying during the air campaign. See Lawrence Freedman, 'Victims and Victors: Reflections on the Kosovo war', *Review of International Studies*, Vol. 26 No. 3, July 2000.
88 *National Security Strategy for a Global Age*, Washington DC: The White House, December 2000, Chapter 1, p. 1.
89 Michael O'Hanlon, 'The Bush Doctrine: Strike First', *San Diego Union-Tribune*, 14 July 2002; also Alan W. Dowd, 'NATO After Kosovo', *Policy Review*, December 1999, No. 98, Web-version, *http://www.policyreview.org/de c99/dowd.html* (accessed 9 May 2003).
90 House of Commons Foreign Affairs Committee, Fourth Report, 1999–2000 session, 23 May 2000, Para 123.
91 NATO Acting Spokesman Mark Laity cited in Jonathan Steele, 'Motivated to believe the worst', *Guardian* (UK), 18 August 2000.

92 See Daya Kishan Thussu, 'Legitimizing humanitarian intervention? CNN, NATO and the Kosovo crisis', *European Journal of Communication*, Vol. 15 No. 3, September 2000, p. 73.

93 Christopher Layne, 'Collateral Damage in Yugoslavia', in Carpenter, *NATO's Empty Victory*, pp. 51–2.

94 Allin, *NATO's Balkan Interventions*, pp. 60–1.

95 Mccgwire, 'Why did we bomb Belgrade?', p. 14.

96 Jonathan I. Charney, 'Anticipatory humanitarian action in Kosovo', *American Journal of International Law*, Vol. 93 No. 3, October 1999, pp. 834–41.

97 Daalder and O'Hanlon, *Winning Ugly*, pp. 12, 207.

98 Cited in Chandler, *From Kosovo to Kabul: Human Rights and International Intervention*, Foreword, p. xiv.

99 Gareth Evans and Mohamed Sahnoun, 'The responsibility to protect', *Foreign Affairs*, November/December 2002, Vol. 81 No. 6.

100 For these two approaches to risk management, see Christopher Hood, Henry Rothstein and Robert Baldwin, *The Government of Risk: Understanding Risk Regulation Regimes*, Oxford: Oxford University Press, 2001, p. 183.

101 Statement by the Prime Minister, Tony Blair, in the House Of Commons, 23 March 1999, Hansard (House of Commons Daily Debates), *http://www. publications.parliament.uk/pa/cm199899/cmhansrd/v0990323/debtext/90323–06.h tm* (accessed 10 April 2003).

102 John Kriendler, 'Anticipating Crises', *NATO Review*, Winter 2002, No. 4, Web-version, *http://www.nato.int/docu/review/2002/issue4/english/art4.html* (accessed 11 May 2003).

103 Quoted in Ralph Crosby Jr, 'The path forward for NATO and EU defence capabilities: information dominance and precision strike', *World Systems Procurement Edition*, Vol. 3 No. 1, January 2001, p. 121.

104 Yahya A. Dehqanzada and Ann M. Florini, *Secrets for Sale: How commercial satellite imagery will change the world*, Washington DC: Carnegie Endowment for International Peace, 2000, p. 7.

105 Jack Smith, 'Eyes over Kosovo', ABCNEWs. com, 7 April 1999.

106 Paul Virilio, *Strategy of Deception*, London: Verso, 2000, pp. 14–15, 21–3.

107 Don DeLillo, 'Human Moments in World War Three', *Esquire*, July 1982.

108 Bacevich, American Empire, p. 192.

109 Thomas Barnett and Henry H. Gaffney, Jr, 'Top ten post-Cold War Myths', *US Naval Institute Proceedings*, Vol. 172/2/1, 176, February 2001, pp. 32–8.

110 Statement by President Clinton on Kosovo, 24 March 1999, Office of the Press Secretary.

111 Andrew Bacevich, 'The bombing: Over-the-top statecraft', *Washington Post*, 28 Mar 1999; also Bacevich and Cohen (eds), *War over Kosovo: Politics and Strategy in a Global Age*, Introduction, p. xi.

112 Bacevich, 'The bombing'.

113 Luttwak, *Strategy*, p. 76 and p. 201.

114 President Clinton, Address to the Nation on Kosovo, 24 March 1999; and Linda D. Kozaryn, 'No silver bullet to stop Serb aggression', *American Forces Press Service*, 31 Mar 1999.

115 Ignatieff, *Virtual War: Kosovo and beyond*, pp. 15–16, 95.

116 Press Conference by Secretary General Dr Javier Solana and SACEUR Gen. Wesley Clark, 25 Mar 1999, NATO HQ, Brussels; Rubin cited in Daalder and O'Hanlon, *Winning Ugly*, p. 69.

117 Mccgwire, 'Why did we bomb Belgrade?', p. 3.

118 See Sabrina P. Ramet, 'The USA: To war in Europe again', in Weymouth and Henig (eds), *The Kosovo Crisis: The last American war in Europe?*, p. 177.

119 RFE/RL Balkan Report, *Confronting Evil*, Vol. 4 No. 52, 14 July 2000, Prague, Czech Republic.
120 Luttwak, *Strategy*, pp. 76 and 201.
121 Daalder and O'Hanlon, *Winning Ugly*, p. 2.
122 Thomas Carothers, 'Ousting Foreign Strongmen: Lessons from Serbia', *Carnegie Endowment Policy Brief*, Vol. 1 No. 5, May 2001, pp. 1–7.
123 Although Milosevic was later put on trial in the Hague for war crimes, this was not the direct result nor stated goal of Allied Force.
124 Quoted in Cilina Nasser, 'Reshaping region is real US goal', *The Daily Star* (Beirut), 4 December 2001.
125 Cited in Daalder and O'Hanlon, *Winning Ugly*, p. 104.
126 Kosovo Post-strike assessment Press Conference, SACEUR HQ, Mons, Belgium, 16 Septmber 1999.
127 Lord Robertson, 'The aims of the air campaign' and 'Could it have been done better?'.
128 Lambeth, *NATO's Air War for Kosovo*, p. 219.
129 Department of Defence, Annual Defence Report to Congress and the President, Chapter 1: The Defence Strategy and the National Security Strategy, Washington DC, 1998.
130 Chapter 1: Fundamentals of the Strategy, A National Security Strategy for a Global Age, Washington DC: The White House, December 2000.
131 Robert Cooper, *The Post Modern State and World Order*, London: Demos, 1996, p. 44.
132 A. Wolfson, 'Humanitarian hawks? Why Kosovo but not Kuwait?', *Policy Review*, Number 98, December 1999/January 2000, Web version, *http://www.policy review.org/dec99/wolfson.html* (accessed 3 May 2003).
133 Zygmunt Bauman, 'Wars of the globalisation era', *European Journal of Social Theory*, Vol. 4 No. 1, 2001, pp. 11–28.
134 Edward Luttwak, 'Atlantic Unbound Roundtable: Picking a good fight', April 11 2000, *http://www.theatlantic.com/unbound/roundtable/goodfight/luttwak2.htm* (accessed 11 April 2003).
135 'American body bag syndrome holding back NATO', *Daily Telegraph*, 21 March 2001.
136 'NATO too timid over guerillas', *Daily Telegraph*, 3 March 2001.
137 Joseph S. Nye, 'Ill-suited for empire', *Washington Post*, 25 May 2003.
138 See Simon Chesterman, *You the People: the United Nations, Transitional Administration and State-building*, Oxford: Oxford University Press, 2004.
139 Strategic Survey 2002/03, Oxford: Oxford University Press for the IISS, May 2003, p. 59; 'Rumsfeld asks NATO to trim Bosnia forces to bolster war on terrorism', *LA Times*, 19 December 2001.
140 Christopher Coker, 'How wars end', *Millennium*, Vol. 26 No. 3, 1997, pp. 615–29.
141 Quoted in 'Verbatim Special', *Air Force Magazine*, Vol. 82 No. 6, June 1999, p. 51.
142 Anthony Cordesman, The lessons and non-lessons of the Kosovo air and missile war, Washington DC: CSIS, July 1999, *http://www.csis.org/kosovo/LessonsExec.pdf* (accessed 25 May 2003).
143 Clark, *Waging Modern War*, p. 421.
144 Ted Galen Carpenter, 'Introduction: A Great Victory?' in Carpenter (ed.), *NATO's Empty Victory: A Postmortem on the Balkan War*, p. 8; Frank Cillufo and George Salmoiraghi, 'And the winner is ... the Albanian mafia', *Washington Quarterly*, Vol. 22 No. 4, Autumn 1999, pp. 21–5.

145 Michael Mandelbaum, 'A Perfect Failure', *Foreign Affairs*, Vol. 78 No. 5, September/October 1999, pp. 2–9; Krauthammer, 'The short unhappy life of humanitarian war', pp. 6–7.

146 Ignatieff, *Virtual War*, pp. 138, 208.

147 William J. Buckley, 'Not losing sight of justice', in Buckley (ed.), *Kosovo: Contending Voices on Balkan Interventions*, p. 238.

148 Unnamed UN official quoted in William G. O'Neil, *Kosovo: An Unfinished Peace*, Boulder, CO: Lynne Rienner publishers, 2002, p. 30.

149 Lord Robertson, 'Could it have been done better?'.

150 Daalder and O'Hanlon, *Winning Ugly*, p. 6.

151 *National Security Strategy for a Global Age*, Washington DC: The White House, December 2000, pp. 41–2.

152 Bacevich, *American Empire*, p. 185.

153 Luttwak, *Strategy*, p. 61.

154 See Anna Matveeva and Wolf-Christian Paes, 'Trapped in its own maze', *The World Today*, sVol. 58 No. 7, July 2002, pp. 19–21.

155 President Clinton, CBS Interview with Dan Rather, 31 March 1999; Kozaryn, 'No silver bullet to stop Serb aggression'.

156 Caygill, 'Perpetual police?', pp. 79–80.

157 Henry A. Kissinger, 'Kosovo and the vicissitudes of American foreign policy', in Buckley (ed.), *Kosovo: Contending Voices on Balkan Interventions*, p. 305.

158 'The Future of Kosovo: An indefinite NATO presence', *IISS Strategic Comments*, Vol. 6 Issue 1, January 2000.

159 Statement by NATO Secretary-General Lord Robertson followings the North Atlantic Council decision to launch Operation Essential Harvest, NATO HQ, Brussels, 22 August 2001.

160 'Bin Laden and the Balkans: the politics of anti-terrorism', International Crisis Group Report, 9 November 2001.

161 'Back to the Balkans', *Jane's Intelligence Digest*, 16 Aug 2002.

162 Allin, *NATO's Balkan Interventions*, p. 9.

163 O'Neil, *Kosovo: An Unfinished Peace*.

164 'Time running out to stop Kosovo's descent into violence', *Guardian*, 27 January 2005.

165 Mandelbaum, 'A Perfect Failure', pp. 2–9.

166 Dowd, 'NATO after Kosovo'.

167 Human Rights Watch, *Civilian Death Toll in NATO's Air Campaign*, February 2000.

5 THE AFGHAN CAMPAIGN AND THE WAR ON TERRORISM

1 An earlier version of this chapter appeared as 'Unravelling the war on terrorism: A risk management exercise in war clothing', *Security Dialogue*, Vol. 33 No. 2, June 2002. I am grateful for permission from SAGE Publications, London, UK to reproduce certain sections of the article.

2 See Max Boot, 'This victory may haunt us', *Wall Street Journal*, 14 November 2001.

3 'Bush tones down talk of winning terror war', *Washington Post*, 31 August 2004.

4 Giles Andreani, 'The war on terror: Good cause, wrong concept', *Survival*, Vol. 46 No. 4, Winter 2004–05, p. 31.

5 Andreani, 'The war on terror', p. 37.

6 Michael Byers, 'Terror and the future of international law', in Ken Booth and Tim Dunne (eds), *Worlds in Collision: Terror and the Future of Global Order*, Basingstoke: Palgrave Macmillan, 2002, p. 124.

7 Kurt M. Campbell, 'Globalisation's first war?', *Washington Quarterly*, Winter 2002, Vol. 25 No. 1, pp. 7–14.

8 Michael Clarke, 'Unpredictable', *World Today*, Vol. 57 No. 11, November 2001, pp. 7–9.

9 Andreani, 'The war on terror'.

10 Susan Sontag, 'Real battles and empty metaphors', *New York Times*, 10 Septmber 2002.

11 Department of Defence (DoD) News Briefing – Secretary Rumsfeld, 20 September 2001.

12 Quoted in Neil King Jr. and Jim VandeHei, 'Allies hope antiterror effort won't ignore local fights', *Wall Street Journal*, 26 September 2001.

13 Jonathan Stevenson, 'Pragmatic Counter-terrorism', *Survival*, Vol. 43 No. 4, Winter 2001–2002, pp. 35–48.

14 Paul Pillar, *Terrorism and US Foreign Policy*, Washington DC: Brookings Institution Press, 2001, p. 29.

15 Michael Ignatieff, 'It's war – but it doesn't have to be dirty', *The Guardian*, 1 October 2001.

16 For this issue, see David Tucker, *Skirmishes at the edge of empire: The United States and international terrorism*, Westport: Praeger, 1997.

17 Cited in Tucker, *Skirmishes at the Edge of Empire*, p. 34.

18 Michael Howard, 'What's in a name?: How to fight terrorism', *Foreign Affairs*, Vol. 81 No. 1, January/February 2002, pp. 22–35.

19 Don Melvin, 'Enemy, victory hard to define', *Atlanta Journal-Constitution*, 18 September 2001.

20 Quoted in Melvin, 'Enemy, victory hard to define'.

21 Howard, 'What's in a name? How to fight terrorism'.

22 Ian O. Lesser, Bruce Hoffman, John Arquilla, David F. Ronfeldt, Michele Zanini, Brian Michael Jenkins, *Countering the New Terrorism*, Santa Monica: RAND, 1999, p. 46.

23 Lesser et al., *Countering the New Terrorism*, p. 70; Daniel Pipes, 'War, not crime: Time for a paradigm shift', *National Review*, 1 October 2001; Caleb Carr, 'Terrorism as warfare', *World Policy Journal*, Vol. XIII, No. 4, Winter 1996–97, pp. 1–13.

24 L. P. Bremer, 'A new strategy for the new face of terrorism', in *The National Interest*, No. 65, 2001.

25 Colin McInnes, 'A different kind of war? September 11 and the United States' Afghan war', *Review of International Studies*, Vol. 29 No. 2, April 2003, pp. 165–85.

26 Stephen Biddle, 'Afghanistan and the future of warfare', *Foreign Affairs*, Vol. 82 No. 2, March/April 2003, pp. 32, 46.

27 Andrew Bacevich, *American Empire*, Cambridge, MA: Harvard University Press, 2002, p. 236.

28 Remarks by the President to the Opening Session of the 53rd United Nations General Assembly, 21 September 1998.

29 Prepared Statement for the House and Senate Armed Services Committees: 'Building a military for the 21st century', 3–4 October 2001.

30 See David Martin Jones and M. L. R. Smith, 'Franchising Terror', *The World Today*, Vol. 57 No. 10, October 2001, pp. 10–12.

31 *National Strategy for Combating Terrorism*, Washington DC: The White House, February 2003, p. 7.

32 Quoted in Jim Garamone, 'Intelligence chief calls Sept 11 first move of post-Cold War struggle', *American Forces Press Service*, 19 March 2002.

33 'President Bush, Colombia President Uribe discuss terrorism', *Office of the Press Secretary*, 25 September 2002.

34 Pillar, *Terrorism and US Foreign Policy*, p. 141.

35 Wolfowitz quoted in Linda D. Kozaryn, 'Wolfowitz says NATO ties are essential', *American Forces Press Service*, 2 Feb 2002.

36 UK Ministry of Defence, 'Public discussion on the new chapter for the Strategic Defence Review', *http://www.mod.uk/issues/sdr/new_chapter/glance.htm* (accessed 1 April 2003), London, February 2002.

37 Zygmunt Bauman, *Society Under Siege*, Cambridge: Polity Press, 2002, p. 101.

38 Kenneth N. Waltz, 'The continuity of international politics', in Booth and Dunne (eds), *Worlds in Collision: Terror and the future of global order*, p. 349.

39 See Bruce Hoffman, 'Terrorism by weapons of mass destruction: A reassessment of the threat', in Carolyn W. Pumphrey (ed.), *Transnational Threats: Blending law enforcement and military strategies*, conference proceedings, Carlisle: Strategic Studies Institute, November 2000, p. 95.

40 *National Strategy for Combating Terrorism*, Washington DC: The White House, February 2003, p. 16.

41 Testimony before Senate Committee on Intelligence, 16 February 2005.

42 O'Hanlon quoted in Bill Miller, 'Study urges focus on terrorism with high fatalities, cost', *Washington Post*, 29 Apr 2002.

43 Ridge cited in 'US tries to guess next terror target', *Guardian Unlimited*, 3 November 2001, *http://www.guardian.co.uk/uslatest/story/0,1282,-1287584,00.html* (accessed 2 May 2003).

44 Rumsfeld quoted in 'Terror prompts huge US military revamp', *BBC News Online*, 1 February 2002, *http://news.bbc.co.uk/1/hi/world/americas/1795102.stm* (accessed 8 April 2003).

45 Edith M. Lederer, 'US rates chance of Al Qaeda WMD attack', *Associated Press*, 9 June 2003, http://www.jsonline.com/news/nat/ap/jun03/ap-un-us-terrorism060903.asp (accessed 20 January 2005).

46 Pillar, *Terrorism and US Foreign Policy*, p. 229.

47 George W. Bush, *Weekly Radio Address*, 15 February 2003, Office of the Press Secretary.

48 Report of the National Commission on Terrorism, *Countering the Changing Threat of International Terrorism*, June 2000, *http://www.fas.org/irp/threat/commission.html* (accessed 16 April 2003).

49 Remarks at Defence Ministers Meeting of the North Atlantic Council, Brussels, Belgium, 06 June 2002.

50 For contrasting views see Daniel Pipes, 'War, not crime: Towards a new paradigm', *National Review*, 1 October 2001; Vaughan Lowe, 'Clear and present danger: responses to terrorism', *International Comparative Law Quarterly*, Vol. 54, January 2005.

51 Former State Department Legal Advisor Michael Scharf's contribution to 'Is this a new kind of war? September 11 and its aftermath', 7 October 2001, *Crimes of War Project*, *http://www.crimesofwar.org/expert/paradigm-scharf.html* (accessed 12 May 2003).

52 Text of a letter from the President to the Speaker of the House of Representatives and President Pro Tempore of the Senate, 22 August 1998; *http://clinton6.nara.gov/1998/08/1998-08-22-text-of-a-letter-on-afghanistan-and-sudan-strikes.html* (accessed 15 May 2003).

53 Andrew J. Bacevich, *American Empire*, Cambridge, MA: Harvard University Press, 2002, pp. 111, 153.

54 Letter dated 7 October 2001 from the Permanent Representative of the United States of America to the United Nations addressed to the President of the Security Council, S/2001/946.

55 Statement for the record on the War on terrorism, before the Congressional Select Committee on Intelligence of the US Senate, Washington DC, 11 Feb 2003.

56 See Walter Laqueur, 'Left, right and beyond – the changing face of terror', in James F. Hoge and Gideon Rose (eds), *How Did This Happen? Terrorism and the New War*, New York: Public Affairs, 2001, p. 81.

57 Gary Hart and Warren Rudman (Co-Chairs), *America Still Unprepared, Still in Danger*, Report of an independent task force sponsored by the Council on Foreign Relations, Washington DC, 22 October 2002, p. 10.

58 Prime Minister's statement on military action in Afghanistan, 7 October 2001.

59 Address to the Nation by the President, 20 August 1998.

60 Press Briefing by Secretary of State Madeleine Albright and National Security Adviser Sandy Berger, 20 August 1998, *http://clinton6.nara.gov/1998/08/1998–08–20-press-briefing-by-albright-and-berger.html* (accessed 19 April 2003).

61 See 'Secretary Rumsfeld Interview with the Telegraph', *DoD News Transcripts*, 23 February 2002; and Kathleen T. Rhem, 'Coalition turning up the pressure, but battle not over', *American Forces Press Service*, 6 March 2002.

62 US Under-Secretary of State for Political Affairs Thomas Pickering, US Information Agency Foreign Press Centre Briefing, Washington DC, 25 August 1998.

63 Michael O'Hanlon, 'The case for a careful military response', *Brookings Institution Analysis Paper 1: America's response to terrorism*, 25 September 2001.

64 Anthony Clark Arend, 'International Law and the preemptive use of force', *Washington Quarterly*, Vol. 26 No. 3, Spring 2003, p. 99.

65 Michael Evans, 'Forces take on anti-terror role', *The Times*, 15 February 2002.

66 Remarks by President Bush, 'President calls for quick passage of defence bill', Office of the Press Secretary, 15 March 2002.

67 Jeremy Paxman interviews Colin Powell, *BBC Newsnight*, 21 September 2001, *http://news.bbc.co.uk/hi/english/events/newsnight/newsid_1563000/1563074.stm* (accessed 22 May 2003).

68 Elisabeth Bumiller, 'Government to cover most costs of insurance losses in terrorism', *New York Times*, 27 Nov 2002.

69 *America Still Unprepared, Still in Danger*, Report of an independent task force sponsored by the Council on Foreign Relations, Washington DC, 22 Oct 2002, p. 32.

70 Anthony Browne, 'UN's smallpox terror alert', *The Observer*, 21 October 2001.

71 'Governments warned on germ warfare attacks', *Ananova*, 25 September 2001, *http://www.ananova.com/news/story/sm_407043.html* (accessed 11 April 2003).

72 Judith Miller, 'US is deploying monitor system for germ attack', *New York Times*, 21 Jan 2003.

73 Edward F. Mickolus, 'How do we know we're winning the war against terrorists? Issues in measurement', *Studies in Conflict and Terrorism*, Vol. 25 No. 3, May–June 2002, pp. 151–60.

74 'Responsibility for the terrorist atrocities in the United States, 11 September 2001 – an updated account', 10 Downing Street, London, *http://www.number-10.gov.uk/output/Page3682.asp* (accessed 26 May 2003).

75 Jonathan Charney, 'The use of force against terrorism and international law', *American Journal of International Law*, Vol. 95 No. 4, October 2001, p. 836.

76 Quotes cited in David von Drehle, 'Uncertainty is sea where all swim', *Washington Post*, 16 Feb 2003.

77 Quoted in Ian Black, 'Rumsfeld tells NATO to face up to terror danger', *Guardian*, 7 June 2002.

78 Remarks to the National Network of Electro-Optical Manufacturing Technologies Conference, 9 February 1998, Tuscon, Arizona.

79 Press Gaggle by Ari Fleischer aboard Air Force One, 5 November 2002, *Office of the Press Secretary*.

80 Richard Norton-Taylor, 'Security services switch to early swoop policy', *The Guardian*, 18 November 2002.

81 This controversial programme was initially called Total Information Awareness until pressure from Congress banned it from spying on Americans and the Pentagon changed it to its present name.

82 Hart and Rudman (Co-Chairs), *America Still Unprepared, Still in Danger*, p. 3.

83 'Plain speaking: the US President talks about plans for New Year, race and prospect of war with Iraq', *US News and World Report*, 13 December 2002.

84 Bacevich, *American Empire*, p. 153.

85 See Mark Bowden, 'The Kabul-ki Dance', *The Atlantic Monthly*, November 2002.

86 Daniel Byman, 'Are we winning the war on terrorism?', *Brookings Institution Middle East Memo #1*, 23 May 2003.

87 Rice cited in 'Bin Laden search brings frustration', *Guardian Unlimited*, 15 February 2002, *http://www.guardian.co.uk/worldlatest/story/0,1280,-1521784,00. html* (accessed 22 April 2003).

88 'President Bush holds Press Conference', 13 March 2002, *Office of the Press Secretary*.

89 Adm. Natter quoted in 'USS Roosevelt returns home', *Washington Post*, 27 March 2002.

90 Remarks of Mike McCurry to the Media Pool, *Office of the Press Secretary*, 20 August 1998.

91 Lesser et al., *Countering the New Terrorism*, p. 132; Walter Pincus, 'Al Qaeda to survive Bin Laden, panel told', *Washington Post*, 19 December 2001; Paul Dibb, 'The future of international coalitions: how useful? How manageable?' *The Washington Quarterly*, Vol. 25 No. 2, (Spring 2002), pp. 131–44.

92 'Secretary Rumsfeld Television interview with MSNBC', *DoD News Transcripts*, 28 March 2002.

93 Remarks at photo opportunity with Prime Minister Koizumi of Japan, 25 September 2001.

94 Quoted in Kathleen T. Rhem, 'Intelligence, not prosecution is US first priority with Padilla', *American Forces Press Service*, 11 June 2002.

95 Brian Jenkins, *Countering Al Qaeda*, Santa Monica: RAND, 2002, Summary, p. ix.

96 Michael Kenney, 'From Pablo to Osama: Counter-terrorism lessons from the war on drugs', *Survival*, Vol. 45 No. 3, Autumn 2003, p. 187.

97 Cited in Christopher Harmon, *Terrorism Today*, London: Frank Cass, 2000, p. 257.

98 Byman, 'Are we winning the war on terrorism?'.

99 Quoted in Walter Pincus, 'Less intelligence role seen for security department', *Washington Post*, 18 July 2002.

100 Geoff Hoon, *The New Chapter: A Blueprint for Reform*, Lecture at the Royal United Services Institute, 30 July 2002, London.

101 Ian O. Lesser, 'Countering the new terrorism: implications for strategy', in Lesser et al., *Countering the New Terrorism*, p. 134.

102 *National Strategy for Combating Terrorism*, Washington DC: The White House, February 2003, pp. 6–11.

103 DoD News Briefing – Secretary Rumsfeld and Gen. Myers, 09 October 2001; Secretary Powell interview with Jeremy Paxman, BBC Online, 21 September 2001.

104 Quoted in Peter Ford, 'Where's Osama and how much should we care?', *Christian Science Monitor*, 27 June 2002.

105 Quoted in Carlotta Gall, 'US-led Afghan sweep yields unclear results', *New York Times*, 5 March 2003.

106 See 'Added Forces Strengthen Horn of Africa Task Force', *American Forces Press Service*, 13 June 2003.

107 Quoted in 'Pentagon seeking new access pacts for Africa bases', *New York Times*, 5 July 2003.

108 See Lesser et al., *Countering the New Terrorism*, p. 134; Steven Simon and Daniel Benjamin, 'The Terror', *Survival*, Vol. 43 No. 4, (Winter 2001), pp. 5–18; Ray Takeyh and Nikolas Gvosdev, 'Do terrorist networks need a home?', *Washington Quarterly*, Vol. 25 No. 3, Summer 2002, pp. 97–108.

109 *Strategic Survey 2002/2003: An Evaluation and Forecast of World Affairs*, Oxford: Oxford University Press for the IISS, May 2003, pp. 9–10.

110 Interview with Tommy Franks, ABC TV, *This Week with Sam Donaldson and Cokie Roberts*, 4 November 2001.

111 Remarks at photo opportunity with Prime Minister Koizumi of Japan, 25 September 2001.

112 'Belated help for Afghanistan', *New York Times*, Editorial, 9 August 2003.

113 Quoted in Richard Crockatt, *America Embattled*, London: Routledge, 2003, p. 152.

114 Testimony of US Secretary of Defence Donald Rumsfeld before the Senate Armed Services Committee on progress in Afghanistan, Washington DC, 31 July 2002.

115 Jeffrey Record, 'Collapsed Countries, Casualty Dread and the New American Way of War', *Parameters*, Summer 2002, pp. 4–23.

116 *National Security Strategy of the United States of America*, Washington DC: The White House, September 2002, Introduction.

117 Michael Ignatieff, 'Nation-building lite', *New York Times Magazine*, 28 July 2002.

118 Simon Chesterman, 'Bush, the United Nations and nation-building', *Survival*, Vol. 46 No. 1, Spring 2004.

119 See Record, 'Collapsed countries, casualty dread and the new American way of war', pp. 4–23.

120 *The National Security Strategy of the United States*, Washington DC: The White House, 20 September 2002, Chapter III.

121 Hoon, *The New Chapter: A Blueprint for Reform*.

122 *National Strategy for Combating Terrorism*, Washington DC: The White House, February 2003, Conclusion p. 29.

123 See an in-depth analysis on defining success by Daniel Byman, 'Scoring the war on terrorism', *The National Interest*, Issue 72, Summer 2003.

124 DoD News Briefing – Secretary Rumsfeld and Gen. Myers, 9 October 2001.

125 Rudi Williams, 'War will continue until Americans live without fear', *American Forces Press Service*, 29 October 2001.

126 Quoted in Robert Kagan and William Kristol, 'Getting Serious', *Weekly Standard*, 19 November 2001.

127 Dr Condoleezza Rice discusses President's National Security Strategy, Waldorf Astoria Hotel, New York, *Office of the Press Secretary*, 1 October 2002.

128 Melvin, 'Enemy, victory hard to define'.

129 'Bush backtracks on terrorism remark', *Washington Post*, 31 August 2004.

130 DoD News Briefing – Secretary Rumsfeld and Gen. Myers, 8 April 2002.

131 DoD News Briefing – Secretary Rumsfeld and Gen. Myers, 3 September 2002.
132 Mickolus, 'How do we know we're winning the war against terrorists? Issues in measurement', p. 152.
133 Rudi Williams, 'Wolfowitz: Al Qaeda is no snake but like a disease', *American Forces Press Service*, 10 July 2002.
134 Geoff Hoon, *The New Chapter to the Strategic Defence Review: A Progress Report*, Speech to the City Forum Roundtable, 23 May 2002.
135 Pillar, *Terrorism and US Foreign Policy*, p. 232.
136 Kurt M. Campbell and Michele A. Flournoy, *To Prevail: an American Strategy for the Campaign Against Terrorism*, Washington DC: CSIS Press, November 2001, p. 300.
137 John Ashcroft speaking on 'Fox News Sunday', 3 August 2003.
138 Jeremy Paxman interviews Colin Powell, *BBC Online*, 21 September 2001, *http://news.bbc.co.uk/hi/english/events/newsnight/newsid_1563000/1563074.stm* (accessed 24 May 2003).
139 Pillar, *Terrorism and US Foreign Policy*, pp. 5–6.
140 Jeremy Shapiro and Benedicte Suzan, 'The French experience of counter-terrorism', *Survival*, Vol. 45 No. 1, Spring 2003, p. 88.
141 Jonathan Stevenson, Review Article, 'Stephen Flynn, *America the vulnerable: how our government is failing to protect us from terrorism*', *Survival*, Vol. 46 No. 2, 2004.
142 Press Briefing by Secretary of State Madeleine Albright and National Security Adviser Sandy Berger, 20 August 1998.
143 *National Strategy for Homeland Security*, Washington DC: Department of Homeland Security, July 2002, p. 64.
144 Quoted in Mark Leibovich, 'The image of security', *Washington Post*, 22 May 2003.
145 'Bush pledges to hunt terrorists, calls for quick budget approval', *American Forces Press Service*, 15 March 2002.
146 Byman, 'Are we winning the war on terrorism?'.
147 *Strategic Survey 2002/2003*, pp. 8–11.
148 Eva Bertram and Kenneth Sharpe, 'The unwinnable drug war: What Clausewitz would tell us', *World Policy Journal*, Vol. XIII No. 4, Winter 1996–97, pp. 41–53.
149 'Congress presses Bush on terror war', *Associated Press*, 4 March 2002.
150 Presidential Address to the Nation, 7 October 2001; 'Address to a Joint Session of Congress and the American People', 20 September 2001, *Office of the Press Secretary*.
151 Clinton cited in Pillar, *Terrorism and US Foreign Policy*, p. 1.
152 Walter Laqueur, *No End to War: Terrorism in the Twenty-First Century*, London: Continuum Press, 2003.
153 Blair quoted in 'a World Transformed', *The Times*, 9 March 2002; Ridge cited in Bill Miler, 'Ridge close to unveiling new warning system', *Washington Post*, 9 March 2002.
154 David Rappoport, 'The Fourth Wave: September 11 in the History of Terrorism', *Current History*, Vol. 100 No. 650, December 2001, pp. 434–7.
155 Jessica Stern, 'The Protean Enemy', *Foreign Affairs*, Vol. 82 No. 4, July/August 2003, Web version, *http://www.foreignaffairs.org/20030701faessay15403/jessica-stern/the-protean-enemy.html* (accessed 29 May 2003).
156 Kenney, 'From Pablo to Osama: Counter-terrorism lessons from the war on drugs', p. 195.

157 Bruce Hoffman, 'The changing face of Al Qaeda and the global war on terrorism', *Studies in Conflict and Terrorism*, Vol. 27 No. 6, November–December 2004, pp. 549–50.
158 Hoffman, 'The changing face of Al Qaeda and the global war on terrorism', p. 556.

6 WAR ON IRAQ

1 Dana Allin and Steven Simon, 'America's Predicament', *Survival*, Vol. 46 No. 4, Winter 2004–05, p. 13.
2 Sia Spiliopoulou Akermark, 'Storms, foxes and nebulous legal arguments: twelve years of force against Iraq, 1991–2003', *International Comparative Law Quarterly*, Vol. 54, January 2005, p. 231.
3 David H. Dunn, 'Myths, motivations and "misunderestimations": the Bush Administration and Iraq', *International Affairs*, Vol. 79 No. 2, April 2003, pp. 279–97.
4 Robert Litwak, *Rogue States and US Foreign Policy: Containment After the Cold War*, Washington DC: Woodrow Wilson Centre Press, 2000, p. 105.
5 Testimony of Paul Wolfowitz, 'Nomination of Paul Wolfowitz to be Deputy Secretary of Defence', Senate Armed Services Committee, 27 February 2001.
6 'Forging a new Iraq policy', *Washington Post*, 4 March 2001.
7 Colin Powell quoted in CNN, *The Survival of Saddam Hussein*, 16 Jan 2001, *http://www.cnn.com/SPECIALS/2001/gulf. war/unfinished/war/index4.html* (accessed 15 April 2003); Remarks by President George W. Bush and President Vicente Fox in Joint Press Conference, *Office of the Press Secretary*, 16 Feb 2001.
8 Michael Klare, *Rogue States and Nuclear Outlaws*, New York: Hill and Wang, 1995, pp. 26–7.
9 Dunn, 'Myths, motivations and "misunderestimations"', p. 294.
10 Christoph Bluth, 'The British road to war: Bush, Blair and the decision to invade Iraq', *International Affairs*, Vol. 80 No. 5, 2004.
11 Condoleezza Rice quoted in David Sanger, 'Debate over attacking Iraq heats up', *New York Times*, 1 Sep 2002, and also *Avenging Terror*, Channel 4 (UK), 31 Aug 2002.
12 Quoted in Thom Shanker, 'Wage war but don't start one', *New York Times*, 24 Nov 2002.
13 Remarks at Tennessee State University, Nashville, Tennessee, 19 February 1998.
14 Andrew Bacevich, *American Empire*, Cambridge, MA: Harvard University Press, 2002, p. 152.
15 Floyd D. Spence, 'US policy toward Iraq', Hearing before the Committee of Armed Services, House of Representatives, 10 March 1999, H.A.S.C. No. 106–10, Washington DC: US Government Printing Office.
16 See 'US air raids in '02 prepared for war in Iraq', *New York Times*, 20 July 2003.
17 Michael Walzer, 'What a little war in Iraq could do', *New York Times*, 07 March 2003.
18 See Robert Samuelson, 'Rediscovering Risk', *Washington Post*, 22 October 2002.
19 Colonel Paul K. White, Airpower and a decade of containment, *Joint Force Quarterly*, No. 27, Winter 2000–01, p. 38.
20 MoD spokesman cited in 'RAF jets bomb Iraqi targets', *Ananova*, 10 August 2001, *http://www.ananova.com/news/story/sm_372069.html?menu=* (accessed 27 April, 2003).

21 See Daniel Byman and Matthew Waxman, *Confronting Iraq: US Policy and the Use of Force Since the Gulf War*, Santa Monica: RAND, 2000. Paul K. White, *Crises After the Storm: an Appraisal of US Air Operations Since the Persian Gulf War*, Washington DC: The Washington Institute for Near East Policy, 1999. Other contributions include Michael W. Isherwood, 'US Strategic Options for Iraq: Easier said than done', *Washington Quarterly*, Vol. 25 No. 2, Spring 2002, pp. 145–60.

22 Adam Roberts, 'Law and the use of force after Iraq', *Survival*, Vol. 45 No. 2, Summer 2003, pp. 31–57.

23 Quoted in 'For old friends, Iraq bares a deep rift', *New York Times*, 14 February 2003.

24 For instance Bob Woodward, *Plan of Attack*, New York: Simon & Schuster, 2004, also John Kampfner, *Blair's Wars*, London: Free Press, 2004. Also see Bluth, 'The British road to war: Bush, Blair and the decision to invade Iraq'.

25 *National Security Strategy of the United States*, Washington, DC: The White House, 2002, Chapter V.

26 Daniel Byman, 'After the storm: US policy toward Iraq since 1991', *Political Science Quarterly*, Vol. 115 No. 4, Winter 2000–01, p. 495.

27 Anthony Cordesman, *Iraq: Sanctions and Beyond*, Boulder, CO: 1997, p. 6.

28 Daniel Byman, Kenneth Pollack, Gideon Rose, 'The Rollback Fantasy', *Foreign Affairs*, Vol. 78 No. 1, January/February 1999, pp. 24–41.

29 Richard Haass, 'Containing Saddam', *Washington Times*, 10 November 1998.

30 Kenneth M. Pollack, *The Threatening Storm: The Case for Invading Iraq*, New York: Random House, 2002.

31 John Mearsheimer and Stephen Walt, 'Keeping Saddam Hussein in a box', *New York Times*, 2 February 2003.

32 'President Bush, Colombia President Uribe discuss terrorism', *Office of the Press Secretary*, 25 September 2002.

33 Prepared Testimony before the House and Senate Armed Services Committee regarding Iraq, Washington DC, 18–19 September 2002.

34 Sandy Berger, 'Building Blocks to Iraq', *Washington Post*, 1 August 2002; Jack Straw, BBC Radio 4 'Today' Programme, 22 August 2002.

35 Jeffrey Record, 'Threat confusion and its penalties', *Survival*, Vol. 46 No. 2, Summer 2004, p. 52.

36 I thank Christopher Coker for discussions on this issue. Also see research project on International Risk Policy at Otto Suhr Institute, Free University Berlin, Germany.

37 President Bush delivers graduation speech at West Point, *Office of the Press Secretary*, 1 June 2002.

38 Tony Blair, Transcript of evidence given to the House of Commons Liaison Committee, 16 July 2002, available at *http://www.publications.parliament.uk/pa/cm200102/cmselect/cmliaisn/1065/106501.htm* (accessed 2 June 2003).

39 Testimony at Budget Hearing before Senate Foreign Relations Committee, 8 March 2001.

40 Bluth, 'The British road to war: Bush, Blair and the decision to invade Iraq', p. 877.

41 Prepared Testimony before the House and Senate Armed Services Committee regarding Iraq, 18–19 September 2002.

42 Pollack, *The Threatening Storm: The Case for Invading Iraq*, pp. 148–9.

43 Thomas E. Ricks, 'Some top military brass favor status quo in Iraq', *Washington Post*, 28 July 2002.

44 Paul Pillar, *Terrorism and US Foreign Policy*, Washington DC: Brookings Institution Press, 2001, p. 104.

45 See Daniel Byman, 'Iraq After Saddam', *The Washington Quarterly*, Vol. 24 No. 4, (Autumn 2001) pp. 151–62.

45 See Daniel Byman, 'Iraq After Saddam', *The Washington Quarterly*, Vol. 24 No. 4, (Autumn 2001) pp. 151–62.
46 Lawrence Freedman, 'War in Iraq: Selling the threat', *Survival*, Vol. 46 No. 4, Summer 2004, p. 9.
47 *Strategic Survey 2002/03*, Oxford: Oxford University Press for the IISS, May 2003, p. 65.
48 Pollack, *The Threatening Storm*, p. 180.
49 Toby Dodge and Steven Simon, Introduction, in Toby Dodge and Steven Simon (eds), *Iraq at the crossroads: state and society in the shadow of regime change*, Oxford: Oxford University Press for the IISS, January 2003, p. 14.
50 Freedman, 'War in Iraq: Selling the threat', p. 17.
51 Statement to Parliament, 18 March 2003.
52 See Dana Priest and Walter Pincus, 'Bush certainty on Iraq arms went beyond analysts' view', *Washington Post*, 7 June 2003.
53 *National Security Strategy of the United States*, Chapter V, Washington DC: The White House, September 2002.
54 Quoted in Andrew Sullivan, 'Clinton talked a good war – Bush has to fight it', *Sunday Times*, 9 March 2003.
55 See Tom Friedman, 'The war over the war', *New York Times*, 03 August 2003.
56 'Bush Administration in denial about lack of Iraqi WMD: Kay', *Agence France Presse*, 7 Oct 2004. http://www.turkishpress.com/news.asp?id=30023 (accessed 11 June 2005)
57 President says Saddam Hussein must leave Iraq within 48 hours, 17 March 2003, *Office of the Press Secretary*.
58 Remarks by Deputy Defence Secretary Paul Wolfowitz, Fletcher Conference, Washington DC, 16 October 2002.
59 Department of Defence (DoD) News Briefing – Secretary Rumsfeld and Gen. Myers, 3 September 2002.
60 Prepared Testimony before the House and Senate Armed Services Committee regarding Iraq, Washington D.C., 18–19 September 2002.
61 Vice President speaks at VFW 103rd National Convention, *Office of the Press Secretary*, 26 August 2002; DoD News Briefing – Secretary Rumsfeld, 03 September 2002.
62 Tony Blair cited in *Campaign Against Terrorism: A Coalition Update*, 11 March 2002, *http://www.number-10.gov.uk/output/page4591.asp* (accessed 26 May 2003).
63 President George Bush discusses Iraq in National Press Conference 6 Mar 2003, *Office of the Press Secretary*.
64 Prime Minister's statement to the House of Commons on US/UK airstrikes on Iraq, 17 December 1998.
65 President Clinton's statement on air strikes against Iraq, 16 December 1998, *Office of the Press Secretary*.
66 William A. Galston, 'Why a first strike will surely backfire', *Washington Post*, 16 June 2002.
67 See US Department of Defense, *DOD Dictionary of Military and Associated Terms*, Joint Publication 1–02, Washington DC: DoD, 12 April 2001, pp. 333, 336.
68 Dr Condoleezza Rice discusses President's National Security Strategy, *Office of the Press Secretary*, 1 October 2002.
69 Walter B. Slocombe, 'Force, pre-emption and legitimacy', *Survival*, Vol. 45 No. 1, Spring 2003, p. 125.
70 Anthony Clark Arend, 'International law and the preemptive use of force', *Washington Quarterly*, Vol. 26 No. 2, Spring 2003, p. 97.

71 House of Commons Select Committee 2002/2003 on Foreign Affairs Second Report, *Disarming Iraq*, 19 December 2002, Line 157.

72 For a detailed discussion of pre-emption and prevention, see Jeffrey Record, 'The Bush Doctrine and War with Iraq', *Parameters: US Army War College Quarterly*, Vol. XXXIII No. 1, Spring 2003, pp. 4–21; Lawrence Freedman, 'Prevention, not preemption', *Washington Quarterly*, Spring 2003, Vol. 26 No. 2, p. 105.

73 Francois Heisbourg, 'A Work in Progress: the Bush Doctrine and its consequences', *Washington Quarterly*, Vol. 26 No. 2, Spring 2003, p. 75.

74 For these issues, see Marc Weller, 'The US, Iraq and the use of force in a unipolar world', *Survival*, Vol. 41, No. 4, Winter 1999–2000, pp. 81–100.

75 Press remarks on military attack on Iraq, 17 December 1998.

76 James. J. Wirtz, 'Counter proliferation, conventional counterforce and nuclear war', *Journal of Strategic Studies*, Vol. 23, No. 1, March 2000, pp. 5–25.

77 Slocombe, 'Force, pre-emption and legitimacy', p. 125.

78 James Rubin, State Department Presentation on Iraq, 29 February 2000.

79 Text of letter available at *http://www.nci.org/c/c81199.htm* (accessed 18 May 2003).

80 Robin Grove-White, Panel remarks on *Do we live in a culture of fear?*, Goodenough College and 21st Century Trust Conference on Risk, 11–12 Apr 2002, London. For Rumsfeld's use of 'unknown unknowns', see DoD News Briefing – Secretary Rumsfeld and General Myers, 12 February 2002.

81 Remarks at the Defence Ministers Meeting of the North Atlantic Council, NATO HQ, 6 June 2002, *http://www.nato.int/docu/speech/2002/s020606d.htm* (accessed 28 April 2003); and DoD News Briefing, 12 February 2002.

82 *National Security Strategy of the United States of America*, Washington DC: The White House, September 2002, Chapter V.

83 Prepared Testimony before the House and Senate Armed Services Committee regarding Iraq, Washington D.C., 18–19 September 2002.

84 Sen. Graham quoted in Joby Warrick, 'In Assessing Iraq's arsenal, the reality is uncertainty', *Washington Post*, 31 July 2002; Cordesman quoted in James Dao, 'Senators want to know the unknowable on Iraq, and time is running out', *New York Times*, 3 August 2002.

85 *Iraq's Weapons of Mass Destruction: The Assessment of the British Government*, London: The Stationery Office, 24 September 2002.

86 President Bush discusses Iraq, *Office of the Press Secretary*, 10 August 2002.

87 President Bush outlines Iraqi threat, *Office of the Press Secretary*, 7 October 2002.

88 Richard Perle, 'Why the West must strike first against Saddam Hussein', *Daily Telegraph*, 9 August 2002.

89 Jack Beatty, 'In the name of God', *Atlantic Monthly*, 5 March 2003.

90 Hans Blix, *Disarming Iraq*, New York: Pantheon Books, 2004, pp. 111–16.

91 US Senate Select Committee on Intelligence, *Report on the US Intelligence Community's Pre-War Intelligence Assessments on Iraq*, Washington DC, July 2004.

92 Testimony to Hearing of the Senate Armed Services Committee, *Iraqi Weapons of Mass Destruction Programs*, 28 January 2004.

93 Michael V. Deaver, *Disarming Iraq: Monitoring Power and Resistance*, Westport: Praeger, 2001, pp. 5, 20.

94 Alexander Bernard, 'Lessons from Iraq and Bosnia on the theory and practice of no-fly zones', *Journal of Strategic Studies*, Vol. 27 No. 3, September 2004, pp. 456, 464.

95 Philip Gibbons, 'US No-fly zones: To what end?', Washington Institute for Near East Policy, *Policy Watch*, No. 632, 1 July 2002.
96 Keith Hall, Remarks to the National Network of Electro-Optical Manufacturing Technologies Conference, 9 February 1998, Tuscon, Arizona.
97 'Statement by the Prime Minister on Iraq', 17 December 1998.
98 Remarks on Iraq by President Clinton to Pentagon personnel, 17 February 1998, *Office of the Press Secretary*.
99 Remarks by President George W. Bush and President Vicente Fox of Mexico in Joint Press Conference, *Office of the Press Secretary*, 16 February 2001.
100 Quoted in Kathleen T. Rhem, 'US, Pentagon attention on Iraq is long-standing', *American Forces Press Service*, 12 February 2002.
101 In May 1999, US F-15Es mistakenly bombed shepherds after analysts misinterpreted water troughs for missile launchers.
102 Gregory Gause III, 'Getting it Backward on Iraq', *Foreign Affairs*, May/June 1999, pp. 54–65. For more sceptical views, see Patrick Clawson, 'Inspections in Iraq: A test for Saddam, not a good solution for WMD', *The Washington Institute for Near East Policy*, Policy Watch 590, 20 December 2001.
103 For analysis of Saddam's tactics, see Deaver, *Disarming Iraq*.
104 John Springer, UN Panel on Iraq recommends 'reinforced' monitoring regime, *Arms Control Today*, March 1999.
105 For detailed analysis of intelligence estimates on Iraq, see 'In Sketchy data, trying to gauge the Iraqi threat', *New York Times*, 20 July 2003.
106 Edward Luttwak, *Strategy: The Logic of Peace and War*, Cambridge, MA: Harvard University Press, 2001, pp. 76 and 201.
107 White, 'Airpower and a decade of containment', p. 38.
108 See one recent attempt to rectify this. Bernard, 'Lessons from Iraq and Bosnia on the theory and practice of no-fly zones', p. 454.
109 Remarks by President Bush and President Vicente Fox of Mexico in joint press conference, *Office of the Press Secretary*, 16 February 2001.
110 Thomas Barnett and Henry H. Gaffney, Jr, 'Top ten post-Cold War Myths', *US Naval Institute Proceedings*, Vol. 172/2/1, 176, February 2001, pp. 32–8.
111 See Howard Kaygill, 'Perpetual Police? Kosovo and the elision of police and military violence', *European Journal of Social Theory*, Vol. 4 No. 1, February 2001, pp. 74–6.
112 The threat of force and aggressive inspections could also have proved a model of multilateral action. See Allin and Simon, 'America's Predicament', p. 11.
113 An idea also raised by Francois Heisbourg, *Warfare*, London: Phoenix, 1997, p. 14. 'Virtual' consent is suggested in Michael Ignatieff, *Virtual War: Kosovo and Beyond*, London: Chatto and Windus, 2000, p. 138.
114 See Ofra Bengio, 'Couldn't be worse?: Iraq after Saddam', *The National Interest*, Issue 66, (Winter 2001–2002).
115 Quoted in Judith Yaphe, 'Iraq: the exception to the rule', *Washington Quarterly*, Vol. 24 No. 1, Winter 2001, p. 126.
116 Cited in Avigdor Haselkorn, *The Continuing Storm: Iraq, Poisonous Weapons and Deterrence*, New Haven: Yale University Press, 1998, Chronology, p. xxii.
117 Cited in Robert S. Litwak, *Rogue States and US Foreign Policy: Containment after the Cold War*, p. 139.
118 Quoted in Barbara Crossette, 'For Iraq, a Doghouse with Many Rooms,' *New York Times*, 23 November 1997.
119 Morton H. Halperin and Geoffrey Kemp, *A Report on US Policy Options toward Iraq*, Council On Foreign Relations, June 2001.
120 Condoleezza Rice quoted in Mike Peacock, 'Key Bush Aide says Saddam must be dealt with', *Reuters*, 15 August 2002.

121 Jessica Matthews, 'The Wrong Target', *Washington Post*, 4 March 2002.
122 Colin Powell, NBC's 'Meet the Press', 20 October 2002; Interview with *USA Today* Editorial Board, 2 October 2002.
123 'President Bush outlines Iraq threat', Cincinnati, 7 October 2002; 'President discusses foreign policy matters with NATO Secretary', 21 October 2002, *Office of the Press Secretary*.
124 Quoted in Michael Evans, 'The last stand of Saddam', *The Times*, 5 April 2003.
125 Quoted in Julian Borger, 'General admits chemical weapons intelligence was wrong', *The Guardian*, 31 May 2003.
126 Philip H. Gordon, 'Bush's Middle East Vision', *Survival*, Vol. 45 No. 1, Spring 2003, p. 155.
127 Quoted in Dana Milbank, 'For Bush, war defines presidency', *Washington Post*, 9 March 2003.
128 Secretary of Defence Cohen's DoD News Briefings, 18 and 21 December 1998.
129 Address to the Nation, 16 December 1998, *Office of the Press Secretary*.
130 Remarks at Y2K and Social Security Event, 28 December 1998, *Office of the Press Secretary*; Bernard, 'Lessons from Iraq and Bosnia on the theory and practice of no-fly zones', p. 467.
131 Formal evidence given to House of Commons Foreign Affairs Select Committee Second Report, 'Foreign Policy Aspects of the War against terrorism', Para104, HC196, published 19 December 2002, London.
132 General Myers Press Conference, Bagram Air Base, Afghanistan, 30 July 2003.
133 Simon Chesterman, 'Bush, the United Nations and nation-building', *Survival*, Vol. 46 No. 1, Spring 2004.
134 Quoted in Thomas E. Ricks, 'Top Iraqis believed targeted in US strike', *Washington Post*, 23 June 2003.
135 Tom Friedman, 'Repairing the world', *New York Times*, 16 March 2003.
136 General Tommy Franks, Address to the House Armed Services Committee, Washington DC, 11 July 2003.
137 'Remarks by the President at Graduation exercise of the United States military academy', West Point, New York, 1 June 2002, *Office of the Press Secretary*.
138 Chesterman, 'Bush, the United Nations and nation-building'.
139 James Dobbins cited in Allin and Simon, 'America's Predicament', p. 19.
140 G. John Ikenberry, 'The end of the neo-conservative moment', *Survival*, Vol. 46 No. 1, Spring 2004, p. 11.
141 See Eugene J. Caroll Jr, 'Bombing Iraq won't solve problem', *Newsday*, 17 December 1998 or Micah Zenko, 'Airstrike on Iraq seeks wrong goal', *The Baltimore Sun*, 21 February 2001.
142 Statement before hearings on US Policy on Iraq, 10 March 1999, US House Armed Services Committee.
143 Richard N. Haass, 'Again, half a loaf may have to do', *The Los Angeles Times*, 9 February 1998; also 'Containing Saddam', *Washington Times*, 11 November 1998.
144 Interview on NBC's Meet the Press with Tim Russert, 20 December 1998.
145 Edward Luttwak, 'Toward post-heroic warfare', *Foreign Affairs*, May/June 1995, Vol. 74 No. 3, pp. 116–20.
146 Richard Haass, *Intervention: The Use of American Military Force in the Post-Cold War World*, Washington DC: Brookings Institution Press, 1999, p. 60; Caygill, 'Perpetual police?', p. 80.
147 See Cordesman, *Iraq: Sanctions and Beyond*, p. 211; Byman, 'After the storm: US policy toward Iraq since 1991', p. 513, and White, *Crises After the Storm*.

148 National Intelligence Estimate, *Foreign Missile Developments and the Ballistic Threat through 2015*, December 2001, *http://www.cia.gov/nic/pubs/other_ products/ Unclassifiedballisticmissilefinal.htm* (accessed 7 May 2003).
149 Freedman, 'War in Iraq: Selling the threat', p. 22.
150 Cited in Byman, 'After the storm', p. 493.
151 Cited in Ian Black, 'Caged but for how long?', *Guardian*, 21 December 1998.
152 Richard Haass, 'An Iraq Attack Ensures Nothing', *Boston Globe*, 15 February 1998.
153 Quoted in Gerard Baker, 'Analysis: Did the Gulf War really end?', *New York Times*, 15 October 2002.
154 Thomas Lippman, 'US warns Iraq of more raids', *Washington Post*, 21 December 1998.
155 Susan Wright, 'The hijacking of UNSCOM', *Bulletin of the Atomic Scientists*, Vol. 55 No. 4, July/August 1999, *http://www.thebulletin.org/issues/ 1999/mj99/mj99wright.html* (accessed 11 April 2003).
156 Micah Zenko, 'Firing Blanks at the Iraqi military', *The Chicago Tribune*, 29 March 2001, described no-fly zones as 'a counterproductive mission in search of an overall strategy'.
157 See testimony of Thomas A. Kearney and John Hillen before the House of Representatives Committee of Armed Services, 'US Policy toward Iraq', 10 March 1999.
158 Bernard, 'Lessons from Iraq and Bosnia on the theory and practice of no-fly zones', pp. 460, 463, 468.
159 See Kaygill, 'Perpetual policing', pp. 74–6.
160 Peter Slevin and Bradley Graham, 'Rolling victory key to US endgame', *Washington Post*, 4 April 2003.
161 See Oliver Burkeman, 'Iraqi weapons general arrested and concern grows over inspection chaos', *The Guardian*, 28 April 2003. Also see the report on 'Nuclear Nightmare in Iraq', *Jane's Intelligence Digest*, 28 May 2003, which highlighted the 'security risks' and the golden opportunity for terrorists amid the chaos; UK Intelligence and Security Committee, *Iraqi Weapons of mass destruction – intelligence and assessments*, London, September 2003.
162 Testimony before Senate Select Committee on Intelligence, 16 February 2005.
163 Jessica Stern, 'How America created a terrorist haven', *New York Times*, 20 August 2003.
164 Bacevich, *American Empire*, p. 199.

7 THE RISE AND FALL OF WAR AS RISK MANAGEMENT?

1 Ulrich Beck, *Risk Society*, Cambridge: Polity Press,1992, p. 46.
2 Deborah Lupton, *Risk*, London: Routledge, 1999, p. 99.
3 See Don Hubert, 'The challenge of humanitarian mine clearance', in Maxwell Cameron, Robert J. Lawson and Brian W. Tomlin (eds), *To Walk Without Fear: The Global Movement to Ban Landmines*, Toronto: Oxford University Press, 1998, p. 321.
4 Bill Purves, *Living With Landmines: From International Treaty to Reality*, Montreal: Rose Press, 2000, p. 126.
5 See Landmine Monitor report 2000, available at *www.icbl.org/lm/2000/ report/LMWeb-25.php3* (accessed 17 April 2003).
6 One interesting footnote to distributing risks occurred during the Kosovo air campaign itself, when USAID funded the NGO International Rescue

Committee's (IRC) relief flights, which NATO had declined to undertake – slow, low-flying risky air drops to refugees in mountains. The IRC has a history of doing hazardous things governments are unwilling to do, such as delivering food under fire to Mostar and Gorazde.

7 See 'Demining in Afghanistan', Foreign Press Centre Briefing by Lincoln Bloomfield, Assistant Secretary of State for Political Military Affairs, 18 December 2001, Washington DC; *http://fpc.state.gov/7453.htm* (accessed 3 May 2003).

8 Andrew Bacevich, *American Empire*, Cambridge, MA: Harvard University Press, 2002, p. 158.

9 David Shearer, *Private Armies and Military Intervention*, Adelphi Paper 316, London: Oxford University Press, 1998, p. 62.

10 'Secrecy in Colombia', *Jane's Foreign Report*, 29 March 2001.

11 Quoted in 'Secrecy in Colombia', *Jane's Foreign Report*, 29 March 2001.

12 A recent analysis would include for example Eugene B. Smith, 'The New Condottieri and US policy: the privatisation of conflict and its implications', *Parameters*, Vol. XXXII No. 4, Winter 2002–03, pp. 104–19.

13 A selection includes Michael Ignatieff, *Empire lite: nationbuilding in Bosnia, Kosovo, Afghanistan*, London: Vintage, 2003; Bacevich, *American Empire*, 2002; Niall Ferguson, *Empire: the rise and demise of British world order and lessons for global power*, New York: Basic Books, 2003.

14 Joseph S. Nye, 'Ill-suited for empire', *Washington Post*, 25 May 2003.

15 Simon Chesterman, 'Bush, the United Nations and nation-building', *Survival*, Vol. 46 No. 1, Spring 2004.

16 See Anna Simons, 'The Death of Conquest', *The National Interest*, Issue 71, Spring 2003, pp. 41–50.

17 For an in-depth discussion of the intelligence assessments and flaws in the run-up the war, see Lawrence Freedman, 'War in Iraq: selling the threat', *Survival*, Vol. 46 No. 2, Summer 2004.

18 Gaddis, *Strategies of Containment*, p. 238; Kissinger quoted in Berdal and Economides, *Strategic Thinking*, p. 143.

19 Pierre Hassner, 'The United States: the empire of force or the force of empire', *Chaillot Papers*, No. 54, September 2002, p. 43.

20 Quoted in Peter Ford, 'Injustice seen as fertile soil for terrorists', *Christian Science Monitor*, 28 November 2001.

21 Dana Allin and Steven Simon, 'America's Predicament', *Survival*, Vol. 46 No. 4, Winter 2004–05, p. 28.

22 Chesterman, 'Bush, the United Nations and nation-building', p. 104.

23 G. John Ikenberry, 'The end of the neo-conservative moment', *Survival*, Vol. 46 No. 1, Spring 2004, p. 12.

24 Ikenberry, 'The end of the neo-conservative moment', p. 18.

25 Chris Brown, 'Ethics, interests and foreign policy', in Karen Smith and Margot Light (eds), *Ethics and foreign policy*, Cambridge: Cambridge University Press, 2001.

26 Peter Beinart, 'Nation building is the best defence', *Pittsburg Post-Gazette*, 18 November 2001. Also see Francis Fukuyama, *State-Building: Governance and Order in the 21st Century*, Ithaca: Cornell University Press, 2004.

27 For more sceptical views, see Gary Dempsey, 'Nation-building's newest disguise', *Orbis*, Summer 2002.

28 Chesterman, 'Bush, the United Nations and nation-building', p. 112.

29 Ibid.

30 Bob Woodward, *Plan of Attack*, New York: Simon & Schuster, 2004, p. 220.

SELECT BIBLIOGRAPHY

1 Books and Journal Articles

Adam, Barbara and Van Loon, Joost, 'Repositioning Risk: the challenge for social theory', in Adam, Barbara, Beck, Ulrich and Van Loon, Joost (eds), *The Risk Society and Beyond: Critical Issues for Social Theory*, London: Sage Publications, 2000.

Adam, Barbara, Beck, Ulrich and Van Loon, Joost (eds), *The Risk Society and Beyond: Critical Issues for Social Theory*, London: Sage Publications, 2000.

Adams, John, 'Frameworks for thinking about risk', Paper presented at *Goodenough-Chevening Conference on Risk*, 11 April 2002, Goodenough College, London.

—— *Risk*, London: UCL Press, 1995.

Akermark, Sia Spiliopoulou, 'Storms, foxes and nebulous legal arguments: twelve years of force against Iraq, 1991–2003', *International Comparative Law Quarterly*, Vol. 54, January 2005.

Allan, Stuart, Adam, Barbara and Carter, Cynthia, *Environmental Risks and the Media*, London: Routledge, 2000.

Allin, Dana H., *NATO's Balkan Interventions*, Adelphi Paper 347, Oxford: Oxford University Press for the IISS, July 2002.

Allin, Dana H. and Simon, Steven, 'America's Predicament', *Survival*, Vol. 46 No. 4, Winter 2004–05.

Andreani, Giles, 'The war on terror: Good cause, wrong concept', *Survival*, Vol. 46 No. 4, Winter 2004–05, p. 35.

Applegate, Melissa, *Preparing for Asymmetry: As Seen through the Lens of Joint Vision 2020*, Carlisle, PA: US Army War College Strategic Studies Institute, September 2001.

Arend, Anthony Clark, 'International Law and the preemptive use of force', *Washington Quarterly*, Vol. 26 No. 3, Spring 2003, pp. 89–103.

Arquilla, John and Ronfeldt, David, 'The advent of netwar revisited', in Arquilla, John and Ronfeldt, David (eds), *Networks and Netwars: The Future of Terror, Crime and Militancy*, Santa Monica, CA: RAND, 2001.

Ash, Timothy Garton, 'Round Table: the global order in the twenty-first century', *Prospect*, August/September 1999, pp. 50–8.

Aubin, Stephen P., 'Operation Allied Force: War or "coercive diplomacy"?', *Strategic Review*, Vol. XXVII No.3, Summer 1999, pp. 4–13.

Auerwald, David, 'Explaining wars of choice: an integrated decision model of NATO policy in Kosovo', *International Studies Quarterly*, Vol. 48 No. 3, September 2004.

Bacevich, Andrew, *American Empire: The Realities and Consequences of American Diplomacy*, Cambridge, MA: Harvard University Press, 2002.

Bacevich, Andrew and Cohen, Eliot (eds), *War Over Kosovo: Politics and Strategy in a Global Age*, New York: Columbia University Press, 2001.

Barnett, Thomas and Gaffney, Jr, Henry H., 'Top ten post-Cold War Myths', *US Naval Institute Proceedings*, Vol. 172/2/1, 176, February 2001, pp. 32–8.

Bauman, Zygmunt, *Post-modern Ethics*, Oxford: Blackwell, 1993.

—— *Society Under Siege*, Cambridge: Polity Press, 2002.

—— 'Wars of the globalisation era', *European Journal of Social Theory*, Vol. 4 No. 1, 2001, pp. 11–28.

Baylis, John and Wirtz, James J., 'Introduction', in Baylis, John, Cohen, Eliot, Gray, Colin, Wirtz, James (eds) *Strategy in the Contemporary World: An introduction to strategic studies*, New York: Oxford University Press, 2002.

Beck, Ulrich, *Democracy Without Enemies*, trans. Mark Ritter, Cambridge: Polity Press, 1998.

—— 'Politics of Risk Society', in Franklin, Jane (ed.), *The Politics of Risk Society*, Cambridge: Polity Press, 1998.

—— 'Risk Society and the Provident State' in Lash, Scott, Szerszynski, Bronislaw, Wynne, Brian (eds), *Risk, Environment and Modernity*, London: Sage, 1996.

—— *Risk Society: Towards A New Modernity*, trans. Mark Ritter, Cambridge: Polity Press, 1992.

—— *The Reinvention of Politics*, Cambridge: Polity Press, 1997.

—— 'Terror and solidarity' in Leonard, Mark (ed.), *Re-ordering the World*, London: The Foreign Policy Centre, 2002.

—— 'The terrorist threat: World Risk Society revisited', *Theory, Culture and Society*, Vol. 19 No. 4, August 2002, pp. 39–56.

—— *What is Globalisation?*, trans. Patrick Camiller, Cambridge: Polity Press, 2000.

—— *World Risk Society*, Cambridge: Polity Press, 1999.

Bengio, Ofra, 'Couldn't be worse? Iraq after Saddam', *The National Interest* No. 66, Winter 2001–2002, pp. 52–9.

Bercovitch, Jacob and Regan, Patrick, 'Managing Risks in international Relations', in Schneider, Gerald, and Weitsman, Patricia, (eds), *Enforcing Cooperation: Risky states and intergovernmental management of conflict*, Basingstoke: Macmillan, 1997.

Berdal, Mats and Economides, Spyros (eds), *Strategic Thinking: An introduction and farewell Philip Windsor*, London: Lynne Rienner, 2002.

Bernard, Alexander, 'Lessons from Iraq and Bosnia on the theory and practice of no-fly zones', *Journal of Strategic Studies*, Vol. 27 No. 3, September 2004.

Bertram, Eva and Sharpe, Kenneth, 'The unwinnable drug war: What Clausewitz would tell us', *World Policy Journal*, Vol. XIII No. 4, Winter 1996–97, pp. 41–53.

Beyerchen, Alan, 'Clausewitz, nonlinearity and the unpredictability of war', *International Security*, Vol. 17 No. 3, Winter 1992–3, p. 71.

Biddle, Stephen, 'Afghanistan and the future of warfare', *Foreign Affairs*, Vol. 82 No. 2, March/April 2003, pp. 31–46.

—— 'The new way of war', Review Article, *Foreign Affairs*, Vol. 81 No. 3, May/June 2002.

Black, Jeremy, *War in the New Century*, London: Continuum, 2001.

—— *Why Wars Happen*, London: Reaktion Books, 1998.

Blix, Hans, *Disarming Iraq*, New York: Pantheon Books, 2004.

Bluth, Christoph, 'The British road to war: Bush, Blair and the decision to invade Iraq', *International Affairs*, Vol. 80 No. 5, 2004.

Boyle, M., 'Utopianism and the Bush foreign policy', *Cambridge Review of International Affairs*, Vol. 17 No. 1, April 2004.

Bremer, L. Paul, 'A new strategy for the new face of terrorism', *The National Interest*, No. 65 (supp), 2001, pp. 23–30.

Brown, Chris, *Understanding International Relations*, (2nd edn), Basingstoke: Palgrave, 2001.

Buckley, Mary and Cummings, Sally N., 'Introduction' in Buckley, Mary and Cummings, Sally N. (eds), *Kosovo: Perceptions of War and Its Aftermath*, London: Continuum, 2001.

Buckley, William J., 'Not losing sight of justice', in Buckley, William J. (ed.), *Kosovo: Contending Voices on Balkan Interventions*, Grand Rapids, MI: William B. Eerdmans Publishing Company, 2000.

Burr, William and Richelson, Jeffrey T., 'Whether to "strangle the baby in the cradle": The United States and the Chinese nuclear program 1960–64', *International Security*, Vol. 25 No. 3, Winter 2000/01, pp. 54–99.

Buzan, Barry, *People, States and Fear: an agenda for international security studies in the post-Cold War era* (2nd edn), Hemel Hempstead: Harvester, 1991.

Byers, Michael, 'Terror and the future of international law', in Ken Booth and Tim Dunne (eds), *Worlds in Collision: Terror and the Future of Global Order*, (Basingstoke: Palgrave Macmillan, 2002).

Byman, Daniel, 'After the storm: US policy toward Iraq since 1991', *Political Science Quarterly*, Vol. 115 No 4, Winter 2000–01, pp. 493–516.

—— 'Iraq After Saddam', *The Washington Quarterly*, Vol. 24 No. 4, Autumn 2001, pp. 151–62.

—— 'Scoring the war on terrorism', *The National Interest*, Issue 72, Summer 2003.

Byman, Daniel, Pollack, Kenneth, and Rose, Gideon, 'The Rollback Fantasy', *Foreign Affairs*, Vol. 78 No. 1, January/February 1999, pp. 24–41.

Byman, Daniel and Waxman, Matthew, *Confronting Iraq: US Policy and the Use of Force Since the Gulf War*, Santa Monica, CA: RAND, 2000.

Campbell, Kurt M., 'Globalisation's first war?', *Washington Quarterly*, Vol. 25 No. 1, Winter 2002, pp. 7–14.

Campbell, Kurt M. and Flournoy, Michele A., *To prevail: An American strategy for the Campaign Against Terrorism*, Washington DC: CSIS Press, November 2001.

Carpenter, Ted Galen, 'Introduction: A Great Victory?' in Carpenter, Ted Galen (ed.), *NATO"s Empty Victory*, Washington DC: CATO Institute, 2000.

—— 'Kosovo as an omen: the perils of a new NATO', in Carpenter, Ted Galen (ed.), *NATO's Empty Victory*, Washington DC: CATO Institute, 2000.

—— 'Relations with Russia and China' in Carpenter (ed.), *NATO's Empty Victory*, Washington DC: CATO Institute, 2000.

Carr, Caleb, 'Terrorism as warfare', *World Policy Journal*, Vol. XIII No. 4, Winter 1996–97, pp. 1–13.

Carter, Ashton B. and Perry, William J., *Preventive Defence: A New Security Strategy for America*, Washington DC: Brookings Institution Press, 1999.

Castel, Robert, 'From dangerousness to risk', in Burchell, Graham, Gordon, Colin, and Miller, Peter (eds) *The Foucault Effect*, Chicago: University of Chicago Press, 1991.

Caygill, Howard, 'Perpetual police? Kosovo and the elision of police and military violence', *European Journal of Social Theory*, Vol. 4 No. 1, February 2001, pp. 73–80.

Chandler, David, *From Kosovo to Kabul: Human Rights and International Intervention*, London: Pluto Press, 2002.

Charney, Jonathan I., 'Anticipatory humanitarian action in Kosovo', *American Journal of International Law*, Vol. 93 No. 3, October 1999, pp. 834–41.

—— 'The use of force against terrorism and international law', *American Journal of International Law*, Vol. 95 No. 4, October 2001.

Chesterman, Simon, 'Bush, the United Nations and nation-building', *Survival*, Vol. 46 No. 1, Spring 2004.

—— *You the people: The United Nations, Transitional Administration and State-building*, Oxford: Oxford University Press, 2004.

Clark, Wesley, *Waging Modern War: Bosnia, Kosovo and the future of combat*, Oxford: Public Affairs, 2001.

Clarke, Michael, 'British perceptions', in Buckley, Mary and Cummings, Sally N., (eds), *Kosovo: Perceptions of war and its aftermath*, London: Continuum, 2001.

—— 'Review Article: War in the New International Order', *International Affairs*, Vol. 77 No. 3, July 2001, pp. 663–70.

—— 'Unpredictable', *World Today*, Vol. 57 No. 11, November 2001, pp. 7–9.

Clarke, Simon and Paul Hoggett, 'The Empire of Fear: The American political psyche and the culture of paranoia', *Psychodynamic Practice*, Vol. 10 No. 1, February 2004.

Cohen, Eliot, 'A strange war', *The National Interest* No. 65 (supp), 2001, pp. 11–22.

Coker, Christopher, *Globalisation and Insecurity in the Twenty-First Century: NATO and the Management of Risk*, Adelphi Paper 345, Oxford: Oxford University Press for the IISS, April 2002.

—— 'How wars end', *Millennium: Journal of International Studies*, Vol. 26 No. 3, 1997, pp. 615–29.

—— *Humane Warfare: The New Ethics of Postmodern War*, London: Routledge, 2001.

—— *Waging War Without Warriors: the Changing Culture of Military Conflict*, London: Lynne Rienner, 2002.

Coles, Eve, Smith, Denis and Tombs, Steve (eds), *Risk Management and Society*, Dordrecht: Kluwer Academic Publishers, 2000.

Cooper, Robert, *The Breaking of Nations: Order and Chaos in the 21st Century*, Cambridge: Polity Press, 2003.

—— *The Post Modern State and World Order*, London: Demos, 2000.

Cordesman, Anthony, *Iraq: Sanctions and Beyond*, Boulder, Colorado: Westview Press, 1997.

—— *Lessons and Non-Lessons of the Kosovo Air War*, Washington DC: Centre for Strategic and International Studies, July 1999.

Crockatt, Richard, *America Embattled: 9/11, Anti-Americanism and the Global Order*, London: Routledge, 2003.

Crosby Jr, Ralph, 'The path forward for NATO and EU defence capabilities: information dominance and precision strike', *World Systems Procurement Edition*, Vol. 3 No. 1, January 2001.

Crouhy, Michael, Galai, Dan and Mark, Robert, *Risk Management*, New York: McGraw-Hill, 2001.

Daalder, Ivo H. and O'Hanlon, Michael E., *Winning Ugly: NATO's war to save Kosovo*, Washington DC: Brookings Institution Press, 2000.

Dandeker, Christopher, 'New times and new patterns of civil-military relations', in Kuhlman, Jurgen and Callaghan, Jean (eds), *Military and Society in 21ˢᵗ Century Europe: A Comparative Analysis*, Hamburg: Lit Verlag, 2000.

—— *Surveillance, Power and Modernity*, Cambridge: Polity Press, 1990.

Daniel, Donald C. F., Hayes, Bradd C., and Oudraat, Chantal de Jonge, *Coercive Inducement and the Containment of International Crises*, Washington DC: United States Institute of Peace, 1999.

Danner, Mark, 'Endgame in Kosovo' in Buckley, William J., (ed.), *Kosovo: Contending Voices on Balkan Interventions*, Grand Rapids, MI: William B. Eerdmans Publishing Company, 2000.

Davis, Lynn E., *Security Implications of Globalisation*, Santa Monica, CA: RAND, 2003.

Deaver, Michael V., *Disarming Iraq: Monitoring Power and Resistance*, Westport: Praeger, 2001.

Dehqanzada, Yahya A. and Florini, Ann M., *Secrets for Sale: How Commercial Satellite Imagery Will Change the World*, Washington DC: Carnegie Endowment for International Peace, 2000.

Dempsey, Gary, 'Nation-building's newest disguise', *Orbis*, Summer 2002.

Der Derian, James, 'Global events, national security and virtual theory', *Millennium*, Vol. 30 No. 3, December 2001, pp. 669–690.

—— *Virtuous War: Mapping the Military-Industrial-Media-Entertainment Network*, Boulder, CO: Westview Press, 2001.

Dibb, Paul, 'The future of international coalitions: how useful? How manageable?' *The Washington Quarterly*, Vol. 25 No. 2, Spring 2002, pp. 131–44.

Dodge, Toby and Simon, Steven, 'Introduction', in Dodge, Toby and Simon, Steven (eds), *Iraq at the Crossroads: State and Society in the Shadow of Regime Change*, Oxford: Oxford University Press for the IISS, January 2003.

Douglas, Mary, *Risk and Blame: Essays in Cultural Theory*, London: Routledge: 1992.

Dowd, Alan W., 'NATO after Kosovo', *Policy Review*, December 1999/January 2000 No.98.

Dunn, David H., 'Myths, motivations and "misunderestimations": The Bush Administration and Iraq', *International Affairs*, Vol. 79 No. 2, April 2003, pp. 279–97.

Dyer, Hugh, 'Environmental security and international relations: the case for enclosure', *Review of International Studies*, Vol. 27 No. 3, July 2001, pp. 441–50.

Erdmann, Andrew, 'The US presumption of quick costless wars', *Orbis*, Vol. 43 Issue 3, Summer 1999.

Ericson, Richard and Haggerty, Kevin, *Policing the Risk Society*, Toronto and Buffalo: University of Buffalo Press, 1997.

Eriksson, Johan (ed.), *Threat Politics: New Perspectives on Security, Risk and Crisis Management*, Aldershot: Ashgate Publishing, 2001.

Evans, Gareth and Sahnoun, Mohamed, 'The responsibility to protect', *Foreign Affairs*, Vol. 81 No. 6, November/December 2002.

Evans, Martin and Lunn, Kevin (eds), *War and Memory in the Twentieth Century*, Oxford: Berg, 1997.

Ewald, Francois, 'Insurance and Risk', in Burchell, Graham, Gordon, Colin and Miller, Peter, (eds), *The Foucault Effect*, Chicago: University of Chicago Press, 1991.

Feeley, Malcolm and Simon, Jonathan, 'Actuarial Justice: the emerging new criminal law' in Nelken, David (ed.), *The Futures of Criminology*, London: Sage Publications, 1994.

Ferguson, Niall, *Empire: The Rise and Demise of British World Order and Lessons for Global Power*, New York: Basic Books, 2003.

Franklin, Jane, 'Introduction' in Franklin, Jane (ed.), *The Politics of Risk Society*, Cambridge: Polity Press, 1998.

Freedman, Lawrence, 'Prevention, not preemption', *Washington Quarterly*, Spring 2003, Vol. 26 No 2, pp. 105–14.

—— *The Revolution in Strategic Affairs*, Adelphi Paper 318, Oxford: Oxford University Press for the IISS, 1998.

—— 'The Third World War?', *Survival*, Vol. 43 No. 4, Winter 2001–2002, pp. 61–88.

—— 'Victims and Victors: Reflections on the Kosovo war', *Review of International Studies*, Vol. 26 No. 3, July 2000, pp. 335–58.

—— 'War in Iraq: Selling the threat', *Survival*, Vol. 46 No. 2, Summer 2004.

Freud, Sigmund, *Beyond the Pleasure Principle*, London: The International Psycho-Analytical Press, 1922, trans. C. J. M Hubback.

Fukuyama, Francis, *State-Building: Governance and Order in the 21ˢᵗ Century*, Ithaca: Cornell University Press, 2004.

Furedi, Frank, *Culture of Fear: Risk-Taking and the Morality of Low Expectation*, London: Cassell, 1998.

Gaddis, John Lewis, *Strategies of Containment: A Critical Appraisal of Postwar American National Security Policy*, New York: Oxford University Press, 1982.

Gallie, W.B., 'Essentially contested concepts', in Black, Max (ed.), *The Importance of Language*, Englewood Cliffs, NJ: Prentice Hall, 1962, pp. 121–46.

Garland, David, *The Culture of Control: Crime and Social Order in Contemporary Society*, Oxford: Oxford University Press, 2001.

Garthoff, Raymond, *A Journey through the Cold War: A Memoir of Containment and Coexistence*, Washington DC: Brookings Institution Press, 2001.

Gause III, Gregory, 'Getting it Backward on Iraq', *Foreign Affairs*, Vol. 78 No. 3, May/June 1999, pp. 54–65.

Gibbons, Philip, 'US No-fly zones: To what end?', Washington Institute for Near East Policy, *Policy Watch* No. 632, 1 July 2002.

Gibson, James W., *The Perfect War: Technowar in Vietnam*, New York: Atlantic Monthly Press, 2000.

Giddens, Anthony and Pearson, Christopher, *Conversations with Anthony Giddens*, Cambridge: Polity Press, 1998.

Giddens, Anthony, *Modernity and Self-identity: Self and Society in the Late Modern Age*, Cambridge: Polity Press, 1991.

Goldman, Emily and Berman, Larry, 'Engaging the world: first impressions of the Clinton foreign policy legacy' in Campbell, Colin and Rockman, Bert (eds), *The Clinton Legacy*, New York: Chatham House Publishers, 2000.

Gordon, Philip H., 'Bush's Middle East Vision', *Survival*, Vol. 45 No 1, Spring 2003. pp. 155–67.

Graham, John D., 'A future for the precautionary principle?', *Journal of Risk Research*, Vol. 4 No. 2, April 2001, pp. 109–13.

—— 'Decision-Analytic Refinements of the Precautionary Principle', *Journal of Risk Research*, Vol. 4 No. 2, April 2001, pp. 127–43.

Gray, Chris Hables, *Post-modern War: The New Politics of Conflict*, New York: Guilford Press, 1997.

Gray, Colin S., *Modern Strategy*, New York: Oxford University Press, 1999.

—— 'World Politics as usual after September 11: Realism vindicated', in Booth, Ken and Dunne, Tim (eds), *Worlds in Collision: Terror and the future of global order*, Basingstoke: Palgrave Macmillan, 2002.

—— *The Sheriff: America's Defence of the New World Order*, Lexington, KY: University of Kentucky Press, 2004.

Grove-White, Robin, Panel remarks on *Do we live in a culture of fear?*, Goodenough College and 21st Century Trust Conference on Risk, 11–12 April 2002, London.

Griner, Shlomo, 'Living in a World Risk Society: A reply to Mikkel V. Rasmussen', *Millennium: Journal of International Studies*, Vol. 31 No. 2, 2002, pp. 149–60.

Haass, Richard, *Intervention: The Use of American Military Force in the Post-Cold War World*, Washington DC: Brookings Institution Press, 1999.

Halperin, Morton H. and Kemp, Geoffrey, *A report on US Policy Options toward Iraq*, New York: Council on Foreign Relations, June 2001.

Harmon, Christopher, *Terrorism Today*, London: Frank Cass, 2000.

Harremoes, Poul, Ge, David, MacGarvin, Malcolm, Stirling, Andy, Keys, Jane, Wynne, Brian, Guedes Vaz, Sofia (eds), *The Precautionary Principle in the 20th Century*, London: Earthscan Publications, 2002.

Hart, Gary and Rudman, Warren, (Co-Chairs), *America Still Unprepared, Still in Danger*, Report of an independent task force sponsored by the Council on Foreign Relations, Washington DC, 22 Oct 2002.

Haselkorn, Avigdor, *The Continuing Storm: Iraq, Poisonous Weapons and Deterrence*, New Haven: Yale University Press, 1998.

Hassner, Pierre, 'The United States: the empire of force or the force of empire', *Chaillot Papers* No. 54, September 2002.

Heisbourg, Francois, 'A Work in Progress: the Bush Doctrine and its consequences', *Washington Quarterly*, Vol. 26 No. 2, Spring 2003, pp. 75–88.

—— *Warfare*, London: Phoenix, 1997.

Hester, R. E. and Harrison, R. M., (eds), *Risk Assessment and Risk Management*, Cambridge: The Royal Society of Chemistry, 1998.

Heurlin, Bertel, *The Threat As a Concept in International Politics*, Copenhagen: The Information and Welfare Service of the Danish Defence, 1977.

Hoffman, Bruce, 'The changing face of Al Qaeda and the global war on terrorism', *Studies in Conflict and Terrorism*, Vol. 27 No. 6, November–December 2004.

—— 'Terrorism by weapons of mass destruction: A reassessment of the threat', in Carolyn W. Pumphrey (ed.), *Transnational Threats: Blending Law Enforcement and Military Strategies*, conference proceedings, Carlisle: Strategic Studies Institute, November 2000.

Holsti, Kalevi, *Peace and War: Armed Conflicts and International Order 1648–1989*, Cambridge: Cambridge University Press, 1991.

Hood, Christopher and Jones, David K. C., *Accident and Design: Contemporary Debates in Risk Management*, London: UCL Press, 1996.

Hood, Christopher, Rothstein, Henry and Baldwin, Robert, *The Government of Risk: Understanding Risk Regulation Regimes*, Oxford: Oxford University Press, 2001.

Howard, Michael, 'What's in a name?: How to fight terrorism', *Foreign Affairs*, Vol. 81 No. 1, January/February 2002, pp. 22–35.

Hubert, Don, 'The challenge of humanitarian mine clearance, in Cameron, Maxwell, Lawson, Robert J., and Tomlin, Brian W., (eds), *To Walk without Fear: The Global Movement to Ban Landmines*, Toronto: Oxford University Press, 1998.

Hudson, Barbara, 'Punishment, rights and difference: defending justice in the risk society', in Stenson, Kevin, and Sullivan, Robert (eds), *Crime, Risk and Justice: The Politics of Crime Control in Liberal Democracies*, Cullompton, Devon: Willan Publishing, 2001.

Hughes, Gordon, *Understanding Crime Prevention: Social Control, Risk and Late Modernity*, Buckingham: Open University Press, 1998.

Ignatieff, Michael, *Empire-lite: Nationbuilding in Bosnia, Kosovo, Afghanistan*, London: Vintage, 2003.

—— *Virtual War: Kosovo and Beyond*, London: Chatto & Windus, 2000.

International Crisis Group Report, 'Bin Laden and the Balkans: the politics of anti-terrorism', 9 November 2001.

Ikenberry, G. John, 'The end of the neo-conservative moment', *Survival*, Vol. 46 No. 1, Spring 2004.

Isherwood, Michael W. 'US Strategic Options for Iraq: Easier said than done', *Washington Quarterly*, Vol. 25 No. 2, Spring 2002, pp. 145–60.

Jenkins, Brian, *Countering Al Qaeda*, Santa Monica, CA: RAND, 2002.

Joas, Hans, *War and Modernity*, Cambridge: Polity Press, 2003.

Johnson, Robert, *Improbable Dangers: US Conceptions of Threat in the Cold War and After*, New York: St Martin's Press, 1994.

Johnston, Les, *Policing Britain: Risk, Security and Governance*, Harlow: Longman Press, 1999.

Jones, David Martin and Smith, M. L. R., 'Franchising Terror', *The World Today*, Vol. 57 No. 10, October 2001, pp. 10–12.

Lowe, Vaughan, 'Clear and present danger: responses to terrorism', *International Comparative Law Quarterly*, Vol. 54, January 2005.

Kaldor, Mary, *New and Old Wars*, Cambridge: Polity Press, 1999.

Kampfner, John, *Blair's Wars*, London: Free Press, 2004.

Kaygill, Howard, 'Perpetual Police? Kosovo and the elision of police and military violence', *European Journal of Social Theory*, Vol. 4 No. 1, February 2001, pp. 74–6.

Keegan, John, *War and our World*, London: Hutchinson, 1998.

Keen, David, *The Economic Functions of Civil Wars*, Adelphi Paper 320, Oxford: IISS, 1998.

Kenney, Michael, 'From Pablo to Osama: Counter-terrorism lessons from the war on drugs', *Survival*, Vol. 45 No. 3, Autumn 2003, pp. 187–206.

Kissinger, Henry, 'Kosovo and the Vicissitudes of American foreign policy', in William J. Buckley (ed.), *Kosovo: Contending Voices on Balkan Interventions*, Grand Rapids, MI: William B. Eerdmans Publishing Company, 2000.

Klare, Michael, *Rogue States and Nuclear Outlaws: America's Search for a New Foreign Policy*, New York: Hill & Wang, 1995.

Klinke, Andreas and Renn, Ortwin, 'Precautionary Principle and discursive strategies: classifying and managing risks', *Journal of Risk Research*, Vol. 4 No. 2, April 2001, pp. 159–75.

Krauthammer, Charles, 'The short unhappy life of humanitarian war', *The National Interest*, Fall 1999 No. 57, pp. 5–8.

Kriendler, John, 'Anticipating Crises', *NATO Review*, Winter 2002 No.4.

Kunreuther, Howard and Slovic, Paul, 'Science, values and risk', in Kunreuther, Howard and Slovic, Paul (ed.), Challenges in risk assessment and risk management: Special Volume, *The Annals of the American Academy of Political and Social Science*, Vol. 545, May 1995.

Laidi, Zaki, *A World Without Meaning: Crisis of Meaning in International Politics*, London: Routledge, 1998.

Lambeth, Benjamin S., *NATO's Air War for Kosovo: A Strategic and Operational Assessment*, Santa Monica, CA: RAND, 2001.

Laqueur, Walter, 'Left, right and beyond- the changing face of terror', in Hoge, James F., and Rose, Gideon (eds), *How did this happen? Terrorism and the New War*, New York: Public Affairs, 2001.

—— *No End to War: Terrorism in the Twenty-First Century*, London: Continuum Press, 2003.

Lasch, Christopher, *Culture of Narcissism: American Life in an Age of Diminishing Expectations*, London: Abacus Press, 1980.

—— *The Minimal Self: Psychic Survival in Troubled Times*, London: Norton, 1984.

Lawrence, Philip K., *Modernity and War*, Basingstoke: Macmillan, 1997.

Layne, Christopher, 'Collateral Damage in Yugoslavia', in Carpenter, Ted Galen, *NATO's Empty Victory*, Washington DC: CATO Institute, 2000.

Lesser, Ian O., Hoffman, Bruce, Arquilla, John, Ronfeldt, David F., Zanini, Michele, Jenkins, Brian Michael, *Countering the New Terrorism*, Santa Monica, CA: RAND, 1999.

Litwak, Robert S., *Rogue States and US Foreign Policy: Containment After the Cold War*, Washington DC: Woodrow Wilson Centre Press, 2000.

Luhmann, Niklas, *Risk: A Sociological Theory*, trans. Rhodes Barrett, New York: Adline de Gruyter, 1993.

Lupton, Deborah, *Risk*, London: Routledge, 1999.

Luttwak, Edward, *Strategy: The Logic of War and Peace*, (revised edition), Cambridge, MA: Harvard University Press, 2001.

—— 'Towards post-heroic warfare', *Foreign Affairs*, Vol. 74 No. 3, May/June 1995, pp. 109–20.

Lyon, David, 'Chapter 1: Surveillance as social sorting' in David Lyon (ed.), *Surveillance As Social Sorting: Privacy, Risk and Digital Discrimination*, London: Routledge, 2003.

—— *Surveillance Society: Monitoring Everyday Life*, Buckingham: Open University Press, 2001.

Mandelbaum, Michael 'A Perfect Failure', *Foreign Affairs*, Vol. 78 No. 5, September/October 1999, pp. 2–9.

—— 'Is major war obsolete?', *Survival*, Vol. 40 No. 4, Winter 1998–9, pp. 20–38.

Mearsheimer, John, Posen, Barry and Cohen, Eliot, 'Reassessing net assessment', *International Security*, Vol. 13 No. 4, Spring 1989, pp. 129–79.

Mccgwire, Michael, 'Why did we bomb Belgrade?', *International Affairs*, Vol. 76 No. 1, January 2000, pp. 1–24.

McDermott, Rose, *Risk-taking in International Politics: Prospect Theory in US Foreign Policy*, Ann Arbor: University of Michigan Press, 1998.

McInnes, Colin, 'A different kind of war? September 11 and the United States' Afghan War', *Review of International Studies*, Vol. 29 No. 2, April 2003, pp. 165–84.

—— 'Fatal attraction? Airpower and the West', in McInnes, Colin and Wheeler, Nicholas (eds), *Dimensions of Western Military Intervention*, London: Frank Cass, 2002.

McInnes, Colin, *Spectator Sport War: The West and Contemporary Conflict*, London: Lynne Rienner, 2002.

McLaughlin, David, *Managing Conflict in the Post-Cold War World*, Aspen, CO: The Aspen Institute, 1995.

Mickolus, Edward F., 'How do we know we're winning the war against terrorists? Issues in measurement', *Studies in Conflict and Terrorism*, Vol. 25 No. 3, May-June 2002 pp. 151–60.

Moss, David, *When All Else Fails: The Government As the Ultimate Risk Manager*, Cambridge, MA: Harvard University Press, 2002.

Mueller, John, *Retreat from Doomsday: The Obsolescence of Major War*, New York: Basic Books, 1991.

—— *The Remnants of War*, Ithaca: Cornell University Press, 2004.

Mutimer, David, 'Reconstituting security? The practices of proliferation control', *European Journal of International Relations*, Vol. 4 No. 1, March 1998, pp. 99–129

Murray, Williamson, 'Clausewitz out, computer in', *National Interest*, Issue 48, Summer 1997.

Nardulli, Bruce R. et al., *Disjointed War: Military Operations in Kosovo 1999*, Santa Monica, CA: RAND Arroyo Centre, 2002.

Neal, Mark, 'Risk Aversion: the rise of an ideology', in Jones, Laura (ed.), *Safe Enough? Managing Risk and Regulation*, Vancouver: Fraser Institute, 2000.

Norris, Clive and Armstrong, Gary, *Maximum Surveillance Society*, Oxford: Berg, 1999.

Olsen, Gorm Rye, 'Europe and Africa's Failed States: from development to containment', Paper presented to conference on The global constitution of failed states: the consequences of a new imperialism?, University of Sussex, 18–20 April 2001.

O'Malley, Pat (ed.), *Crime and the Risk Society*, Aldershot: Dartmouth Publishing, 1998.

O'Neil, William G., *Kosovo: An Unfinished Peace*, Boulder, CO: Lynne Rienner Publishers, 2002.

O'Riordan, Tim, Cameron, James, Jordan, Andrew, 'The Evolution of the Precautionary Principle', in O'Riordan, Tim, Cameron, James, Jordan, Andrew (eds), *Reinterpreting the Precautionary Principle*, London: Cameron May, 2002.

—— (eds), *Reinterpreting the Precautionary Principle*, London: Cameron May, 2002.

O'Tuathail, Gearoid, 'Understanding Critical Geopolitics: Geopolitics and Risk Society', *Journal of Strategic Studies*, Vol. 22 No. 2/3, June/Sep 1999, pp. 107–24.

Pillar, Paul, *Terrorism and US Foreign Policy*, Washington DC: Brookings Institution Press, 2001.

Pollack, Kenneth M. *The Threatening Storm: The Case for Invading Iraq*, New York: Random House, 2002.

Purves, Bill, *Living With Landmines: From International Treaty to Reality*, Montreal: Rose Press, 2000.

Ramet, Sabrina P., 'The USA: To war in Europe again', in Weymouth, Tony and Henig, Stanley (eds), *The Kosovo Crisis: The Last American War in Europe?*, London: Pearson Education Limited, 2001.

Rappoport, David, 'The Fourth Wave: September 11 in the History of Terrorism', *Current History*, Vol. 100 No. 650, December 2001, pp. 434–7.

Rasmussen, Mikkel Vedby, *9–11: Globalisation, Security and World Order*, DUPI Working Paper 2002/2, Copenhagen: Danish Institute of International Affairs, 2002.

—— 'Reflexive security: NATO and International Risk Society', *Millennium*, Vol. 30 No. 2, 2001, pp. 285–310.

—— 'It sounds like a riddle: Security studies, the war on terror and risk', *Millennium*, Vol. 33 No. 2, March 2004, p. 381.

Record, Jeffrey, 'Collapsed countries, casualty dread and the new American way of war', *Parameters: US Army War College Quarterly*, Vol. XXXII No. 2, Summer 2002, pp. 4–23.

—— 'The Bush Doctrine and War with Iraq', *Parameters: US Army War College Quarterly*, Vol. XXXIII No. 1, Spring 2003, pp. 4–21.

—— 'Threat confusion and its penalties', *Survival*, Vol. 46 No. 2, Summer 2004.

Redd, Steven B., 'The influence of advisers and decision strategies on foreign policy choices: President Clinton's decision to use force in Kosovo', *International Studies Perspectives*, Vol. 6 No. 1, February 2005.

Renn, Ortwin, 'Three decades of risk research: accomplishments and new challenges', *Journal of Risk Research*, Vol. 1 No. 1, 1998, pp. 49–73.

Roberts, Adam, 'Law and the use of force after Iraq', *Survival*, Vol. 45 No. 2, Summer 2003, pp. 31–57.

—— 'NATO's Humanitarian war over Kosovo', *Survival*, Vol. 41 No. 3, Autumn 1999, pp. 102–23.

Rogers, Paul, *Losing Control: Global security in the 21st century*, London: Pluto Press, 2000.

Royal Society, *Risk: Analysis, perception and management*, London: Royal Society, 1992.

Rupp, Richard, 'NATO 1949–2000: from collective defence toward collective security', *Journal of Strategic Studies*, Vol. 23 No. 3, September 2000, pp. 154–76.

Schelling, Thomas, *Arms and Influence*, New Haven, CT: Yale University Press, 1966.

—— *Strategy of Conflict*, Cambridge, MA: Harvard University Press, 1960.

Shapiro, Jeremy and Suzan, Benedicte, 'The French experience of counter-terrorism', *Survival*, Vol. 45 No. 1, Spring 2003, pp. 67–99.

Shearer, David, *Private Armies and Military Intervention*, Adelphi Paper 316, London: Oxford University Press, 1998.

Simon, Steven and Benjamin, Daniel, 'The Terror', *Survival*, Vol. 43 No. 4, Winter 2001, pp. 5–18.

Simons, Anna, 'The Death of Conquest', *The National Interest*, Issue 71, Spring 2003, pp. 41–50.

Slocombe, Walter B., 'Force, pre-emption and legitimacy', *Survival*, Vol. 45 No. 1, Spring 2003, pp. 117–31.

Smith, Denis and Tombs, Steve, 'Conceptualising issues of risk management within the Risk Society', in Coles, Eve, Smith, Denis and Tombs, Steve (eds), *Risk Management and Society*, Dordrecht, Netherlands: Kluwer Academic Publishers, 2000.

Smith, Eugene B., 'The New Condottieri and US policy: the privatisation of conflict and its implications', *Parameters*, Vol. XXXII No. 4, Winter 2002–03, pp. 104–19.

Stanbury, William T., 'Reforming risk regulation in Canada: the next policy frontier?', in Jones, Laura (ed.), *Safe Enough? Managing Risk and Regulation*, Vancouver: Fraser Institute, 2000.

Steinbrunner, John, *Principles of Global Security*, Washington DC: Brookings Institution Press, 2000.

Stern, Jessica, 'The Protean Enemy', *Foreign Affairs*, Vol. 82 No. 4, July/August 2003.

Stevenson, Jonathan, 'Pragmatic Counter-terrorism', *Survival*, Vol. 43 No. 4, Winter 2001–2002, pp. 35–48.

Stothard, Peter, *Thirty Days: Tony Blair and the Test of History*, New York: Harper Collins, 2003.

Takeyh, Ray and Gvosdev, Nikolas, 'Do terrorist networks need a home?', *Washington Quarterly*, Vol. 25 No. 3, Summer 2002, pp. 97–108.

Toffler, Alvin and Heidi, *War and Anti-war: Making Sense of Today's Global Chaos*, London: Warner Books, 1995.

Tucker, David, *Skirmishes at the Edge of Empire: The United States and International Terrorism*, Westport: Praeger, 1997.

Van Creveld, Martin, *On Future War*, London: Brassey's, 1991.

Vertzberger, Yaacov, *Risk-Taking and Decision-Making: Foreign Military Intervention Decisions*, Stanford: Stanford University Press, 1998.

Virilio, Paul, *Strategy of Deception*, London: Verso, 2000.

Von Clausewitz, Karl, *On War*, translated and edited by Michael Howard and Peter Paret, Princeton: Princeton University Press, 1976.

Wallander, Celeste and Keohane, Robert, 'Risk, threat, and security institutions' in Haftendorn, Helga, Keohane, Robert and Wallander, Celeste (eds), *Imperfect Unions: Security Institutions over Time and Space*, New York: Oxford University Press, 1999.

Walt, Stephen, 'Rational choice and international security' in Brown, Michael E., Cote Jr, Owen R., Lynn-Jones, Sean and Miller, Steven E. (eds), *Rational Choice and Security Studies: Stephen Walt and his Critics*, Cambridge, MA: MIT Press, 2000.

Waltz, Kenneth N., *Theory of International Politics*, Boston: Addison-Wesley, 1979.

—— 'The Continuity of international politics', in Booth, Ken and Dunne, Tim (eds), *Worlds in Collision: Terror and the Future of Global Order*, Basingstoke: Palgrave Macmillan, 2002.

Waring, Alan and Glendon, A. Ian, *Managing Risk: Critical Issues for Survival and Success into the 21st Century*, London: Thomson Learning, 1998.

Weller, Marc, 'The US, Iraq and the use of force in a unipolar world', *Survival*, Vol. 41 No. 4, Winter 1999–2000, pp. 81–100.

Weymouth, Tony, 'Why war, why NATO?', in Weymouth, Tony and Henig, Stanley (eds), *The Kosovo Crisis: The Last American War in Europe?*, London: Pearson Education Limited, 2001.

Wheeler, Nicholas, *Saving Strangers: Humanitarian Intervention in International Society*, Oxford: Oxford University Press, 2003.

White, Paul K., 'Airpower and a decade of containment', *Joint Force Quarterly*, No. 27, Winter 2000–01, pp. 35–40.

—— *Crises after the Storm: An Appraisal of US Air Operations Since the Persian Gulf War*, Washington DC: The Washington Institute for Near East Policy, 1999.

Wilkinson, Iain, *Anxiety in a Risk Society*, London: Routledge, 2001.

Wirtz, James J., 'Counterproliferation, conventional counterforce and nuclear war', *Journal of Strategic Studies*, Vol. 23 No 1, March 2000, pp. 5–24.

Wolfson, Adam, 'Humanitarian hawks? Why Kosovo but not Kuwait?', *Policy Review*, Number 98, December 1999/January 2000.

Woodward, Bob, *Plan of Attack*, New York: Simon & Schuster, 2004.

Woolacott, Martin, 'The Politics of Prevention' in Franklin, Jane, (ed.), *The Politics of Risk Society*, Cambridge: Polity Press, 1998.

Yaphe, Judith, 'Iraq: the exception to the rule', *Washington Quarterly*, Vol. 24 No. 1, Winter 2001, pp. 125–40.

Yost, David, *NATO Transformed: the Alliance's new roles in international security*, Washington DC: United States Institute of Peace, 1998.

Zeckhauser, Richard J., Viscusi, W. Kip, 'The Risk Management Dilemma', in Kunreuther, Howard and Slovic, Paul (ed.), Challenges in risk assessment and risk management: Special Volume , *The Annals of the American Academy of Political and Social Science*, Vol. 545, May 1996.

2 Official Publications

Cabinet Office Strategy Unit, *Risk: improving government's capacity to handle risk and uncertainty*, London, November 2002.

European Commission, *Communication from the Commission on the Precautionary Principle*, Brussels, 2 February 2000.

General Accounting Office (US), *Combating Terrorism: Threat and Risk assessments can help prioritise and target program investments*, Report Number NSIAD-98–74, 9 April 1998, Washington DC.

NATO, *Kosovo One Year On*, Brussels, Belgium, 21 March 2000.

NATO, *The Alliance's Strategic Concept agreed by the Heads of State and Government participating in the meeting of the North Atlantic Council*, Rome, 08 November 1991.

NATO, *The Alliance's Strategic Concept agreed by the Heads of State and Government participating in the meeting of the North Atlantic Council in Washington DC*, 23 and 24 April 1999.

The White House, *A National Security Strategy for a New Century*, Washington DC, December 1999.

The White House, *National Security Strategy of the United States*, Washington DC, September 2002.

The White House, *National Strategy for Combating Terrorism*, Washington DC, February 2003.

The White House, *National Strategy to Combat Weapons of Mass Destruction*, Washington DC, December 2002.

US Department of Defence, *Annual Defence Report to Congress and the President*, Washington DC, 1998.

US Department of Defence, *Annual Defence Report to the President and the Congress*, Washington DC, 2002.

US Department of Defence, *DOD Dictionary of Military and Associated Terms*, Joint Publication 1–02, Washington DC, 12 April 2001.

US Department of Defence, *Quadrennial Defence Review*, Washington, DC, September 2001.

US Department of Defence, *Nuclear Posture Review*, Washington DC, December 2001

US Department of Homeland Security, *National Strategy for Homeland Security*, Washington DC, July 2002.

US National Intelligence Council, *Global Trends 2015: A dialogue about the future with non-government experts*, Washington DC, December 2000.

US National Intelligence Council, *National Intelligence Estimate: Foreign Missile Developments and the ballistic Threat through 2015*, Washington DC, December 2001.

US Senate Select Committee on Intelligence, *Report on the US intelligence community's pre-war intelligence assessments on Iraq*, Washington DC, July 2004.

UK Government, *Iraq's weapons of mass destruction: The Assessment of the British Government*, London, September 2002.

UK House of Commons Foreign Affairs Select Committee Second Report, *Foreign Policy Aspects of the War against terrorism*, HC196, 19 December 2002, London.

UK Ministry of Defence, *The Future Strategic Context of Defence*, London, February 2001.

UK Ministry of Defence, *Strategic Defence Review*, London, July 1998.

UK Ministry of Defence, *The Strategic Defence Review: A new chapter*, London, 2002.

UK Ministry of Defence Joint Doctrine and Concepts Centre, *Strategic Trends*, London, March 2003.

United Nations, *Ninth Quarterly Report of the Executive Chairman of the United Nations Monitoring, Verification and Inspection Commission under Paragraph 12 of Security Council Resolution 1286 (1999)*, 31 May 2002, S/2002/606.

3 Newspapers, Magazines and Web-only articles

Air Force Magazine
Armed Forces Information Service News (US Military)
Arms Control Today
Atlanta Journal-Constitution
Boston Globe
Brookings Institution Analysis Papers
Brookings Institution Middle East Memorandums
Christian Science Monitor
IISS Strategic Comments
IISS Strategic Survey 2002/03: An evaluation and forecast of world affairs
Jane's Foreign Report
Jane's Intelligence Review
National Review (US)
New York Times
New York Times Magazine
New Yorker
Newsday
San Diego Union-Tribune
The Atlantic Monthly
The Daily Telegraph (London)
The Guardian (London)
The LA Times

The New Yorker
The Times (London)
US News and World Report
Wall Street Journal
Washington Post
Washington Times
Weekly Standard

Conetta, Carl and Knight, Charles, 'Inventing Threats', *Bulletin of the Atomic Scientists*, Vol. 53 No. 2, March/April 1998, *http://www.thebulletin.org/issues/ 1998/ma 98/ma98conetta.html* (accessed 10 February 2003)

CNN, The Survival of Saddam Hussein, 16 January 2001, *http://www.cnn.com/ SPECIALS/2001/gulf.war/unfinished/war/index4.html* (accessed 23 May 2002)

'Through the Realist lens: Conversation with John Mearsheimer', Institute of International Studies, University of California, Berkeley, 8 April 2002, *http:// globetrotter.berkeley.edu/people2/Mearsheimer/mearsheimer-con5.html* (accessed 3 April 2003)

Der Derian, James, '9.11: Before, After, and in between' , Social Science Research Council, *http://www.ssrc.org/sept11/essays/der_derian.htm* (accessed 11 December 2001)

International Campaign to Ban Landmines, Landmine Monitor Report 2002, *www.icbl.org/lm/2002/intro/mre.html* (accessed 5 February 2003)

Kaldor, Mary, 'Terror in the US', *Fathom*, September 13 2001, *http://www.fathom. com* (accessed 1 November 2001)

Luttwak, Edward, 'Atlantic Unbound Roundtable: Picking a good fight', 11 April 2000, *http://www.theatlantic.com/unbound/roundtable/goodfight/luttwak2.htm* (accessed 20 November 2001)

Reed, Amy Charlene, 'Federal Commission Proposes Risk Management Framework', RiskWorld News, *http://www.riskworld.com/NEWS/96Q1/nw5aa010.htm*, 13 June 1996, (accessed 23 March 2003)

Scharf, Michael, Untitled contribution to 'Is this a new kind of war? September 11 and its aftermath', 7 October 2001, Crimes of War Project, *http://www. crimesofwar.org/expert/paradigm-scharf.htm* (accessed 23 March 2003)

Wright, Susan, 'The hijacking of UNSCOM', *Bulletin of the Atomic Scientists*, Vol. 55 No. 4, July/August 1999, *http://www.thebulletin.org/issues/1999/mj99/ mj99wright.html* (accessed 23 March 2003)

INDEX